IN SEARCH OF

ALMIGHTY VOICE

RESISTANCE AND RECONCILIATION

BILL WAISER

Published in Canada by Fifth House Publishers, 195 Allstate Parkway, Markham, ON   L3R 4T8

Published in the United States by Fifth House Publishers, 311 Washington Street, Brighton, MA   02135

Library and Archives Canada Cataloguing in Publication
Title: In search of Almighty Voice : resistance and reconciliation / Bill Waiser.
Names: Waiser, W. A., author.
Description: First edition. | Includes bibliographical references and index.
Identifiers: Canadiana 20200189034 |
ISBN 9781771770019 (softcover)

Subjects: LCSH: Almighty Voice, 1874-1897. |
LCSH: Almighty Voice, 1874-1897—
Influence. | LCSH:
    Almighty Voice, 1874-1897—In mass media. |
LCSH: Indigenous peoples—
Canada—Social conditions. |
    LCSH: Canada—Race relations.
Classification: LCC E99.C88 W35 2020 |
DDC 305.897/323—dc23
Publisher Cataloging-in-Publication Data (U.S.)

Names: Waiser, W. Λ., author.

Title: In Search of Almighty Voice : Resistance and Reconciliation / Bill Waiser.

Description: Markham, Ontario : Fifth House Publishers, 2020. | Includes index. | Summary: "In May 1897, Almighty Voice, a member of the One Arrow Willow Cree, died violently when Canada's North-West Mounted Police shelled the fugitive's hiding place. Since then, his violent death has spawned a succession of conflicting stories. Almighty Voice has been maligned, misunderstood, romanticize, celebrated, and invented. What these stories have in common is that the Willow Cree man mattered. Understanding why he mattered has a direct bearing on reconciliation efforts today" -- Provided by publisher.

Identifiers: ISBN 978-1-77177-001-9 (paperback)

Subjects: LCSH: Almighty Voice, 1874-1897. | Cree Indians -- Biography. | Indians, Treatment of – North America. | Indians of North America – Government relations. | BISAC: HISTORY / Native American.
Classification: LCC E92.W357 |
DDC 970.004970922 – dc23

Maps: Articulate Eye
Editor: Charlene Dobmeier
Proofreader: Jan Coleman
Indexer: Adrian Mather
Text and cover design: hundreds & thousands

Printed in Canada by Friesens

10 9 8 7 6 5 4 3 2 1

Canada Council   Conseil des Arts
for the Arts   du Canada

ONTARIO ARTS COUNCIL
CONSEIL DES ARTS DE L'ONTARIO
an Ontario government agency
un organisme du gouvernement de l'Ontario

Fifth House Publishers acknowledges with thanks the Canada Council for the Arts and the Ontario Arts Council for their support of our publishing program.

www.fifthhousepublishers.ca

FIFTH
HOUSE

for Fraser Seely

the guy I want
in the bow of my canoe
crossing rough waters

Contents

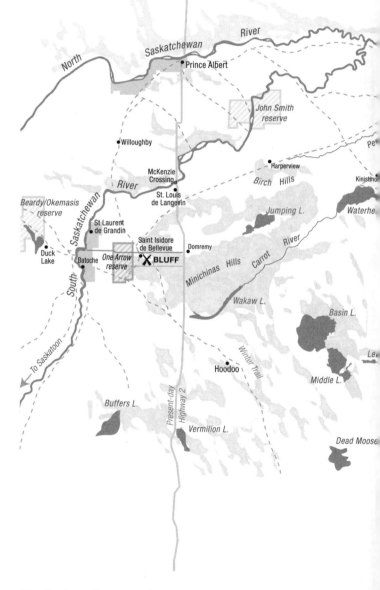

The Almighty Voice search area

PREFACE

It Involves All of Us

It's a drive rich in Saskatchewan history. Highway 41, heading north from the east side of Saskatoon, is popularly known as the "back way" to Prince Albert. Ten minutes up the highway is a sign for the "Old Trail Road," a reference to the Carlton Trail that once served as the major cart thoroughfare from Winnipeg to Edmonton in the mid-nineteenth century. The few surviving sections of the trail, which have never been ploughed nor disturbed in any way, are still deeply rutted. Then, there are a series of highway turn-offs to rural roads named after immigrant families, such as Laniwci, Hyshka, and Bayda, who settled the district in the early 1900s. The Ukrainian legacy also lives on in their distinctive community churches topped by onion-shaped domes. Those at Smuts and Alvena are visible from the highway, but many more can be found today in isolation—seemingly in the middle of nowhere—in the surrounding countryside. The highway also cuts through the middle of the Rural Municipality of Fish Creek (#402). It was along the western edge of the RM, in a coulee where Fish Creek enters the South Saskatchewan River, that Métis forces ambushed the North-West Field Force on 24 April 1885 during the North-West Rebellion and shattered the confidence of its cocksure British commander.

At Alvena, where Highway 41 bends slightly northeast for Wakaw, the Third Meridian road leads north, following one of the major survey lines against which the land was measured into standard homestead quarters, regardless of the geography. The cultivated fields here are slightly undulating with pockets of standing water. But after leaving the grid road, jogging west a short distance along secondary Highway 312 before turning north again, the landscape changes dramatically. Rolling hills covered with scruffy bush often give way to small stands of trees, interspersed with large sloughs that lick at the edges of the gravel road. A welcome sign soon announces that the land is the home of the One Arrow First Nation, one of the Willow Cree bands that was assigned reserve #95 in 1881. Houses, no more than simple bungalows, dot the high ground on both sides of the road. A large, two-storey band office and new recreational/community facility stand side-by-side in what would be main street in any other Saskatchewan village or town. The apparent poverty of the community is hard to ignore, but what defines the One Arrow Cree is a strong sense of identity, an unshakeable belief in tradition, and a quiet resiliency. These values have helped the band deal with life under treaty with the Canadian state.

It was here, in a small meeting room on the second floor of the band office, that I met Peter Almightyvoice,[1] the great grandson of Almighty Voice. One Arrow Chief Tricia Sutherland arranged the meeting with the family as the first step in working with the band. After presenting Peter with tobacco, I explained that I was writing about the Almighty Voice incident—wanted to sort out as best I could what really happened. He smiled and nodded in response. He later privately told Chief Sutherland that the book project made him "very proud."

Another meeting followed, this time with the community Elders who come together every first Tuesday of the month. After the blessing and meal, I talked about the project and then answered several questions. One of the Elders was particularly concerned with the exoneration of Chief One Arrow, the namesake of the band and one of three Cree chiefs imprisoned after the 1885 North-West Rebellion. With assistance from Chief Sutherland, I also provided enlarged photographs of Almighty Voice's descendants in the 1930s and 1940s and placed them on the table for examination. The Elders took turns pausing over the pictures, nodding at those they recognized and smiling at the memories.

The same photographs greeted band members as they entered the hall for a community meeting. Some people quickly pointed out family members and talked about the kin connections, while others tried to identify those who hadn't been named yet. After accepting my tobacco offering, former One Arrow chief and Elder Stewart Prosper opened the gathering with a prayer. Those in attendance, including some senior students from the band school, then sat around a large round table. A few people wandered in during the meeting to see what was going on and stayed to listen. My research findings generated a wide-ranging discussion about the band history in the late nineteenth century and the Almighty Voice story in particular—and lots of questions. Chief Sutherland was concerned that the incident had cast her community in a negative light and said it was important to understand what exactly happened and why. There was also general agreement about the need to keep talking and sharing information. The meeting closed with another prayer and then everyone shook hands.

Moving forward together is fundamental to Canada's reconciliation process. Former Saskatchewan Premier Roy Romanow said as much at the signing of the Treaty Land Entitlement Agreement with several First Nations communities in September 1992. "We have great reason to be proud—great reason to celebrate," he told the audience at Saskatoon's Wanuskewin Heritage Park. "We're acknowledging our shared destiny."[2] But that shared destiny will be compromised, if not lost, unless accompanied by an uncomfortable understanding of what happened in the colonial past. It's not enough to work towards a common future without confronting some hard truths and recognizing and addressing past wrongs. Getting involved as an historian has meant interrogating the past, looking at accepted versions through other lenses, listening to marginalized voices, and pushing interpretations in new directions.

Reconciliation must be a collective undertaking to have lasting meaning and resonance across generations. As Senator Murray Sinclair observed in June 2015 in his capacity as chair of the Truth and Reconciliation Commission, "Reconciliation is not an Aboriginal problem—it is a Canadian problem. It involves all of us."[3] It's not something that should be the exclusive domain of Indigenous people—or non-Indigenous people for that matter—for the simple reason that there were no separate Indigenous and non-Indigenous histories after newcomers arrived in the western interior, but a common or shared story. This relationship was not necessarily a balanced or equal one. Nor was it simply one-sided. Native-newcomer relations were always shifting, sometimes complicated, if not downright messy. The one constant was that they were interwoven. Telling the story of one without the other would consequently be incomplete, if not blinkered. Keeping people and their stories apart also works against cooperation and partnership. Just as reconciliation is a shared journey, understanding the history of Native-newcomer relations must be a shared story.[4]

Almighty Voice was a galvanizing figure in Native-newcomer relations. In October 1895, the Willow Cree man was arrested for killing a settler's cow. He escaped from custody and killed a pursuing North-West Mounted Police sergeant rather than surrender. With help from family and friends, Almighty Voice eluded capture for the next nineteen months. Then, in May 1897, he was surrounded in a bluff only a few miles from his home reserve and defiantly held off the mounted police, killing three more people before his refuge was shelled by cannon.

The Almighty Voice incident might appear to be the sorry outcome of one crime (taking private property) escalating into a bloody firefight (the killing of several people). But the story has larger significance. There was a profound gulf between the Indigenous and non-Indigenous understanding of the incident, and the reasons for it. Government officials arrogantly insisted they were working in the best interests of the Indigenous population, while Cree bands resented the repressive and coercive policies of the Indian Affairs department. Because of these different filters, Almighty Voice was either a "bad Indian" or a powerful symbol of Indigenous resistance.

In Search of Almighty Voice offers a fresh account of the incident—a difficult task because of the conflicting source material about the man and the need to separate fact from fiction, truth from rumour. Cree oral history challenged the accepted story and provided a more plausible and persuasive interpretation that laid bare non-Indigenous assumptions and attitudes about Almighty Voice and his actions. The overriding question that kept coming up about the incident was not why did it happen, but why did it happen only once?

The book also examines how the story has been told over the past 120 years: from newspaper columns, magazine articles, and pulp fiction to poetry, music, plays, and film. Almighty Voice has been maligned, misunderstood, romanticized, celebrated, and invented. Trying to find the Willow Cree man in this popular material can be just as frustrating as the mounted police search for him from 1895 to 1897. Who he might have been was less important than who he became; there have been many Almighty Voices over the years.

What these stories have in common, though, is that the Willow Cree man mattered. Understanding why he mattered has a direct bearing on reconciliation efforts today.

INTRODUCTION

Temptation to Starving Men

It started with the butchering of a cow. At dawn on 22 October 1895, North-West Mounted Police Sergeant Colin Colebrook and Constable William Hume left the Batoche detachment in a double buckboard for the hour-long trip to the One Arrow reserve. It was treaty payment day,[1] and, as customary, the mounted police were to serve as observers and ensure that everything went smoothly. Indian Agent Robert S. McKenzie commenced payments shortly after the two policemen arrived. For the next several hours, he handed five dollars, in new one-dollar bills,[2] to everyone on the treaty list who came forward. The agent took a break at dinner time—there were 107 band members—and then continued payments until 3:30 p.m. Colebrook and Hume then headed back to Batoche. But they did not return alone. While the payments were underway, the police had taken into custody a woman, Kâ-miyo-oskinîkiskwêw (Good Young Woman), for theft, and two men, Kisê-manitouwêw (Almighty Voice or Voice of the Great Spirit), and Kâ-môskwâsiw (Flying Sound), for killing a cow belonging to a Métis rancher.[3] The manacled prisoners were taken first to Batoche and then across the South Saskatchewan River by ferry to Duck Lake (originally named Stobart), where they were to be held overnight before appearing in court the following morning. Their date with justice would be swift and punitive. Indian Agent McKenzie doubled as justice of the peace and had not only issued the arrest warrant but would preside over their hearing.

≈

The Cree people and the North-West Mounted Police had a respectful, though at times uneasy, relationship. The mounties, as they were popularly known, had been formed in 1873 to ensure the peaceful, orderly settlement of the western interior and, at the same time, make clear to the United States that Canada controlled the territory. Backstopping the police presence was the popular belief that the Canadian frontier was different from its wild and woolly American counterpart, and that there could be no British justice without the fair and consistent application of law and order. That's why the mounted police wore red tunics to differentiate the force from the blue-uniformed American cavalry.

The North-West Mounted Police, shown here at its Regina headquarters in the 1880s, was formed to ensure the peaceful, orderly settlement of the western interior. LIBRARY AND ARCHIVES CANADA PA 118754

It would take more than red serge, though, to successfully bring the Cree of present-day central Saskatchewan into Canadian confederation, including a new legal system that the young dominion unilaterally imposed on the North-West in 1870. Nor was the region immune from the kind of indiscriminate violence that characterized the American West simply because of the presence of the mounted police.[4] The Cree chose to cooperate with the NWMP because of their treaty relationship with the Crown. Without their acquiescence, especially their treaty pledge not to take up arms, the history of Native-newcomer relations in the Canadian West could have been quite different—perhaps written in blood. Instead, the Cree accepted settlers in their territory on the understanding that Treaty Six (1876) represented a long-term reciprocal agreement—one that would constantly be renewed—and that Canada would provide generous assistance in the coming years and decades. The Canadian government, on the other hand, wanted to avoid costly Indian[5] wars and looked to treaty negotiation as the cheaper course of action in dealing with the Cree. The merits of this policy were clearly borne out by the experience south of the border, where the United States spent more money fighting Indian wars in 1870 than the entire Canadian budget for that year.[6]

Even with the treaty, trouble could be expected between the resident Indian population and the tens of thousands of white settlers expected to engulf the region in the 1870s and 1880s. The NWMP were consequently to serve as an "on-the-ground" buffer between immigrants and Indians, while performing a wide range of civil duties on behalf of the Canadian state. In working out a viable relationship with the Cree people, the police had to use discretion, sometimes exercise toleration, even show compassion. These dealings were sometimes fraught with tension and misunderstanding. But confrontations rarely descended into violence because Indian leaders counselled restraint and the police did not push matters. Indeed, the Cree knew that the "Queen's soldiers" were not like the "Long Knives" south of the border. During the eleven-year period between the arrival of the police and the start of the 1885 North-West Rebellion, only one mountie was killed on duty—and even then, under mysterious circumstances.[7]

The Cree chose to cooperate with the North-West Mounted Police because of their treaty relationship with the Crown. BURPEE, *THE SEARCH FOR THE WESTERN SEA*

What undermined the police-Indian relationship was the growing Canadian reluctance to meet the costs of its treaty obligations, a reluctance that translated into a drastic reduction in Indian Affairs spending after the economy slid into recession in the early 1880s. For many Canadians, Indians were deadbeats standing in the way of progress, and it did not make sense to waste money trying to keep a dying race alive. These cutbacks could not have come at a worse time. By 1879, except for a few small herds that sometimes drifted into Canadian territory, the bison were gone from the northern plains. Hungry Cree bands looked to Ottawa for famine assistance, as solemnly promised in the treaty, until they could begin successful farming on their reserves. But the Indian Affairs department, through its front-line employees on reserves, arrogantly insisted that rations be minimal and provided only to those who worked for them. One particular Indian agent, renowned for his single-minded toughness, is said to have "extract[ed] from his Indians as much work as possible in exchange for minimum rations," and boasted about it.[8]

The police soon found themselves confronted with several potentially explosive incidents. In July 1880, Willow Cree Chiefs One Arrow, Beardy, and Cutnose told their men to butcher the cattle intended for rations when treaty annuities were paid at Duck Lake. A NWMP party was sent to arrest the three chiefs. As the leaders were taken into custody, a defiant One Arrow shouted at his men to shoot the police. Fortunately, they only fired in the air.[9] Indian Affairs officials demanded that the Willow Cree be punished for destroying government property. But at their trial, headman Omenakaw explained, "Some of us, I among the number, killed the cattle as we had nothing to eat and we were told they belonged to us."[10] The jury acquitted the chiefs. It is not known whether they sympathized with their plight or believed that a warning would suffice. Edgar Dewdney, lieutenant governor for the North-West Territories, warned Ottawa to count on more unrest. "Indians dissatisfied," he wired the deputy superintendent general of Indian Affairs. "If assured plenty of food this winter, all will be well, otherwise trouble, for they have suffered."[11]

The disappearance of the bison from the northern plains in the late 1870s led to starvation among Cree bands. BILL WAISER

Hunger was also at the heart of an incident on the Sakimay reserve. In February 1884, Yellow Calf and several followers knocked the farm instructor aside and raided the government storehouse. When the police arrived to apprehend the culprits, the starving Cree refused to give up the food, prepared to defend it with their lives, insisting they had taken only what rightfully belonged to them. "If ... the provisions were not intended to be eaten by the Indians," Yellow Calf reportedly asked, "why were they stored on our reserve?" [12] In the end, the Indian Affairs department increased rations without admitting that hunger had been the cause of the trouble.

Four months later, two of Lucky Man's sons assaulted the farm instructor on the Little Pine reserve when he refused to provide rations. When the mounted police attempted to arrest the two brothers, only the most strenuous efforts of Cree leaders, who offered to give themselves up in place of the two young men, prevented the tense showdown from reaching a bloody conclusion. "It would seem," Superintendent Leif Crozier mused, "as if there was a wish to see upon how little a man can work and exist." [13]

These confrontations placed the police in an awkward situation. They also marked a significant departure from past dealings with "unlawful" Indian behaviour. In a major study of criminal cases on the prairies between 1878 and 1885, [14] it was found that the crime rate for Indian peoples was unexpectedly low (18 per cent). White people were five times more likely than Indians to be charged with a criminal offence in all crime categories—except one. That exception was livestock theft (horse stealing or cattle killing), which represented about 11 per cent of the cases reported by the NWMP during the study period. Fifty-seven per cent of the defendants in those cases were Indian.

These findings are not surprising. One of the few remaining ways for Indian warriors to secure prestige and honour was to steal horses, especially from their enemies. And with the demise of the bison, killing cattle became a ready substitute for hungry Indians—whether they belonged to a settler or rancher or were part of the reserve livestock. The NWMP did their best to bring an end to this activity and the "wild ways" it represented. Horse stealing and cattle rustling were not in keeping with the kind of society and values the mounties sought to impose and nurture in the prairie west. This crackdown meant that Indians were more likely to be convicted in this category, in contrast to the leniency for other crimes before the territorial court.

The growing Canadian reluctance to fulfil its treaty responsibilities in the early 1880s undermined the relationship between the Cree and the mounted police. This statue is located at Fort Walsh national historic park, the former NWMP headquarters in present-day south-western Saskatchewan. BILL WAISER

By the mid-1880s, Indian horse raiding was no longer a serious problem. But cattle killing persisted—and the mounties blamed government policy. In the aftermath of the 1885 North-West Rebellion, the Indian Affairs department decided that the Cree needed a firm government hand and adopted a number of draconian measures under the deceptively mundane title, "future management."[15] One of the most controversial policies was a pass system that effectively forbade individuals from leaving their reserves without securing permission. Indian Affairs officials had first floated the idea of ending Indian freedom of movement in November 1883. But NWMP Commissioner A. G. Irvine had dissuaded the government, warning strenuously that "such a system would be tantamount to a breach of confidence with the Indians." And why was that? Indians had been promised during treaty negotiations, Irvine reminded Ottawa officials, "that compulsory residence on reservations would not be required ... and that they would be at liberty to travel about for legitimate hunting and trading purposes."[16]

After 1885, though, Indian Affairs was determined to impose its will on Indian peoples and compel them to embrace a new, government-directed way of life. And the best way to do that was to keep Indians separate and apart from white settlers. To ensure that treaty bands behaved accordingly, rations were given only to those who cooperated with Indian agents and farm instructors and diligently worked their reserve lands without complaint. They were much like serfs in the medieval world.[17] Roman Catholic bishop Vital-Justin Grandin called it "a state of slavery."[18]

Even then, Indian Commissioner Hayter Reed, known to the Battleford Cree as "Iron Heart,"[19] steadily cut back on the amount of food assistance, especially meat. An accounting of the reductions, in tabular form, was routinely published in the department annual reports. Reed also threatened to reduce or delay payment of band annuities if it appeared that they were not labouring hard or producing enough. Either step was a violation of the treaties. This callous attitude reflected an Indian Affairs culture that believed the department's first duty was to establish authority over the Indians. One scholar has suggested that "the Government's policy could be summed up in six words: feed one day, starve the next."[20]

The mounted police and Indian Affairs officials often disagreed over treatment of destitute bands in the aftermath of the 1885 North-West Rebellion. PRINCE ALBERT HISTORICAL SOCIETY, BILL SMILEY ARCHIVES, MODERN SERIES 91-715

There were also political realities at play. In the House of Commons, the government and opposition constantly wrangled over Indian Affairs expenses. In April 1882, for example, in response to persistent Liberal complaints about "generous" government spending on Indians, Conservative Prime Minister John A. Macdonald admitted that his officials "are doing all they can, by refusing food until the Indians are on the verge of starvation, to reduce expenses."[21] That Canada had treaty obligations seemed, at best, irrelevant.

The NWMP, for its part, keenly appreciated the need to keep a watchful eye on Indian peoples and their whereabouts. It was one way of removing the potential for trouble with white settlers. But the force did not become simple enforcers of state policy. Although the Indian Affairs department implemented the new pass system to control, if not stop, off-reserve movement, the mounted police regularly questioned its legality and were reluctant to retrieve those who left their community without permission, especially if they were away hunting. The police also complained that the spike in cattle rustling in the early 1890s was directly linked to the short rations policy and not some "primitive" Indian lust for glory. "The temptation to starving men to help themselves," NWMP Superintendent Sam Steele reasoned, "will be very great."[22] In fact, the police often sided with hungry Indians in protesting department policy because the mounties had to deal with the fallout: butchered cattle carcasses and upset settlers and ranchers.

Indian Affairs, though, would brook no interference and chastised the NWMP for being soft on Indians and unsupportive of department policy. It was even suggested that the mounted police should stay off reserves and away from Indians unless their services were needed. Superintendent A. B. Perry countered that "no injury has been done" by patrols through Indian communities—that the police had a duty to "make their state known" because "Indian officials are oft'times not liked by the Indians." He also acknowledged that the Cree had come to "fear the police ... we have developed into the men who arrest them." This distrust was worrisome to Perry and could be overcome only if police could freely visit bands as friends and talk to them. Otherwise, Indians will become "strangers to us" and that will be a "great loss."[23]

During his command of the Prince Albert district ("F" division),

NWMP Superintendent A. B. Perry (centre) warned in the late 1880s that the Cree had come to "fear the police ... we have developed into the men who arrest them." RCMP HISTORICAL COLLECTIONS UNIT, REGINA, SK 1933.7.8A

Superintendent Perry was particularly troubled by the Indian Affairs department treatment of the One Arrow band. "Their suffering [is] a notorious fact," he advised the NWMP commissioner in the late winter of 1886, "rations ... not being very ample."[24] Hunger forced people to leave the reserve in a desperate search for food in the nearby Minichinas Hills (hills that stick out).[25] One-quarter to one-third of the band members were reported away hunting in the annual department reports after the rebellion. No mention is made of whether the individuals first secured permission. Nor would not having a pass have deterred them. Starvation drove the band to seek out food wherever they could find it, especially when local Indian Affairs officials would not or could not distribute rations on reserve.

These absences from One Arrow were not as frequent in the early 1890s according to official records. But that did not mean that band members ceased to slip away, ceased to live by the hunt, especially when reserve farming enjoyed more bad years than good. That was especially true in 1895. In his monthly report for July, Indian Agent McKenzie noted that crops were stunted because of drought. There was not even enough hay to feed the agency horses.[26] Crop failures were common in the early years of western agriculture, when pioneer homesteads struggled to come to terms with the vagaries of the semi-arid environment. But the blind desire of Indian Affairs to have treaty bands become more self-reliant left little room for poor harvests.

For hungry Cree, the temptation was to poach fresh meat. And the One Arrow people did not have to look far. "There are so many cattle owned close to the reserve," McKenzie grumbled in May 1895, "that straying onto reserve is difficult to prevent."[27] Wandering bulls were a particular nuisance. McKenzie told Louis Marion, the resident One Arrow farm instructor, that the Indians should tie up any settler's cattle found on the reserve and then notify the owner. It was a ridiculous order, tellingly naive—unless, of course, he believed that Indian fear of him outweighed their hunger. Almighty Voice and his brother-in-law Flying Sound were not intimidated and butchered a stray cow at first opportunity. The two men undoubtedly knew it was wrong; Almighty Voice later offered a horse to the settler as compensation.[28] But the beef would have fed many, in much the same way a bison kill would have been shared in the past.

Treaty payment day at the Whitecap reserve, south of Saskatoon, in the late nineteenth century. The North-West Mounted Police served the arrest warrant for Almighty Voice on treaty payment day at the One Arrow reserve in 1895. UNIVERSITY OF SASKATCHEWAN, UNIVERSITY ARCHIVES AND SPECIAL COLLECTIONS, DEPARTMENT OF PHYSICS FONDS, RG 2043 F8

Almighty Voice and Flying Sound, along with Almighty Voice's sister Good Young Woman, were arrested on 22 October 1895—curiously, five months after the killing of the steer. Because court was to be held at Duck Lake the next morning, NWMP Sergeant Colin Colebrook sent the three prisoners there in the late afternoon instead of holding them at Batoche. The decision was one of convenience, not security. There was no mounted police gaol at Duck Lake, only a crude, two-storey log structure that served as office and sleeping quarters for the detachment.

Sergeant Harry Keenan, one of the original members of the NWMP, took charge of the incoming prisoners. He had beds made up for them in one of the corners of the office and then organized a night watch with the men on hand. There were to be five shifts. The constable on duty was to keep the front door locked and not leave the room or the prisoners unattended. If someone slept through the start of his shift, the guard was to knock on the ceiling with a broom and try to rouse the person and get him to come downstairs.

Keenan took no other precautions. Nor did he see a need to shackle the prisoners with a ball and chain, even though the recently updated guard room regulations required Indians to be held in irons if not confined to a cell. The veteran mountie, with more than two decades of service in police scarlet, looked upon their crimes as minor and expected them to receive light sentences.[29]

There was no gaol cell in the North-West Mounted Police barracks at Duck Lake, where Almighty Voice was held the night of 22 October 1895. PROVINCIAL ARCHIVES OF SASKATCHEWAN S-B11136

Constable Samuel Carter, followed by Constable Gerald O'Kelly (one of two brothers on duty that night), handled the first two shifts without incident. Constable Robert Dickson, a former Winnipeg steamboat agent who had joined the force the previous year at age thirty, was scheduled to take over just before midnight. But when he did not come down to the office, O'Kelly called Dickson from the door at the bottom of the stairs and then went up a few steps and called him again. When the dozing constable finally answered, O'Kelly returned to his watch over the prisoners until Dickson appeared for duty.

The six foot, five inch Dickson spent the better part of the next two hours reading a newspaper at a table, when not getting up to stretch his long frame, walk around the office, or inspect the prisoners. When his relief failed to appear at 2 a.m., Dickson checked that the three Indians were still asleep and then climbed the stairs to the sleeping quarters, leaving the key to the front door under the newspaper on the table. When Dickson entered the room, Constable Andrew O'Kelly was getting ready for his shift. The two men exchanged a few words before O'Kelly headed downstairs to the office. He immediately felt a draft. Finding the front door ajar with the key in it, O'Kelly looked over at the prisoners and counted only two. Almighty Voice was gone.[30]

CHAPTER ONE

Miserable Beyond Description

He was going to hang. That's the popular explanation for Almighty Voice's late-night escape from the Duck Lake barracks. Sometime during his two-hour watch over three Indian prisoners, North-West Mounted Police Constable Robert Dickson supposedly told Almighty Voice that he faced certain death for killing a stray cow. And when the constable slipped away for a few minutes, blithely leaving the front-door key under a newspaper on the table, the Willow Cree man fled in fear rather than face the hangman's noose. The story makes for good drama and has been repeated so many times that it has to be true. But in the exhaustive mounted police investigation of Almighty's Voice escape, especially the disciplinary hearings for Dickson and his commanding officer, Sergeant Harry Keenan, the hanging threat was never mentioned. Nor is it found in Department of Indian Affairs records or any of the other contemporary sources, including interviews with Indigenous people. In fact, until Almighty Voice's escape none of three guards on duty that night reported any interaction with the three Indians in custody, including any request to use the outside bathroom. The prisoners were all asleep in their makeshift beds in the corner of the office. Constable Dickson would never have left the office if he believed any of the Indians were awake and feigning sleep. He may have been careless, but he would not have chanced going upstairs if he had given the unshackled Indians a reason to try to escape. Almighty Voice, for his part, was not stupid. He would have known that killing cattle was never severely punished. Some form of restitution was usually required but never hanging. Almighty Voice did, however, have good reason for running. He was afraid of suffering the same treatment as his grandfather and father at the hands of government authorities.

≈

Almighty Voice was officially known to the Canadian government as One Arrow band member #57. Probably born in 1874, two years before the Willow Cree entered Treaty Six, he was the first son (one of eight children) of Nanâcohkonâkos (Spotted Calf or Appears in Various Ways) and Seenokesick (John Sounding Sky or The Sounding Sky). Spotted Calf was the daughter of One Arrow headman Kâ-namahcît (Left Hand) and adopted daughter of his brother Chief One Arrow (Kā-pêyakwaskonam or Single One Shaft). John Sounding Sky, a Saulteaux, was from the Nut Lake (Yellow Quill) band that lived north of the Quill Lakes (near present-day Kelvington). He met Spotted Calf when he was working for the Hudson's Bay Company, as a trader for the Fort Qu'Appelle post, travelling out on the plains to the camps of hunting bands and bringing back meat and bison robes.[1]

John Sounding Sky (Seenokesick), Almighty Voice's father, probably at Fort Carlton before 1885. PRINCE ALBERT HISTORICAL SOCIETY

This cooperation and intermarriage were quite common among Indigenous groups in the mid-nineteenth century. The Cree, Assiniboine, and Saulteaux often came together—sometimes with Métis—in mixed bands to hunt the dwindling bison herds. The ethnic composition of these "hybrid" bands greatly varied. The Willow Cree, for example, were descended from George Sutherland, a late-eighteenth-century HBC servant whose mixed-descent son (known as the "Englishman") took three Indigenous wives and fathered eighteen children (ten boys and eight girls). One Arrow was the son of Sutherland's second wife, Pasikus. Two other band members and future leaders, Kamīyistowesit (Beardy) and Saswaypew (Cutnose), had married into the family.[2] Their identification as Parkland or Prairie Willow Cree derived from their home territory, south and east of Fort Carlton, in the Saskatchewan country.

Little is known about Almighty Voice's childhood. He would have travelled with the band on its seasonal round from present-day Duck Lake to Goose Lake (North Battleford) on the west to Round Prairie (Dundurn) on the south and Little Manitou Lake (Watrous) to the east. The Willow Cree spent their summers on the northern plains hunting bison either by gun from horseback or the more traditional method of pounding. Come winter, they retreated to the shelter of river valleys and subsisted on a wider range of game and food resources.

Métis trader Norbert Welsh provided a rare snapshot of the One Arrow band before treaty in his memoirs, of how these "fine hunters" were at home on the plains and had a dependable source of furs and bison robes. During his first winter at Round Prairie in 1865, Welsh was invited to participate in a communal bison kill. He watched the men, women, and children of the band build a large, sturdy pound from poplar logs. Spirit offerings were placed on a solitary tree that had been left standing in the middle of the corral. Riders on horseback then expertly guided a nearby bison herd into the enclosure. So many animals crowded into the pound that they could not move. Once the captive bison were killed—using guns, bows and arrows, and knives—Welsh counted 170 carcasses. The meat was shared among families.[3]

Almighty Voice would have grown up with stories of the glory days of the bison hunt, glory that contrasted sharply with the bitter reality of reserve life under treaty. Weakened by disease, exhausted by intertribal warfare, and grappling with the loss of the bison, the Willow Cree had entered Treaty Six at a site halfway between Fort Carlton and Duck Lake in late August 1876. The discussions had been difficult. Beardy had not only insisted on a separate meeting with Treaty Commissioner Alexander Morris but wanted something done to protect the bison in order to avoid starvation. In response, Morris had repeatedly pledged, using kinship terms, that the Crown wanted to enter into a long-term reciprocal relationship and would provide much-needed help in making the transition to agriculture. This promise of security convinced the Willow Cree to enter treaty, but their determination to get what was best for them and their future—including a copy of the treaty document—did not sit well with the treaty commissioner. Morris later reported that they "gave me great trouble and were very difficult to deal with."[4]

Conservative Prime Minister John A. Macdonald was also Canada's longest-serving minister of Indian Affairs (October 1878 to October 1887). LIBRARY AND ARCHIVES CANADA PA027002

The One Arrow band's relationship with Canada was a troubled one. In the first few years after treaty, Ottawa did little, if anything, to assist the Willow Cree, maintaining that the Indians could fend for themselves until the expected rush of settlers made it necessary to take up their reserve land. In 1878, there was only one Indian agent for the entire Treaty Six area (121,000 square miles in present-day central Saskatchewan and Alberta). It consequently took five years from the signing of Treaty Six before the

One Arrow reserve (#95) was surveyed: sixteen square miles of undulating, gravelly land, dotted with treed bluffs and sloughs, four miles east of the South Saskatchewan River.[5] Three years later, the band was still awaiting delivery of some of the promised agricultural items, including livestock. Nor was a resident farm instructor, someone who could help the band bring the land under cultivation, assigned to the reserve.

Adjusting to settled life in a confined area was not easy for One Arrow and his followers. Palmer Clarke, Indian agent for the Carlton district, found the Cree who had come in from the plains to be "insolent."[6] But these hungry people chafed at local Indian Affairs officials' refusal to provide rations unless they performed some form of labour, no matter how demeaning or degrading. They also showed little inclination to take up farming, preferring to hunt game and harvest other foods in the Minichinas Hills to the east. The young Almighty Voice would

Edgar Dewdney, who doubled as lieutenant governor of the North-West Territories and Indian commissioner, was prepared to use "sheer compulsion" in dealing with Cree bands. LIBRARY AND ARCHIVES CANADA PA026668

have learned to be at home in these brush-riddled hills, would come to know the ravines and ridges as he honed his survival skills under the guidance of his father and grandfather. But his family's and others' stubborn adherence to traditional ways was equated with backwardness—all the more so because of their refusal to speak English or be converted to Christianity.

Indian Affairs constantly bemoaned the One Arrow band's delinquency in bringing reserve land into production. In June 1882, the start of a new crop year, Indian Agent J. M. Rae charged that "they will do nothing unless starved to it."[7] Things were little better, in the eyes of the department, the following year. "They make very slow progress, the chief being old and past work," a government official reported. "Their case is as bad as ever."[8] That was an understatement. Not only did the band continue to depend on government rationing when not foraging along the river or the nearby hills, but its numbers were in decline, dropping below one hundred in the early 1880s. Sickness regularly carried away members, especially the young. The crude death rate on One Arrow over the winter of 1883–84 was 141.3 per thousand. Ten of the thirteen deaths were children.[9]

Indian Affairs finally named a resident farm instructor, Michel Dumas, to the One Arrow reserve in the fall of 1884. Eight years after treaty, the department suddenly wanted "to have an Instructor constantly with them until they can see their way to look after themselves."[10] The educated, acculturated Dumas was from the nearby Métis community of Saint-Louis de Langevin and could speak Cree. Chiefs had constantly asked for people who knew their language. But Dumas was one of the leaders of a local movement that had invited exiled Métis leader Louis Riel, quietly working as a schoolteacher in Montana, to the Saskatchewan country in June 1884 to help resolve outstanding land issues.

Riel seemed intent at first to pursue traditional protest strategies: holding meetings with the disaffected, calling for cooperative action, and drafting petitions. Then, on 19 March 1885, opting for more forceful measures to shake the federal government of its lethargy, Riel declared a provisional government at Batoche and demanded the surrender of Forts Carlton and Battleford in order to force Canada to address Métis grievances. A negotiated

The North-West Mounted Police at Duck Lake in 1884.

settlement became impossible when a NWMP patrol clashed with a Métis party, led by Riel's redoubtable general, Gabriel Dumont, near Duck Lake one week later.

From the start of the North-West Rebellion,[11] Riel expected Indian support. Not only were many Willow Cree in the Duck Lake area of mixed ancestry, but some Métis men from the South Branch communities (along the South Saskatchewan River) had married Cree women and become part of their extended families.[12] A growing number of Cree chiefs were also disillusioned with their treaty partner and began working together to lobby Ottawa for the support and assistance that had been promised by Canada's negotiators in 1876. To that end, Beardy had called a meeting at Duck Lake in July 1884 to discuss a range of grievances, from the lack of schools and healthcare to poor farming equipment, clothing, and rations. One Arrow was one of the participating chiefs. "[I]t is almost too hard for them," reported the local Indian agent, "to bear the treatment received at the hands of the Government after its 'sweet promises' made in order to get the country from them."[13]

Riel sensed an opportunity, and over the winter of 1884–85, sent messengers among the local bands with presents and an invitation to take up arms alongside the Métis. Cree leaders, however, repeatedly rebuffed Riel's overtures. They sought a peaceful resolution to their grievances and knew that any violence would lead to retribution, thereby wrecking their plans to get Ottawa to honour the treaty. That left Riel only one option—forcibly gathering up supporters. Dumas, a member of Riel's governing council (Exovedate), ordered the Willow Cree band to slaughter their cattle and join the Métis camp at Batoche. Gabriel Dumont's presence with a contingent of armed horsemen ensured that the Indians complied. Eleven-year-old Almighty Voice would have been among the captives. "Surrounded by rebels and influenced by their own Instructor," a government official later concluded, "it was almost impossible to expect Indians to act differently to 'One Arrow's' Band."[14]

General Frederick Middleton, commander of the North-West Field Force (second from left), interrogates Willow Cree Chief Beardy (sitting, with decorated hat) after the fall of Batoche in May 1885. PROVINCIAL ARCHIVES OF SASKATCHEWAN R-B2064

One Arrow's presence at Batoche during the rebellion seemed irrefutable proof of his duplicity. The Willow Cree chief appeared to have broken his word. On the eve of the declaration of Riel's provisional government, when Indian Agent J. B. Lash visited the reserve to ascertain the band's intentions, One Arrow "spoke in glowing terms of [his] loyalty."[15] The next day, he had apparently enlisted in Riel's army. Exactly how many One Arrow men, including the chief, actually participated in the fighting is not known.

When it came to assigning guilt, General Frederick Middleton, the commander of the North-West Field Force, considered anyone appearing to assist Riel to be the enemy and took One Arrow into custody after the fall of Batoche in mid-May 1885. The general also confiscated his treaty medal. "Think it will be a good thing for the country," Middleton informed the minister of Militia, "if I can chastise a body of rebel Indians."[16]

One Arrow was held in Prince Albert for more than a month before being taken south to Regina for trial. The elderly chief was probably confused by his incarceration, if only because he had refused to break his treaty pledge and been compelled to join Riel and the rebellion. Now, he found himself back in gaol for something far more serious than ordering the killing of a few government cattle. The wagon trip to the territorial capital would also have been unsettling. One Arrow was manacled to Will "Crank" Jackson, a so-called white rebel from Prince Albert and Riel's secretary, who had become unhinged during the rebellion. Jackson defied the military escort at every opportunity, including soiling himself to the disgust of the other prisoners. When he was forced to take a bath in a slough because the stench had become unbearable, he disappeared under the surface, then bolted from the water and ran naked across the prairie. From that time forward, he remained shackled to One Arrow.[17]

One Arrow appeared before the territorial court in Regina on 13 August 1885. He was one of four chiefs charged with treason-felony for their part in the rebellion.[18] His trial started badly. The elderly chief found the proceedings bewildering, even more so when the indictment was translated as "knocking off the Queen's bonnet and stabbing her in the behind with the sword." There was no Cree equivalent for words such as conspiracy, traitor, or rebellion. "Are you drunk?" a perplexed One Arrow reportedly asked the court interpreter.[19]

The case against One Arrow rested on the contention that he had openly associated with the Métis at Batoche and thereby breached his treaty "allegiance to the Government, the country, and the Queen."[20] Not one prosecution witness was able to say, however, that the Willow Cree leader had actually fired a shot or was even directing his band at Batoche. But whether the chief had actively participated or not was irrelevant. One Arrow's mere presence in the rebel camp sufficed. The six-man jury required only a few minutes to return with a verdict of guilty.

Lawrence W. Herchmer, future commissioner of the North-West Mounted Police (second from right, head cocked) with Whitecap (standing third from left) and probably Chakastaypasin (standing first from left) in May 1885. Almighty Voice could be the young man lying on the ground on the far left. LIBRARY AND ARCHIVES CANADA C000752

Before he was sentenced, an overwrought One Arrow tried to explain through the court interpreter that he could not have taken up arms because he was grieving for a lost grandchild, likely one of Almighty Voice's siblings. He also claimed that his fighting days were long past and that he would never break his treaty pledge. "I was taken to the place, Batoche's, to join Riel by Gabriel [Dumont]," he asserted. "They took me there ... I know that I have done nothing wrong ... I beg of you to let me go, to let me go free."[21] One Arrow's plea probably sounded like a last-minute fabrication to save himself, and the seventy-year-old chief was sentenced to three years in Manitoba's Stony Mountain penitentiary. He might as well have been condemned to death.

One Arrow was taken by train to Winnipeg in mid-August 1885. The disembarkation of the Indian "rebels," shuffling with their heavy chains along the station platform, created quite a stir. "A more lawless looking set can hardly be imagined," reported one newspaper.[22] One Arrow was transferred by wagon to Stony Mountain the next day and assigned prisoner #29. The admission ledger also listed his vital statistics: he stood five foot, eight inches; was a hunter by occupation; and had no religion.[23] Because the warden insisted that inmates learn some practical trade, seventy-year-old One Arrow was placed in the shoemakers' shop. He also received lessons from l'abbé Gabriel Cloutier, the penitentiary Catholic chaplain, who was determined to convert the "infidels" through baptism.[24]

What One Arrow and other prisoners desperately needed, though, were better living conditions. As a federal inspector gloomily noted: "Anything more unsuited to the purpose of a penitentiary [would be] difficult to conceive."[25] Stony Mountain was designed to house only one hundred, and with the arrival of those convicted of rebellion crimes, the prison population ballooned. Officials with the Department of Justice had actually recommended that the prison be enlarged before the trials got underway, but the new wing was just under construction when One Arrow arrived. The severe overcrowding was exacerbated by the wretched sanitary conditions, especially the lack of a sewage system for human waste. Respiratory and intestinal ailments pervaded the prison population, but the mortality rate was particularly high among the Indians, including the relatively young. "The idea of their detention was for them something very heavy and hard," Father Cloutier remarked on their deaths. "I often heard them saying ... If I were not here, if I were with my people, I would surely recover."[26]

One Arrow was not the only band member to face government justice in the wake of the rebellion. That the Métis had forcibly taken the Willow Cree to Batoche was inconsequential, especially to Assistant Indian Commissioner Hayter Reed, who argued that Indians had to be reined in and subdued "so as to prevent [them] reverting back into their old state."[27] There consequently had to be punishment for being found in the rebel camp. One Arrow members Atimwâyow (Dog Tail), Left Hand, and Nâpêsis (Little Man) were also found guilty of treason-felony and imprisoned at Stony Mountain.[28] Nor was a new chief named in One Arrow's absence. Indian Affairs wanted the band leaderless so that officials could act with impunity. That's also why the department, on Reed's recommendation, identified the One Arrow people as disloyal—for breaching the treaty by their apparent rebellion participation—and stripped them of their annuities. The punishment would be lifted and treaty payments restored only when Indian Affairs said so. Until then, the band was at the mercy of the department if it wanted government help.

Hayter Reed, who succeeded Edgar Dewdney as Indian commissioner in 1888, sought to minimize Canadian assistance to Cree bands. LIBRARY AND ARCHIVES CANADA PA212538

Some of One Arrow's people decided it was not safe to remain in the area or even Canada. Among them was John Sounding Sky, who slipped away for several months. Another six members, last paid in 1884, would be away for at least five years. For those families who returned to the One Arrow reserve after the rebellion, the situation was bleak, especially since they were now regarded as a rebel band. Almighty Voice was likely traumatized by what had befallen the band. Both his natural grandfather, Left Hand, and adoptive grandfather, One Arrow, had been taken away to prison, while his father had temporarily left the region out of fear of government retribution.[29] He may also have been getting over the shock of witnessing the intense fighting at Batoche, replaying in his mind how Canadian troops had shown no mercy in over-running Métis defences and then exacting revenge by destroying what could not be confiscated as war booty. And he would have heard about what had happened to other Cree people who had been caught up in the trouble and how government officials had responded to their plight without compassion or understanding. Any one of these things would have been harrowing for the eleven-year-old boy. What happened next to the band would only harden his mistrust and resentment.

Once the rebellion was over, Indians Affairs decided that the One Arrow band should be amalgamated with the Beardy's & Okemasis reserve on the other or western side of the South Saskatchewan River near Duck Lake. The "bad & lazy Indians," according to Hayter Reed, required "constant supervision" and that could be achieved only by grouping all the Willow Cree together.[30] The hard-bitten Reed did not care that the One Arrow band had a treaty right to its own reserve. That right, in his opinion, had been forfeited by involvement in the rebellion. Nor did Reed think it necessary to follow legislative guidelines for the release or surrender of a reserve (as stipulated in sections 25 and 26 of the 1876 Indian Act). In fact, the department was so confident about the One Arrow relocation that it officially reported in October 1885 that "this band has been joined to that of Beardy."[31]

But the roughly ninety band members steadfastly refused to move, prompting Indian officials to starve the Willow Cree into submission. It was not long before rumours of hardship and privation began circulating around the Prince Albert district. Indian Agent J. M. Rae scoffed at these reports, vociferously claiming that "the destitution [is] altogether exaggerated in my opinion. The rebels are impudent and will not work when rationed."[32] Despite his assurances, the stories persisted.

The NWMP decided to send a small patrol, under Inspector A. R. Cuthbert, to the Duck Lake area on 14 January 1886. What the mounties found were instances of acute distress in the Métis communities, but nothing prepared them for the horrifying scene on the One Arrow reserve. When the band balked at moving to Beardy's & Okemasis and giving up their land, they were left to cope on their own, with no more than bows and arrows and snares. "Their state ... would be impossible to exaggerate," Cuthbert told his supervisor, "& the Halfbreeds pity them more than they do themselves ... They are miserable beyond description ... poorly clothed and huddled in their huts like sheep in a pen ... Last summer they lived on gophers and this winter on rabbits."[33]

Cuthbert went on to describe how the wife of the imprisoned chief would often have to walk the ten miles to Duck Lake in the dead of winter to get a few pounds of flour for her sick daughter. He also reported how a few old horse blankets had been welcomed like priceless gifts. Perhaps the most telling finding was who was not there. When Cuthbert asked about the number of band members present, he was told sixty-seven. But he counted far fewer. A third, maybe even half, of the band had apparently left the reserve in a desperate search for food in the nearby hills. Almighty Voice, a noted hunter from a young age, was likely among them.

L. W. Herchmer, inspector of Indian Agencies for the North-West Territories, arrived in the area a few days later. He had been sent "to get at the bottom of [the rumours]."[34] But Herchmer was more concerned with getting his assignment done. It was brutally cold, and he did not want to be there. Herchmer found the One Arrow band "in a bad state, almost destitute of clothing" and determined that neither Indian Agent Rae nor the farm instructor had visited the reserve for several weeks. He offered no help, though, not even the distribution of rations to the band. Instead, in his official report on the situation, Herchmer confessed that he disliked being an inspector "excessively," when not grumbling about the cold and how it made travel "most disagreeable."[35] He did not seem to make any connection between the frigid temperatures and the poorly clothed One Arrow people.

It was not surprising. Just months earlier, before Herchmer had been promoted to inspector of Indian agencies, three Sioux chiefs had petitioned Ottawa to remove Herchmer as Indian agent at Birtle, Manitoba, because he was "always cross ... complaining and scolding ... will not listen to or talk to us."[36] This complaint against Herchmer underscored how Indian Affairs employees were generally unsuited for the job. They were patronage appointees and had little understanding or sympathy for the Indians

A studio portrait of Almighty Voice, probably taken at Duck Lake in the early 1890s. PROVINCIAL ARCHIVES OF SASKATCHEWAN R-B4512

under their charge and the adjustments they faced. Herchmer, for example, had been a supply officer for the 1872–74 boundary commission and then a Winnipeg brewer before being named an Indian agent in 1876. Local Indian officials also had a reputation for laziness, incompetence, but most of all, brutality. One senior Hudson's Bay Company trader reported that resident farm instructors regularly dealt out "kicks and blows, accompanied with showers of profanity."[37]

Lieutenant Governor Edgar Dewdney, who doubled as Indian commissioner for the territories, was furious with Herchmer's report. It was not the sorry condition of the One Arrow band that angered him. He was annoyed that a police patrol had visited the reserve and distributed presents (old horse blankets) to the Willow Cree without first informing the Indian Affairs office in Prince Albert or consulting with the local Indian agent or farm instructor. In a brusquely worded letter—essentially, a reprimand—he bluntly told NWMP Commissioner A. G. Irvine that rebel Indians were to be treated as such and that police interference had "weakened ... the furtherance of [government] policy."[38] Dewdney's message was clear: the mounted police were to leave the oversight and care of Indians to the department.

The One Arrow people, though, refused to give in. On 30 March 1886, Charles Adams, yet another new Indian agent, glumly reported that the band had repeatedly ignored his requests to relocate across the river to the Beardy's & Okemasis reserve. Herchmer failed as well. During a second visit to the One Arrow community in early February, as part of his official review of the reserves in the agency, Herchmer suggested that moving was in their best interests. Cooperation might help win the release of Chief One Arrow from prison. When that did not work, he cut off rations. "We feed only the Aged the Sick & little ones, leaving the men out," was how Adams explained Herchmer's orders to Dewdney. Almighty Voice, now twelve, would have been among those who went without food.

It was at this point that the Indian agent began to question whether the push for relocation should be put on hold while he attended to the sick and dying. "I took up some simple medicine," he wrote, "but can't do much for them."[39] Adams made two more visits to the reserve in early April 1886 and found band members still resistant to moving to the Beardy's & Okemasis reserve. He reported on 5 April that they would "rather be left to shift for themselves than go anywhere else," and then three days later, that "they would rather be on their own resources" if it meant not having to move.[40] Two people had died between his visits. Adams attributed the band's intransigence to the "Saulteaux Sinnookeesick," Almighty Voice's father, now back on the reserve and speaking out against the move.[41] He believed the One Arrow people would go along with the department's wishes if Sounding Sky's influence could be negated.

Indian Affairs, meanwhile, did not abandon its campaign to get the One Arrow band to relocate. Nor did the department have any qualms about how it was achieved. Taking advantage of Chief One Arrow's early release from Stony Mountain penitentiary, Edgar Dewdney visited the gravely ill chief in St. Boniface on 19 April 1886. With Archbishop Alexandre-Antonin Taché serving as translator, the lieutenant governor asked the chief to send word to his band that it should move to Beardy's reserve. One Arrow countered with his own request: that his people be protected "from mistreatment by the White race."[42]

There was also continued pressure at the band level. In the spring of 1886, Louis Marion, the new One Arrow farm instructor, became the latest Indian official to try "to get them to quietly move over toward Beardy's Reserve."[43] Marion, a Métis from Duck Lake, likely had past dealings with the band because of the close ties between the Willow Cree and the South Branch Métis communities. He had also defied Riel in 1885 by refusing to join his army and knew that "many [Indians at Batoche] were forced to join" the rebellion.[44] But Marion was no more successful than those who had tried before him. The band was determined to remain on its reserve.

By mid-June 1886, Indian Agent Adams was at a complete loss about "how we shall manage them" and asked for further instructions.[45] Hayter Reed responded almost a full month later that "there is nothing to add upon the subject." Even though it was "most desirable" that the One Arrow band be "induced if possible to make the change," the assistant Indian commissioner said there was to be no compulsion or "any suffering."[46] What Reed conveniently forgot, though, is that the One Arrow people, including Almighty Voice, had suffered. He also failed to appreciate that attempting to get the Willow Cree to leave their reserve was ironically what had made them rebels during the North-West

Indian Agent Robert S. McKenzie (far right) was responsible
for the One Arrow band. UNIVERSITY OF SASKATCHEWAN, UNIVERSITY
ARCHIVES AND SPECIAL COLLECTIONS, MORTON MANUSCRIPTS COLLECTION,
C555-2-10-5-m-p01

Rebellion. Indian Affairs may not have forcibly rounded up the
One Arrow people and led them away, as the Métis had done in
March 1885, but it did try to starve the band into abandoning
its reserve.

This insidious policy was never mentioned in the annual
department report for 1886. It was simply stated that the rebel
bands in the Prince Albert agency "are all quiet and behaving
very well, are working hard and doing all they can to redeem
the past."[47] Their redemption, though, would be decided by the
Canadian government. Indian Affairs may have abandoned its
attempt to relocate the One Arrow people, but it still believed
that they had to earn the resumption of their annuity payments.

Food remained a key weapon in reforming—subjugating might
be closer to the truth—the One Arrow people. Because of the
disruption caused by the rebellion, no crop was planted on the
reserve in the spring of 1885. The situation was much the same
the following year because of the push to relocate. Those band
members who remained on reserve consequently had to subsist
on garden produce, mostly potatoes and turnips, supplemented
by government rations. It's little wonder that T. P. Wadsworth, the

new inspector of Indian Agencies, counted only thirty-five people when he visited the reserve in December 1886. The rest of the band, probably including Almighty Voice, was "away hunting."[48]

What made things worse was the reappointment of J. M. Rae as Indian agent after Charles Adams was dismissed in the fall of 1886 because of "poor judgement."[49] That poor judgement evidently included giving the band fifty bushels of potatoes during one of Adams' visits to the reserve, a violation of department standing orders. Rae resumed his past practice of refusing to provision the band, sometimes for weeks. But he soon became a liability—not simply because of his heavy drinking and irascible behaviour—but because of a number of administrative irregularities.

Wadsworth's on-site review of Rae's books and inventory in April 1887 resulted in a whopping seventy-five-page indictment of the Indian agent's practices. He questioned, for example, the agent's habit of feeding his family with rations intended for bands under his direction. He also highlighted Rae's infrequent and short-lived visits to the agency reserves. "If the agent would stay longer," Wadsworth sarcastically observed, "the novelty of his presence would soon wear off." The damning document was sent to Indian Commissioner Dewdney who repeatedly scribbled in the margins, "Agent asked to explain, followed by his initials, "ED."[50] But no explanation could save Rae—not even the fact that he was the prime minister's cousin—and he was dismissed and replaced by Robert Sutherland McKenzie in December 1887.

McKenzie's appointment as Indian agent coincided with some administrative changes. The Indian agency for One Arrow had been based at Fort Carlton until the rebellion and then headquartered at Prince Albert. In 1887, Indian Affairs created two smaller agencies so that agents oversaw fewer Indians, and, theoretically, could exercise more direct control over them. The new Duck Lake agency, situated on Beardy's reserve, was responsible for about 650 Indians in seven bands (Beardy's & Okemasis, One Arrow, John Smith, James Smith, Cumberland or Fort à la Corne, and Chakastaypasin).

Despite the reorganization, McKenzie seemed cast from the same mould as his predecessor. In his first report after assuming

Métis Louis Marion served as farm instructor for the One Arrow
band. PROVINCIAL ARCHIVES OF SASKATCHEWAN R-A70

his duties, he called the One Arrow people a "worthless lot" who
were "never satisfied" and had to be "well-watched."[51] This opinion only hardened during his tenure. Two years later, he derided
them as the "most backward in the agency."[52] Farm instructor
Louis Marion apparently shared this view and refused to live on
the One Arrow reserve until ordered to do so in the fall of 1888.
The department realized, yet again, that the band needed practical help in breaking the land and bringing it under cultivation.
Otherwise, band members, like Almighty Voice, would continue
to leave the reserve to pursue subsistence activities. Indeed, the
band's slow agricultural progress, according to Indian Affairs, was
largely attributable to its failure to tend to its fields. Starvation
apparently had nothing to do with its uncooperative effort.

Indian Affairs seemed to lessen its vise grip on the One Arrow
people when it restored annuity payments in the late 1880s. Some
members were paid in 1888 for "good behaviour," and then, the
entire band was paid in 1889. But the restoration of annuities
ironically coincided with a new Indian Affairs initiative to reduce
spending as much as possible.

In October 1890, Hayter Reed, who had been promoted to
Indian commissioner upon Edgar Dewdney's election to the House
of Commons in 1888, sent a blistering letter to Indian Agent
McKenzie when he asked for lanterns, kettles, and some agricul-

tural tools. Reed charged that McKenzie did "not quite realize the Department's policy towards the Indians, and for the sake of your own success in the service, it is absolutely essential that you should do so." He then demanded to know how the requested items "would make them [Indians] self supporting." McKenzie, according to Reed, should confine his requests "to the narrowest limits ... the time has arrived ... [for] throwing in a large measure the burden of their maintenance upon themselves." He concluded by warning the Indian agent that "[t]he expenses of your agency must be materially lessened, and if this cannot be done ... some radical change will have to be devised."[53]

The message was not lost on McKenzie, who tried to find savings wherever possible, while submitting positive reports about his agency. In 1895, for example, he now boasted: "I am pleased to say that throughout this agency every thing is satisfactory. In fact I have no hesitation in expressing my opinion today that my agency is second to none in the territory. I am proud to say this, as when I took charge it was one of the worst."[54]

Almighty Voice came of age during these years. He was a renowned hunter, deadly with a gun. This skill became ever more important as government rations were "increasingly reduced" in the early 1890s. (Hayter Reed had once suggested to Agent McKenzie that bands should be encouraged to hunt game, even if it meant leaving the reserve.) He also found work in nearby communities. It was probably the priests at Duck Lake who gave him his other name, Jean Baptiste, even though he never converted to Catholicism. In November 1888, Almighty Voice, then fourteen, was listed in the agency financial records as a freighter ("Baptist Indian") for the merchant Stobart and Company in Duck Lake.[55] He might have been hauling hay, something the One Arrow reserve supplied to local communities. The work would have made him familiar to the police, who needed winter feed for their horses.

At some point, likely during one of his visits to Duck Lake, he was photographed, although the circumstances or photographer are not known. The image also did not surface until half a century later. The studio portrait captures a young man, about six feet tall, with strong features, staring straight ahead with piercing dark eyes. His wrap-around coat, over a light shirt, appears to have been made from an old blanket and is held closed by his right hand. There is a wide beaded choker around his neck; strings of the same beads are used to tie his ornately decorated braids. Even more striking are his hide leggings, an interplay of geometric patterns in alternating bright colours, featuring a tomahawk motif. He clearly took pride in his appearance, especially the bead work on his clothing—and others noticed.

Almighty Voice's distinctive facial scar—a bullet graze running from his left ear to the corner of his mouth—might have been the result of a hunting accident. Or it could have been caused by a fight. Pee-yeh-chee of the Red Pheasant band told police guide and interpreter Sam Ballendine that Almighty Voice helped with the preparations for a sun dance at the west end of Duck Lake in late May 1895. "The bead work on his clothing," he remembered, "drew my attention to him." After the ceremony started, Pee-yeh-chee caught Almighty Voice "molesting my wife … he was a very wild young man."[56] This youthful recklessness might explain why the Willow Cree man had once threatened to kill Indian Agent McKenzie. The reasons for the threat are not known—maybe McKenzie tried to intimidate the young man or withheld rations—but other Indian Affairs officials and the local NWMP knew about it. McKenzie was said to be wary of Almighty Voice, but the Willow Cree man was equally distrustful of the Indian agent.[57]

In 1890, sixteen-year-old Almighty Voice married the daughter of Napace (ticket #17) and was with the young girl (described as "under age") for two years. He then took the daughter of Rock Child (ticket #60) as his wife. They had a son in May 1893 who died a little more than a year later of "consumption." Although some accounts suggest that Almighty Voice took a third wife, the daughter of The Rump, the treaty annuity pay lists for One Arrow document only two consecutive marriages in the early 1890s. He was not a polygamist.[58]

The death of Almighty Voice's infant son was reflective of the poor health of the One Arrow population, something that the young father knew from personal experience. Four of his siblings had died in the 1880s.[59] Scrofula (cervical tuberculous

The Canadian government wanted to abolish traditional Cree practices, such as this Grass Dance on the Beardy's & Okemasis reserve in the early 1890s. PROVINCIAL ARCHIVES OF SASKATCHEWAN R-B980

lymphadenitis), according to McKenzie, was the big killer among the "very young." But other diseases took their toll as well. In July 1894, the Indian agent admitted to the new Indian Commissioner Amedée Emmanuel Forget that "the health of the Indians ... under my charge has not been so good." Over the past winter and spring, German measles, influenza, and scarlet fever were "prevalent" in the district.[60] Whether Almighty Voice blamed the sickness on newcomers is debatable, but death certainly came with reserve life and the impoverished living conditions.

The need for fresh meat might have been one of the reasons Almighty Voice killed the stray cow in the spring of 1895. He would have made the obvious link between starvation and sickness. But there are other possible reasons for his action. Almighty Voice, as the oldest son, might have been supporting his family. His second wife was also pregnant at the time and his brother-in-law Flying Sound, the son of Rock Child, was with him. Almighty Voice might also have killed the cow to help feed the participants at the sun dance on Beardy's & Okemasis reserve. He and his male relatives attended the ceremony and would have needed food.[61]

Almighty Voice was not the first to "illegally" kill a cow. There had been several reported instances on Treaty Six reserves over the past few years. In January 1891, for example, John Mahakis of the Pakan band (Whitefish Lake First Nation) had killed a government cow without the Indian agent's approval. The matter was quickly resolved when Mahakis agreed to replace the cow.[62] A similar situation arose in March 1895 when Joseph Badger of the John Smith reserve (Muskoday First Nation) butchered a government cow without permission. In his defence, Badger maintained that the animal belonged to the band and that no harm had been done because he planned to replace it. Indian Agent McKenzie wanted Badger punished for destroying department property, even though the real crime was that the band was not receiving any rations or supplies at the time.[63]

What made the Almighty Voice case different is that he and Flying Sound had killed a settler's cow. But that still doesn't explain why the pair were arrested on 22 October 1895, especially when Almighty Voice had offered to give the settler a horse for the butchered cow. Why wasn't Almighty Voice allowed to resolve the matter in traditional fashion by compensating the aggrieved rancher? And why was the warrant issued five months after the cow met its death? Perhaps the arrest had more to do with the frustration of the Indian Affairs department—and Indian Agent Robert McKenzie in particular—with the One Arrow people's slow adoption of agriculture, Christianity, and education, especially in comparison to other Cree bands.

In June 1895, the Conservative government had come under withering criticism in the House of Commons for its mishandling of Indian Affairs. Too much money was being expended for too few results.[64] Two months later, in August 1895, Prime Minister Mackenzie Bowell, with Hayter Reed at his side, toured the Duck Lake agency after his official duties at the Regina Territorial Exhibition. The ideal of progressive, industrious Indians would have been challenged by reality on the One Arrow reserve. It was not the kind of image the Department of Indian Affairs sought to project about its work and its Indigenous charges.[65] At least Bowell, Reed, and others could take some solace in the steps already taken to end "heathen" cultural practices. In July 1895, the Canadian government had amended the Indian Act to prohibit prairie Indian ceremonies, such as the recent sun dance on Beardy's & Okemasis reserve.

Conservative Prime Minister Mackenzie Bowell (seated in wagon on far right) visited the Duck Lake area in September 1895, just one month before the start of the Almighty Voice incident.
GLENBOW ARCHIVES NA919.1

At the local level, Indian Agent McKenzie became extremely aggressive in getting the One Arrow Cree to send their children to school. Attendance at the reserve day school, organized and run by the Roman Catholic church since 1890, was spotty at best. Parents were reluctant to send their children because they associated the school with baptism and conversion, which they actively resisted. The school was also a bare-bones operation. In her report for 1891, teacher P. L. Lafond stated that she had issued 219 13/16 biscuits to ten students during the entire school year.[66]

At McKenzie's urging, the One Arrow school was closed in September 1893 in favour of sending children to Catholic residential schools at Lebret and Duck Lake. Once again, parents refused to cooperate, prompting the Indian agent to threaten to withhold rations. Then, in early 1895, an exasperated McKenzie called for more "compulsive measures"—namely, forcibly taking children from parents and placing them in schools and arresting those parents who interfered with their child's removal. Both Indian Commissioner A. E. Forget and NWMP Commissioner L.

43

W. Herchmer (the former inspector of Indian agencies) refused to support this course of action. It was too drastic.

McKenzie consequently settled on an alternative tack. He sought to remove those individuals—so-called "troublemakers"—who had influence over the band and effectively held back "advancement." And he was able to move against these band members because of another amendment (section 117) to the Indian Act in 1894 that empowered Indian Affairs employees, in their capacity as justices of the peace, to pursue Criminal Code violations.[67]

The first to be arrested was Almighty Voice's father. John Sounding Sky appeared before One Arrow farm instructor Louis Marion in Duck Lake on 18 October 1895 on charges of stealing a coat, containing some money and papers, from Louis Couture, the farm instructor for the Ahtahkakoop band in the Carlton Agency. In other words, a farm instructor from one agency swore an affidavit before a farm instructor in another agency. Sounding Sky was genuinely puzzled by Couture's accusation and could not understand why he was sentenced to six months' hard labour in the Prince Albert police barracks. He continued to proclaim his innocence to Indian Agent McKenzie after his incarceration, while letting it be known that Couture would be held personally accountable.[68]

Almighty Voice was taken to Duck Lake after his 22 October 1895 arrest and scheduled to appear in court the next morning for cattle killing. PROVINCIAL ARCHIVES OF SASKATCHEWAN S-B10214

On 19 October 1895—coincidentally, the day after Sounding Sky's theft conviction—McKenzie issued an arrest warrant for Almighty Voice and Flying Sound for killing the cow. The charge against the men was based on information provided by another, unnamed band member. The warrant also called for the arrest of Good Young Woman, the sister of Almighty Voice and wife of Larocque (ticket #61), for stealing a blanket and some cups and saucers from the police barracks at Batoche. NWMP Sergeant Colin Colebrook, a fourteen-year veteran of the force, lodged that complaint.

Colebrook and Constable William Hume executed the warrant three days later when treaty payments were made at One Arrow on 22 October. The mounties expected the three to be there; it was standard police practice to apprehend individuals at these kinds of gatherings. It's also why they travelled to One Arrow by wagon and not horseback. But before the arrests were made, the identity of those wanted was quietly confirmed by François Dumont, another band member and apparently, an informant.[69] Dumont may also have been the person who reported the killing of the cow to Indian Agent McKenzie.

The three prisoners were taken first to Batoche and then on to Duck Lake, where they were to appear before Agent McKenzie the next morning. But Almighty Voice would miss his court date because of his escape from custody during the night. If he feared for his life, because of a supposed hanging threat, why did the Willow Cree man not take his brother-in-law with him? After all, Flying Sound was arrested for the same crime and would have faced the same punishment. There is no evidence, though, that NWMP Constable Dickson ever uttered any such threat or even spoke to the sleeping Indians. And if anyone was going to be threatened, it was Sounding Sky, who not only had repeated run-ins with the law but been a thorn in the side of local Indian officials for years.

Almighty Voice did have reason to flee, though, choosing "freedom" over "slavery."[70] His elderly grandfather One Arrow had been sent away to Stony Mountain penitentiary for his supposed part in the 1885 North-West Rebellion, only to be never seen again. And then, just days before Almighty Voice's own arrest, his

father, Sounding Sky, had been brought before the court on questionable charges and taken away to serve six months in the Prince
Albert gaol. Was Sounding Sky going to survive his imprisonment
or suffer the same fate as One Arrow? It's not difficult to imagine
what was roiling through Almighty Voice's head as he lay in the
makeshift bed in the Duck Lake barracks. He feared confinement,
whether on the reserve or in a cell. It meant sickness and loss. He
also deeply distrusted Indian Affairs officials. They brought suffering and hardship. In a few hours he was about to face the white
man's justice in the form of Indian Agent McKenzie, someone he
had threatened to kill. No wonder he ran when he got the chance.

CHAPTER TWO

Come On, Old Boy

"Worse than bloodhounds ... they fetch their men every time."[1] That's how Montana's *Fort Benton Record* applauded the North-West Mounted Police for their dogged pursuit of three smugglers along the international border in April 1877. This reputation to always get their man quickly became part of mountie lore. It was one of the reasons why the police were so admired and respected: that unerring ability to bring criminals to Canadian justice. And members of the force believed in the saying, too. They had every confidence that the fugitive Almighty Voice would be re-arrested within days, if not hours, of his escape from the Duck Lake barracks. His flight was a rash, spur-of-the-moment decision encouraged by the carelessness of one of his guards. And he would probably be found on the One Arrow reserve with his family. It was only a matter of sending a lone policeman to retrieve him. But Almighty Voice was not prepared to surrender, not prepared to be manacled like some trapped animal. Indeed, the lengths to which he would go to evade capture were demonstrated by his early morning crossing of the South Saskatchewan River near St. Laurent de Grandin. Grabbing some discarded wood to keep himself afloat, he somehow navigated the frigid water to the other side and then made his way on foot to his family's home for help. Almighty Voice knew, though, that he couldn't find safety there, that the mounted police would come looking for him, and he sought refuge in the hills where he had hunted since his boyhood. A chance encounter with his pursuer would lead to a bloody showdown that transformed Almighty Voice from a petty criminal into the most wanted man in Canada. He would never really be free again.

≈

NWMP Sergeant Colin Colebrook, the non-commissioned officer in charge of the Batoche detachment, took it upon himself
to find Almighty Voice. He was the mountie who had made the
original arrest on 22 October 1895, and when he learned that the
Willow Cree man had slipped away from the Duck Lake barracks
that night, he led a small patrol in a sweep through the One Arrow
reserve early the next evening. Colebrook didn't find the fugitive
Indian. But he knew Almighty Voice was hiding there, or at least
that's what an informant said.

The English-born Colin Colebrook (regimental #605)
enlisted in the North-West Mounted Police in 1881.

Superintendent George Moffatt, in the meantime, travelled by train to Duck Lake to personally investigate the circumstances behind Almighty Voice's escape. The officer commanding Prince Albert's "F" division was annoyed that Sergeant Harry Keenan had removed the irons from the three prisoners when he took custody of them at Duck Lake. But the twenty-seven-year veteran of the force was angrier with Constable Robert Dickson for allowing Almighty Voice to steal away during his watch and formally charged the constable with negligence. Moffatt suggested to the NWMP commissioner that Dickson had either fallen asleep or went outside, allowing the prisoner "to walk off without any trouble or hurry."

Moffatt also interviewed Colebrook about the search for Almighty Voice and instructed him to offer a ten-dollar reward for the man's capture or information that would lead to his arrest. The police superintendent was convinced that Almighty Voice would probably remain close to the reserve and his family. But if he left the area, Colebrook was authorized to go after him. "I think we will catch the man sooner or later," Moffatt assured the commissioner. "He subsists by travelling."[2]

On Friday, 25 October, three days after the escape, Colebrook was tipped off that Almighty Voice was on the move. He wasn't alone. He had a young woman with him: thirteen-year-old Small Face from the James Smith reserve, located about eighty-five miles to the northeast, straddling the Saskatchewan River. Colebrook hurriedly left Batoche that afternoon, taking along a pack pony to carry the few supplies he could find in the reserve storehouse. No other men from the detachment went with him, though he hired François (Frank) Dumont from One Arrow to serve as his guide.

Colebrook wanted to get on the trail as soon as possible to take advantage of the first autumn snowfall as he tracked the fugitive. There was no need for a larger police search party because Colebrook expected Almighty Voice to willingly give himself up once he was located. And that was Dumont's job. A Métis who had entered treaty as a "straggler" in 1884 and then participated in the North-West Rebellion the following year (he was related to Louis Riel's general, Gabriel Dumont), Dumont had spent five years in the United States before returning to One Arrow in

1890 and rejoining the band (ticket #58). He and Almighty Voice apparently didn't like each other, probably because farm instructor Louis Marion used Dumont as a snitch.[3] He had identified Almighty Voice at his arrest—as the person who had killed the cow—and probably told Colebrook that the escapee had left the reserve. Now, he was helping the mounted police track him down.

Sergeant Colin Campbell Colebrook rode east that late October day with a decade-and-a-half experience on the force. A former clerk from London, England, with no previous military service, Colebrook was a rakish, black-haired, brown-eyed nineteen-year-old when he was engaged in Ottawa in September 1881 and given regimental #605. He was posted throughout present-day Saskatchewan for various terms of duty: Fort Qu'Appelle, Moosomin, Regina, Battleford, and Prince Albert. Colebrook had a checkered police career, much like other mounties at the time. His service record contains frequent references to minor breaches of discipline. He was promoted to corporal and then sergeant by 1887 but demoted three years later for being absent without permission. He had also purchased his discharge in August 1886, seemingly intent on leaving the force to return to England, but he re-engaged two months later.

During the North-West Rebellion, Colebrook accepted the surrender of Chief Big Bear at Fort Carlton on 4 July 1885. In the staged photograph of the event, the mustached corporal stands resolutely behind the old chief in a dirty khaki uniform with his rifle at the ready. He was also involved in the capture of a big-time criminal in 1890. By October 1895, Colebrook, once again a sergeant, was married with a four-year-old son, Kenneth, and stationed at Batoche. His wife, Ida, worked as cook for the detachment. Just the week before his arrest of Almighty Voice, his application for re-engagement was heard before Superintendent Moffatt in Prince Albert and approved for one year. At his medical examination, he stood 5 feet, 9½ inches and weighed 138 pounds, with good eyesight and sound feet. Most notably, his temperament was given as "cool."[4]

The NWMP assumed that Almighty Voice and his young companion would flee southeast along the winter section of the Carlton Trail to the Touchwood Hills (south of the Quill Lakes)

Colebrook (second from left), in a dirty khaki uniform, accepted
the surrender of Chief Big Bear at Fort Carlton in July 1885.
PROVINCIAL ARCHIVES OF SASKATCHEWAN R-A8812

and the Cree reserves there. Detachments in the area were alerted
to watch for the fugitive Indian. But Almighty Voice planned to
go east, through the less accessible Carrot River country, to elude
capture. He and Small Face slipped away on foot late Thursday
night, 24 October, as the first snow of the season started to fall, and
walked a short distance the next day. Later accounts had the pair
fleeing the reserve in a cart, but that would have attracted attention—something Almighty Voice wanted to avoid. A cart would
also limit where he could go. When it became dark, Almighty
Voice disappeared for a few hours and returned with a stolen grey
horse. The pair rode through the night along the Carlton Trail
(known as the Hoodoo Trail in that area) before picking up a
smaller trail sometime on Saturday and striking east through the
rolling parkland, dotted with clumps of trees and small saline lakes
and sloughs. Once among the isolated, sparsely populated hills,
Almighty Voice took time to camp and rest the horse.

Colebrook and Dumont were not far behind. By Sunday, they
had reached Hoodoo, a stopping place and mail station on the
Carlton Trail, just northwest of present-day St. Benedict, and
determined that Almighty Voice had not come that way. That

afternoon, they were joined by NWMP interpreter Tom McKay, who had been sent by Superintendent Moffatt to assist with the search. Working together, they located the place where Almighty Voice and Small Face had left the main trail. The three tracked the man and woman through the brush-riddled country, southeast of the Carrot River, until it became too dark. Early next morning before sunrise (Monday, 28 October), Colebrook and Dumont readied to resume the search, while McKay doubled back to Batoche with Colebrook's packhorse for more food rations. Once back on the Hoodoo Trail, McKay met a police constable and his team hauling supplies from the Batoche detachment for the search. McKay grabbed what he needed and then set off again to find the mountie and his scout, now a day ahead and getting closer to their quarry.

The searchers were in the saddle early again Tuesday morning, anxious to get going as soon as the sun started to come up. It had been almost one week since the escape of Almighty Voice. Dumont had carefully inspected every campsite they came across and told Colebrook the night before, "I am sure we will see him tomorrow."[5] They were probably just east of Waterhen Lake, near present-day Beatty, about sixty miles from One Arrow. The land was etched by deep, heavily timbered ravines that sheltered shallow creeks running northeast to the Saskatchewan. Because of the thick brush, the pair stumbled upon Almighty Voice and Small Face almost by accident. Colebrook spotted them a short distance away and quietly called out to Dumont, who was looking for their tracks, "Here they are."

Almighty Voice had just shot a prairie chicken for breakfast and was tying it to a bundle on the pony, behind where Small Face was sitting. Neither saw the policeman and his scout approaching. Dumont pulled out a service revolver that Colebrook had given him and then called out after them not to run. "I want to ask you something," he said in Cree. Almighty Voice told Small Face that it was a trap and started loading his double-barrelled shotgun. Dumont expected Colebrook to rush the couple and gave his horse a sharp whip with the reins to get going. But the mountie calmly walked his horse forward, and Dumont had to stop and wait for him. Colebrook didn't want to alarm the fugitive but was nonetheless confident he would surrender.

Once together, the pair slowly trotted towards their quarry about 150 yards away. Almighty Voice, still busy loading his shotgun, shouted to Dumont to tell the policeman, "I want to shoot the sergeant." Dumont translated the warning for Colebrook. Small Face, now crying, pleaded with Almighty Voice not to use his gun. Dumont also told him not to shoot. But Almighty Voice ignored them as he capped his shotgun. "He's going to shoot, he's going to shoot," Dumont repeated, his voice betraying his fear.

Colebrook stopped his horse about twenty feet from Almighty Voice and calmly said in his English accent, "Come on, old boy." But the fugitive, with his shotgun now primed, started walking backwards. He stopped two or three times, dropped to one knee and took aim at the mountie. Each time, he yelled in Cree, "Go away, go away." Colebrook's horse was spooked by the shouting and reared up, nearly spilling his rider to the ground. The horse then refused to move.

NWMP Sergeant Colebrook took it upon himself to find Almighty Voice after he had fled from the Duck Lake barracks. GLENBOW ARCHIVES PA-3807-7

After Colebrook got control of his horse, he continued to ride towards Almighty Voice, while Dumont swung wide to try to get behind him. They passed Small Face, who sat frozen on her pony, but were losing ground to Almighty Voice, who had scurried to a nearby bluff about fifty yards away. Colebrook now picked up the pace, with his gloved right arm raised in the halt signal, saying over and over, "Come on, old boy." Almighty Voice knelt down again by the bluff and took aim at the policeman, but then stood up. Colebrook kept coming. Almighty Voice slipped into the bush and trained his shotgun on the mountie. Colebrook was about twenty-five feet away when the blast threw him from his horse. The sergeant was dead before he hit the ground.

Hearing the gunshot, Dumont cautiously rode around the bluff and spotted Colebrook lying motionless with blood seeping out of his upper chest. Almighty Voice was looking down at the mountie but then scrambled back into the bush. Dumont watched for a few nervous minutes to see if Colebrook was still alive. But he detected no movement, not even breathing. The eerie silence was broken only by the policeman's horse, busily feeding as if nothing had happened.

Dumont decided to get help—he remembered passing a house about six miles back—and rode past Small Face, who had not moved since he had first called out to them. He was worried, though, that Almighty Voice might come after him, and in his panic, accidentally discharged his revolver when he tried to cock the hammer while riding off. The shot startled Small Face out of her trance-like state and digging her heels into the side of her pony, she galloped after Almighty Voice, who was running away from the bluff. She followed, looking back occasionally, until he grew tired and got on the pony with her. The pair rode for some time before deciding it was safe to stop. Almighty Voice gave Small Face a few things to live on, telling her that she couldn't go on with him and that she should walk to the nearest place. "They won't leave me alone," he said, "for what I have done to them." He promised to try to meet her at "the closed rock" (Barrier Lake)[6] near Nut Lake and then rode off. Small Face never saw Almighty Voice again.

Dumont found another house, closer to the place of the murder, and frantically told the two occupants (one of them E. B. Cay) what had happened. They weren't sure, at first, what he was talking about. One of the men set off for the mountie stationed at Flett Springs, east of Goose Hunting Creek, and returned more than two hours later with Constable Charles Tennant, who was on fire duty in the area. Dumont repeated his story—how he was certain that Colebrook had been killed—and then led Tennant to the slain sergeant.

In examining the body and the mortal shotgun wound, they found the left hand open, without a glove, and a small, non-regulation-issue revolver within reach. Colebrook had apparently concealed the weapon, at the ready, inside his coat. It could explain why Almighty Voice fired: he might have caught a glimpse of the gun when the mountie's horse reared. Colebrook's corpse was loaded into a wagon brought by the two men from the house. Tennant asked them to take the dead sergeant to Kinistino, while he and Dumont tried to pick up the trail of Almighty Voice, now a murderer on the run.

Word of Colebrook's death reached Prince Albert late the next day, 30 October. Constable Tennant had hurriedly scribbled a few lines in pencil on a scrap of paper and asked the two men transporting the body to hand the note to Corporal William J. Bowdridge at the Kinistino detachment. The news was then relayed to Superintendent Moffatt, who in turn telegraphed the NWMP commissioner in Regina that Colebrook had been killed by "the escaped Indian prisoner" and that Tennant was "on trail of a murderer." That's all he knew. "I have no particulars," he confessed in a follow-up letter that same night. "I am very much in the dark as yet."[7]

The commissioner's office immediately distributed a circular letter to all divisions across the prairies, imploring them to be on the lookout for "a young man, tall, slim, known as Jean Baptiste or Almighty Voice ... what would be considered a good looking Indian."[8] Superintendent Moffatt was convinced, though, that Almighty Voice would seek out help in one of two directions: he would either head north to the James Smith and Big Head (Cumberland) reserves near Fort à la Corne on the Saskatchewan River or east to the Nut Lake (Yellow Quill) reserve. He consequently dispatched a three-man search team, under Inspector

NWMP Commissioner L. W. Herchmer (seated third from left) and
Superintendents Sévère Gagnon and George Moffatt (seated next to
Herchmer, respectively, on his left) would lead the search for Almighty
Voice. RCMP HISTORICAL COLLECTIONS UNIT, REGINA SK 1972.68.72

John Beresford Allan, to Kinistino at daybreak on 31 October
to look for the fugitive Indian. Getting there would not be easy
because of the early arrival of winter. The South Saskatchewan
River, the same river that Almighty Voice had crossed during his
escape only a week earlier, was heavy with floating ice, and the
mounted policemen and their horses had to be ferried across in a
skiff. Even then, they got caught in an ice jam and landed about
a mile below their starting point.

Moffatt also ordered a second group of mounties from Batoche
to Harperview (near present-day Birch Hills) on the Prince Albert–
Kinistino–Melfort trail to retrieve the body of Colebrook and take
it to Prince Albert. Out of respect for their fallen colleague, they
brought Colebrook's wife, Ida, with them. She had answered the
phone at the Batoche detachment when news of her husband's
death was called in. When the party reached William Harper's
home, they were shocked to find the mountie's frozen corpse in a
makeshift coffin in the outhouse. It was being kept there until it
was safe to cross the river.[9]

Several members of NWMP "F" Division in Prince Albert were involved in the search for Almighty Voice. PROVINCIAL ARCHIVES OF SASKATCHEWAN R-B894

Inspector Allan and his men reached Kinistino the same day they left Prince Albert and found Small Face already held there. She had been found on her home reserve and was probably still quite shaken by the shooting and fearful of what might happen to her. Through an interpreter, Small Face told Allan that Colebrook had "flushed them suddenly" and that Almighty Voice had shouted at Dumont "to tell him to go away or he would shoot ... he would not be taken by a Policeman." But the mountie would not listen—"merely held up his gloved hand as a warning not to shoot"—and kept on coming until stopped dead by the shotgun blast.[10] At no part in her account, dutifully taken down by Allan, did Small Voice say anything about Almighty Voice being threatened with hanging or why he refused to surrender to Colebrook.

Once the interview was over, the inspector sent Small Face with one of the constables to Harperview and then on to Prince Albert, where Moffatt charged her with being an accessory to murder and placed her in the guard room. Allan and his party left that same evening—"destination unknown"[11] in Moffatt's words—in a desperate effort to find Almighty Voice before he vanished into the landscape. The inspector knew that the elapsed time since Colebrook's shooting was working against the police in the search for his killer.

Indian Agent Robert McKenzie, by contrast, was in no hurry to inform his superiors about the tragedy, even though he admitted, "I have not the slightest doubt that he [Almighty Voice] would shoot me if he got the chance."[12] McKenzie probably felt partly responsible, if not embarrassed by what had happened. It was not until 1 November that he wrote Indian Commissioner A. E. Forget in Regina about arresting Almighty Voice for cattle killing and how he had escaped before his trial. Colebrook's death was not mentioned until almost the end.

The letter was also surprising for what was not in it. He was silent about how two other One Arrow people had been taken into custody at the same time and held in the same gaol. He also said nothing about how he proceeded with their trials the next morning and gave Good Young Woman a warning and handed Flying Sound, Almighty Voice's companion, a suspended sentence. Nor did he inform Forget that Almighty Voice's father, Sounding Sky, had been sentenced to six months' hard labour just days before his son's arrest. When McKenzie finally provided this information to Indian Commissioner Forget eleven days later, after Almighty Voice was taken into custody, he sheepishly confessed, "I did not think it necessary to bother you."

Senior Indian Affairs officials had been informed by telegram about Colebrook's shooting. In fact, they had already extended their condolences to the police leadership. But they were still annoyed by McKenzie's delay and the lack of information. Someone wrote, "Agt has had ample time to report facts" in the margin of his letter.[13] The incident also made a mockery of the department's insistence, in its annual reports, that Indians increasingly appreciated "the benefits which they receive under the humane and wise policy of the Government."[14] Almighty Voice certainly didn't look upon the relationship that way.

Indian Affairs had also lost control of the situation. The capture of the murderer Almighty Voice was a mounted police matter. And it was in the best interests of the department to help the mounties apprehend the fugitive as soon as possible. To that end, acting on his own initiative, McKenzie confiscated the guns of One Arrow band members. That it was fall hunting season—and the band depended on game—did not matter. He wanted to ensure that Almighty Voice's home community did not help him. Beyond that, McKenzie did not know what else to do.

The village of Kinistino, near where Almighty Voice killed Sergeant Colebrook, served as temporary NWMP search headquarters during the late fall of 1895. WWW.PRAIRIE-TOWNS.COM.

Advice was soon forthcoming from the farm instructor for the Big Head and James Smith bands, based at the Hudson's Bay Company post at Fort à la Corne, just below or east of the Saskatchewan River forks.[15] On 31 October, two days after Colebrook's death, John Gordon reported that the local Cree already knew what had happened and believed that Almighty Voice would remain in the Carrot River country. Gordon, though, expected the murderer to seek out the Saulteaux to the east at Stony Creek (also known as Beatty, southeast of present-day Melfort) or even go as far as Nut Lake, the home of his paternal grandfather. The mounted police, he suggested, could probably intercept Almighty Voice if a patrol was hurriedly dispatched to the region.

Gordon also warned that bands hunting in the area would

give refuge to the fugitive and recommended they be rounded up, by force if necessary, so that Almighty Voice was on his own. "It will have a very bad effect," Gordon cautioned, "if he manages to escape." The farm instructor found it "strange" that Dumont did not "fire at once" after the mounted policeman had been shot. The scout needed to be interviewed about the circumstances behind Colebrook's death and explain why he had allowed Almighty Voice to get away.[16]

The beginning of November passed without any more news about the search, let alone whether the murderer had been apprehended. And NWMP Commissioner Lawrence W. Herchmer grew increasingly frustrated with each day of silence. Despite having no police experience, Herchmer had replaced the ineffectual A. G. Irvine as commissioner in April 1886. The appointment of an outsider alienated many senior mounties who coveted the position. But Conservative Prime Minister John A. Macdonald knew the Herchmer family and looked to Lawrence for steady, efficient leadership.[17] There was also the expectation that, as a former Indian Affairs official, Herchmer would ensure that the mounted police would enforce the government's "management" of Indians. He did that, in large part, by introducing an interconnected network of regular patrols through the western interior, ostensibly to reinforce the police presence, but also to remove the potential for trouble by keeping Indian peoples separate and apart from white settlers. Now, he had a mountie murderer on the loose.

The shooting could not have come at a worse time. Herchmer's leadership was coming under greater scrutiny after almost a decade at the helm. In 1893, an official investigation of his so-called "mistakes and apprehensions" found that the commissioner often acted with "too much zeal." That was an obtuse way of saying, in the words of two mounted police historians, that he was "overbearing, vindictive, and ill-tempered."[18] If Herchmer's political enemies did some digging, they would have learned that he was the same government official who had downplayed the stories of hardship and privation on the One Arrow Reserve—coincidentally, Almighty Voice's home community—just before he was named commissioner. Herchmer realized that Almighty Voice's flight from justice was damaging to the reputation of the force—and his own—and exhorted Superintendent Moffatt, who was coordinating the manhunt from Prince Albert, to "keep every available man out, and give the murderer no chance to rest."[19]

Colebrook's body was temporarily held at Harperview (near present-day Birch Hills) before being taken across the Saskatchewan River for burial at Prince Albert. PRINCE ALBERT HISTORICAL SOCIETY, JAMES COLLECTION J-300

While senior police officials waited for any new information about the search, the administrative machinery of the force had ground on. The disciplinary hearing for Constable Robert Dickson, the man who had allowed Almighty Voice to escape, was held Wednesday, 30 October, before Superintendent Moffatt in Prince Albert. Dickson was fortunate that word of Colebrook's death did not reach the community until late that same day or his punishment could have been worse.

Moffatt had already collected sworn statements from the mounties on duty that night, including one from Dickson, when the superintendent visited Duck Lake and charged the constable with disobeying an order "thereby allowing an Indian prisoner to escape from custody." But when Dickson appeared before Moffatt in Prince Albert a week later, Moffat had—for some unknown

A NWMP honour guard with Colebrook's body at the Prince Albert barracks. KNUCKLE, *IN THE LINE OF DUTY*

reason—divided the original charge into two parts. The hearing lasted less than half an hour. The constable was not given an opportunity to respond to the amended charge after it was read aloud. Nor was any other evidence presented. Moffatt sternly rebuked Dickson for falling asleep on duty and then sentenced him to two months' hard labour and dismissal from the force.

Months later, Dickson would complain—all the way to the Canadian cabinet—that his hearing was "a farce" and "a scandalous abuse of authority." Not only was he denied a chance to speak, especially after the charge had been altered, but Moffatt's sleeping comment was opinion, not established fact. An internal review, though, found no wrongdoing and concluded that "under all circumstances he [Dickson] got off with a light sentence."[20]

Colebrook's body arrived in Prince Albert the day after the Dickson hearing. His police escort had to wait until late afternoon, 31 October, before attempting the treacherous river crossing. Acting Assistant NWMP Surgeon Dr. H. A. Lestock Reid performed the autopsy the next morning. His post-mortem findings were presented that afternoon at a hurriedly called coroner's inquest, chaired by Dr. Hugh U. Bain, a former mayor of Prince Albert. The shotgun blast had broken Colebrook's right collarbone and severed his carotid artery. Death was instantaneous. Bain then adjourned the inquest until the witnesses to the shooting could give testimony.

Superintendent Moffatt delayed the sergeant's funeral until Sunday, 3 November, to ensure that Mrs. Colebrook could get across the river from Batoche. Starting from the Prince Albert barracks at 2 p.m., a seven-pound-gun carriage carried Colebrook's casket to St. Mary's Church. Reverend William Moore conducted the service, using his address to remind the assembled townspeople that they should be thankful for the security provided by the police, especially the slain constable. The body was then taken to the graveyard and placed in a plot next to the mounted policemen and civilian volunteers who had died during the Battle of Duck Lake at the start of the North-West Rebellion in March 1885. Several local members of the Independent Order of Foresters performed a burial ceremony in honour of their lost brother, followed by three volleys by a police firing party. Ironically, Constable Dickson had helped dig Colebrook's grave. It was standard practice for the police to call on prisoners in the guard room to do this kind of work, and the disgraced mountie had just started his sentence. He would add this "piece of refined cruelty worthy of Russia" to his list of grievances.[21]

Over the next few days, Colebrook's tenure with the force was formally brought to an end. His earnings for his last fourteen days—at a dollar per day—were turned over to his widow. Mrs. Colebrook also secured the commissioner's permission to remain with her son at the Batoche detachment over the winter, where she would continue to cook and do other domestic tasks. Then, there was the hearing to discharge Colebrook from the force, effective the date of his death. The half-page certificate, form 84b, described the late sergeant's conduct during his police service as "very good."[22] Colebrook's kit was also returned to stores, including his long black boots, stable jacket and trousers, tunic, towel, and cotton sheets—even his woollen drawers. But his horse, saddle, and rifle were assumed to have been taken by Almighty Voice—and that rankled the police commissioner. No one knew otherwise.

This lack of news about the progress of the search was a

Colebrook was buried in the St. Mary's church cemetery in Prince Albert in early November 1895. His death at the hands of Almighty Voice sent shockwaves through white settlements in the Saskatchewan country. BILL WAISER

problem. By 4 November 1895, Assistant Commissioner J. H. McIllree had grown tired of waiting for information to reach Regina and sent a blistering telegram to Moffat: "If you have no parties out looking for the murderer you have better rectify the matter at once."[23] It was a puzzling comment—of course, there were people searching for Almighty Voice—but it underscored how anxiously the police leadership wanted Colebrook's killer brought to justice. The sergeant was only the second mountie to be murdered on duty since 1874.

The isolation of the country only added to the frustration. Search updates were often several days old. By Friday, 1 November, Constable Tennant and scout Dumont, along with NWMP interpreter McKay, who had joined them after Colebrook's shooting, had tracked Almighty Voice to the Big Head reserve but then lost him. He might have been trying to make contact with Small Face's grandfather, Old Dusty (or LaPoussier). The following Monday, the fugitive, riding the stolen grey pony, approached an old woman near her tent and asked about the local trails and where they led.[24]

Inspector Allan and his search party reached Fort à la Corne two days after the police scouts. He was relieved to hear that Almighty Voice was close at hand but wondered if he could be caught. It was an assessment based on years of experience as an officer in the Canadian militia prior to joining the mounted police. "We ... are terribly handicapped in every way," he sized up the situation. "It is a terrible country to ride through, and unless they [Indians] can be prevented giving him help he could hide for all time in the face of 100 men in pursuit."[25]

After conferring with farm instructor Gordon, Allan decided to call in any Indians out on the land hunting. The James Smith and Big Head bands were brought together at Gordon's home and ordered to camp there with the assurance that they would be fed. The police inspector reasoned they would have a better chance of locating Almighty Voice—a better chance of tracking him—if there were no other people in the search area. He also wanted to deny Almighty Voice any assistance, while small police parties fanned out in an attempt to flush him out. The mounties knew he was out there. Some of the Cree returning from their hunting camps reported seeing Almighty Voice. He was not hard to recognize in his distinctive white leggings.[26]

Inspector Allan also prepared a backup plan if Almighty Voice managed to slip from his grasp. "He will attempt to head back to his own reserve," he warned Superintendent Moffatt, "when he finds himself blocked here." That's where Almighty Voice could expect help, especially from his mother and wife. And the One Arrow people would shelter and protect him, according to Allan, because the reserve was "made up of a d_ _n [damn] bad lot of Indians" and Almighty Voice was "one of the worst." Revenge might also dictate the fugitive's movements. Allan reminded Moffatt that Almighty Voice had once threatened to shoot Indian Agent McKenzie, something he might carry out now that he was

As the search for Almighty Voice extended into late November 1895, NWMP Superintendent George Moffatt began to wonder if the fugitive would ever be captured. RCMP HISTORICAL COLLECTIONS UNIT, REGINA SK

"fighting with a halter round his neck." The only One Arrow Indian that Allan trusted was François Dumont, Colebrook's hired scout. And he sent him back to the reserve from Fort à la Corne so that he could "keep a keen eye peeled" for the mountie murderer.[27]

Superintendent Moffatt seized upon the report that Almighty Voice had been sighted as a call to action. All he had done to assist with the search—while anxiously waiting for any news—was to send another mounted police party, headed by Corporal Richard Vickers, to Kinistino and beyond if necessary. Now, he decided to send out yet another search party in that direction. The ice-choked river remained a problem, though. The ferry men were not only reluctant to put their boats out but refused to take across wagons and horses. Moffatt also tried to improve communication between Fort à la Corne and Prince Albert so that he was better able to stay on top of the search and posted a man at the Saskatchewan forks to relay any messages from Allan. He placed other men at Hoodoo Station to conduct regular patrols of the One Arrow reserve and Carlton Trail, and at Candle Lake, north of the Saskatchewan River, to monitor the trail between there and Fort à la Corne.[28]

These moves were part of a coordinated plan meant to ensnare Almighty Voice, to take him "by strategy."[29] But there was an opening in the police dragnet to the east, towards Nut Lake. And if the fugitive wanted to put distance between himself and his pursuers, he would likely go in that direction. That seemed to be a reasonable conclusion after several days of fruitless thrashing around in the Fort à la Corne area. Even though Allan maintained that Almighty Voice would head back home, it made more sense for the fugitive to push deeper into the bush, northeast into the forested Pasquia Hills (now a provincial reserve), where he could literally get lost. Corporal Bowdridge and Constable Tennant, along with interpreter McKay, consequently decided to extend their search to the east.

Their hunch was confirmed by Small Face. Almighty Voice's companion had refused to cooperate with the police or their interpreters during her first few days in custody in Prince Albert. But then, on 5 November, Moffatt brought in two other interpreters from her home territory, and Small Face opened up. She not only described the deadly encounter on the other side of Waterhen Lake but disclosed that she was supposed to rendezvous with Almighty Voice at a small river, "the closed rock," near Nut Lake. Both interpreters affirmed that Small Face was telling the truth.[30]

As the mounted police scrambled to chase down Almighty Voice, they expected unquestioning assistance from local Indian Affairs officials. After all, Indian Agent Robert McKenzie, who was behind Almighty Voice's arrest, also had responsibility for the James Smith and Big Head bands in the Fort à la Corne area. But when Superintendent Moffatt formally asked McKenzie to approve the distribution of rations to the approximately 125 Indians camped at the HBC post, the agent balked. He told the NWMP that he couldn't grant any such request without authorization from the Indian commissioner in Regina. This bureaucratic delay did not sit well with the Cree families who been called in from their hunting grounds. They are "not very well pleased," farm instructor Gordon declared, "with being corralled here."[31]

McKenzie, though, was not at all sympathetic to their situation. He looked upon the Indians of his agency as weak and vulnerable—easily intimidated by Almighty Voice—and considered their forced congregation around the farm instructor's residence a way to assert government authority over their lives. "I have not the slightest doubt," he told Moffatt, "the murderer will be assisted by some ... not because they approve of his actions but ... fear ... him."[32] McKenzie also grumbled about feeding the Indians. When he informed Indian Commissioner Forget about the situation at Fort à la Corne, he was more concerned about the "large expense" to the department. McKenzie did, however, believe that the rounding up of the Cree presented a wonderful opportunity to confiscate their guns, whatever the cost to their livelihood. "I do not think they should be allowed to have them, especially at the present time," he told Forget. "It would be better than further murders ... committed."[33] Six years later, in reflecting back on his tenure in the Duck Lake agency, an unrepentant McKenzie insisted, "I was not as bad to them [Indians] as they thought I was."[34]

Indian Commissioner Forget was not particularly pleased with McKenzie's handling of the Almighty Voice incident. The former

NWMP Commissioner L. W. Herchmer was determined
to devote whatever police resources were necessary to
find Almighty Voice. PROVINCIAL ARCHIVES OF SASKATCHEWAN
S-B10680

long-time clerk to the North-West Territories Council was an
unlikely survivor in the partisan politics of the period. Despite
his Liberal party affiliation Forget was appointed assistant Indian
commissioner in 1888 and then assumed Hayter Reed's duties
as commissioner—but not his title—in 1893. He would not be
confirmed in the position until October 1895, the very month that
Almighty Voice had escaped custody and then shot a mounted
policeman.

Colebrook's murder had blindsided Forget. It's not that the
new Indian commissioner did not support the hard-line policies of
the Conservative government, but he was at a loss to understand

how an apparent arrest for cattle killing had resulted in "this regrettable affair." And he demanded an explanation. In a tersely worded letter, Forget reminded McKenzie that "this office is as yet quite uninformed" about what happened.[35] He was also perturbed that the agent questioned the cost of feeding the Indians camped at Fort à la Corne when such action was taken "to isolate the fugitive and cut off his means of support." If anything, McKenzie should ensure that Gordon had "sufficient supplies" in order to avoid stirring up the Cree at this critical time.[36]

Whatever the mounted police or Indian officials did, though, made no difference to finding Almighty Voice. And the search was only getting more difficult as winter tightened its grip on the country. On 9 November, Superintendent Moffatt advised Regina that it was no longer possible to cross the river. Those relief parties who managed to get over to the other side had to hire horses and requisition supplies and food. It was also snowing in the search area, making tracking and travel more difficult. "I am not at all sanguine of catching the Indian," Moffatt suggested for the first time, "both on account of his having sympathizers and from the nature of the country."[37]

Inspector Allan's continuing search efforts bore out this opinion. The local Cree were asked to help locate Almighty Voice, but understandably balked when Allan refused to pay them. "I think most of them will tell if they hear of or see him," Gordon wished, "but it is hard to tell."[38] The police inspector did manage to secure the services of several Métis scouts, apparently courtesy of the local HBC manager, but their involvement made no difference. For two days, small parties scoured the country east of the James Smith/Big Head reserves, along both sides of the Carrot River, stymied by thick marshes and heavily timbered bluffs. Several horses went lame. "This was the worst piece of Country I have ever ridden over," Allan lamented.[39] Ironically, while the police were away searching for Almighty Voice, a calf went missing from the Big Head reserve. The animal was taken from an area where the tracks of the fugitive had been found days earlier.

On Saturday, 9 November, Inspector Allan and his fatigued men straggled into Kinistino for fresh horses and supplies. The next morning, he divided his force into two search parties, incorporating mounties who had recently arrived from Prince Albert. There would be one last push to find the murderer—more of a symbolic gesture that the police would not rest until they captured Almighty Voice. Sergeant-Major James Weeks, who had served during the 1885 North-West Rebellion, led one party southeast towards Flett Springs and Stony Creek. If he found any evidence that Almighty Voice was headed to Nut Lake, then Weeks was to go there; otherwise, the party was to sweep back southwestward around Lake Lenore and Basin Lake and then up to Hoodoo Station. Allan, on the other hand, followed the Carrot River valley southwestward, travelling through some of the same rough country as Almighty Voice and Small Face before the fatal shooting. It was a miserable few days. A heavy snowstorm from the north greeted their departure, and they had to stop regularly to rest their horses, who struggled through the drifts.

Indian Commissioner A. E. Forget, shown here at the 1895 Regina Territorial Exhibition, was upset with Indian Agent Robert McKenzie's handling of the Almighty Voice incident. PROVINCIAL ARCHIVES OF SASKATCHEWAN R-B514

Inspector Allan's destination was the Minichinas Hills, directly east of the One Arrow Reserve. He still had this nagging feeling that Almighty Voice would seek help from his family. That appeared to be the case when Louis Marion, the farm instructor for One Arrow, reported that Almighty Voice's mother, Spotted Calf, had left to go hunting in the hills. Sergeant Nichol Jeffrey, temporarily stationed at Hoodoo, immediately sent a few men to follow and watch her. "There is no doubt," Superintendent Moffatt told the commissioner of this promising lead, "that she saw her son after his escape and is well acquainted with his proposed movements."[40] Indian Agent McKenzie also acted on this new development and, once again on his own initiative, instructed Marion to call in any One Arrow Cree who were away hunting. He also brazenly asked Moffatt to lend police assistance in rounding up the Indians if any offered resistance.

Almighty Voice was not to be found in the area. By Wednesday, 13 November, Allan was at Hoodoo and decided to stop in at the reserve with interpreter McKay on his way to the Batoche detachment. He learned from an "old Indian" (name is unknown) that Almighty Voice had told his mother he would first seek help from Small Face's grandfather at Fort à la Corne, and, failing that, he would seek out his paternal grandfather at Nut Lake. Allan tried to telephone this information to Prince Albert, but the line was not working. The inspector visited the reserve again the next day—just in case the fugitive was hiding there—and then set off cross-country with a few men for Kinistino, telling settlers along the way to be on the lookout for Almighty Voice. His search party then took the trail back to Prince Albert, crossing the now frozen South Saskatchewan River on horseback and arriving at Prince Albert in the late afternoon of Sunday, 17 November.

Superintendent Moffatt had called Inspector Allan back to divisional headquarters because his men were getting nowhere three weeks into their search for Almighty Voice. He knew it was time to come up with another scheme to apprehend the fugitive. The mounted police were clearly at a disadvantage. The Cree may not have countenanced Almighty Voice's shooting of Colebrook—that was going too far—but they identified with his defiance of authority and were not about to turn in one of their own. NWMP Superintendent A. B. Perry had warned about this very situation less than a decade earlier when he spoke of the police becoming simply "men who arrest them [Indians]" and the Indians, in turn, "strangers to us."[41] The search was a sad commentary on the breakdown of police-Indian relations.

The police directly involved, meanwhile, tried to justify their failure. In reflecting on his unsuccessful hunt for the Willow Cree man, Inspector Allan conceded that "every [police] movement [had] been watched ... by his friends."[42] Moffatt agreed, adding that Almighty Voice's familiarity with the country meant he was "comfortably hidden as to defy detection or discovery for an unlimited time."[43] But if the mounties couldn't get their man—something they would never admit publicly—then who could do the job? Both policemen believed that local settlers, trappers, and traders who interacted with the Indian population should be enlisted to keep a lookout. There should also be a reward for tipping off the police. Given the circumstances, it seemed the best course of action. As it stood, the only breakthrough was the return of Colebrook's horse. Somehow, the animal had found its way back to Batoche on its own.

CHAPTER THREE

Regarded as a Hero

He was Canada's version of Australia's notorious Ned Kelly. That's how North-West Mounted Police Commissioner L. W. Herchmer likened the search for Almighty Voice in December 1895. In defending the force's failure to arrest "at once" the Willow Cree fugitive, Herchmer argued that the state of Victoria faced "the same difficulty" in tracking down Ned Kelly and his three henchmen. It took "two whole years" to end the criminals' reign of terror "even though all the efforts of the police were directed to their capture." The police commissioner raised the Australian example to offer some perspective on the challenges in bringing Almighty Voice to justice—and plead for some patience. "It is a very difficult undertaking," the usually over-confident Herchmer admitted. The police search had been compromised by "Indians [who] had just scattered out for their fall hunt," many of whom were "more or less related to the murderer." Almighty Voice had also knowingly taken refuge in a "difficult country," extensive, isolated, and in the grip of winter. "People [seem to] think because there are so few people in it," Herchmer responded to his critics, "any individual should easily be found." But the mounties would get their man. They had already captured Almighty Voice for cattle killing and then successfully tracked him down after he escaped from the Duck Lake gaol. It was only a matter of time before Canada's most wanted criminal was flushed out of hiding and "easily taken."[1]

≈

The shooting death of NWMP Sergeant Colin Colebrook made front-page news across the prairie west. Newspapers scrambled to report what facts were known—that an escaped Indian had murdered a policeman—and promised readers more information in the coming days. The *Saskatchewan Herald*, no friend of Indian peoples, confidently assured readers on 1 November 1895 that Almighty Voice would "not likely ... be at large very long."[2] Other papers agreed. The Moose Jaw *Times* even suggested the murderer might already be in custody and that the news of his capture was delayed by the isolation of the search area.[3]

The only strident voice was that of the Regina *Standard*. In an emotionally charged report on Colebrook's death, the headline screamed, "Are We on The Verge of Another Indian Outbreak?"[4] This reference to the 1885 North-West Rebellion would have resonated with the white territorial population and renewed questions about whether Indian peoples remained a menace to the settlement of the region and whether more repressive measures against them were needed.[5] Had not Almighty Voice killed a mountie, the embodiment of law and order in the region?

More details about Colebrook's death and the search for his killer were published in the first two weeks of November. But the earlier certainty about Almighty Voice's capture gave way to concerns about the continuing role and place of the mounted police in the territorial west. By the mid-1890s, both federal political parties were committed to reducing and possibly disbanding the NWMP as the prairie region was settled. Commissioner Herchmer consequently had to make do with a smaller operational budget at the very time that Almighty Voice was on the run. And westerners used the incident, and the continuing failure to apprehend the fugitive, to push back.

From its perch in Prince Albert, the Saskatchewan *Times* said it was "foolhardy and dangerous to send one policeman after an escaped prisoner," but the police force was not to blame when it was being "kept so short of men."[6] Not to be outdone, the Prince Albert *Advocate* used Colebrook's murder to cry out against "heathenism and lawlessness" on civilization's frontier. "If the force were withdrawn," it cautioned, "life in the Northwest would be unsupportable."[7]

The competence of the mounted police also came under scrutiny as Almighty Voice's flight from justice stretched from days into weeks. The Regina *Leader* publicly reminded Commissioner Herchmer of the "necessity" of catching "this Indian" and making "an example" of him. "No precaution or expense should be spared to make sure of that," it lectured.[8] The Saskatchewan *Times* also went from defending the police to questioning, "Why the delay in rounding him up?" If the mounties did not have the manpower to handle the job, then offer a reward.[9]

The Manitoba *Free Press* endorsed this suggestion in a lengthy editorial that explored the larger significance of the Almighty Voice incident. Railing against the "apparent apathy" in hunting down Colebrook's "cold-blooded assassin," the paper charged that the ongoing failure to avenge his death led to the unfortunate conclusion "that killing [a mountie] is of so little consequence." Indeed, "if those [Indians] who are inclined to violence get the impression," the editorial continued, "that they may shoot down a Policeman with impunity, there is danger that the number of murders may become alarmingly great."[10] The implication was unmistakable. As long as Almighty Voice remained at large and unpunished, settlers were not safe in the region.

The North-West Mounted Police believed that Almighty Voice was being secretly assisted by family and relatives in the Duck Lake area and Carrot River country. UNIVERSITY OF SASKATCHEWAN, UNIVERSITY ARCHIVES AND SPECIAL COLLECTIONS, CANADIANS PAMPHLETS COLLECTION, 32

Herchmer was stung by the criticism. Even though the western press understood that the search for Almighty Voice was handicapped by diminished police resources, the commissioner knew a larger force would not necessarily lead to his capture. He was nowhere to be found. He had simply disappeared.

While the police figured out their next move, Herchmer took out his frustration by travelling to Duck Lake and personally investigating the circumstances behind Almighty Voice's escape and, indirectly, Colebrook's death. Constable Robert Dickson had already been sentenced and dismissed from the force. But Herchmer believed that Sergeant Harry Keenan should also be held accountable for not keeping the three Indian prisoners in irons the night of the escape. At a disciplinary hearing on 18 November, coincidentally the day after Inspector J. B. Allan had returned to the Prince Albert barracks from his aborted search, Herchmer found Keenan guilty and reduced him to the ranks.

This finding led to more negative publicity about the mounted police, especially when the public learned the disgraced sergeant was being transferred to the Yukon. The popular Keenan, a member of the first mountie contingent in 1873,[11] was stoutly defended in the Prince Albert newspapers. The real culprit was the dominion government for not providing suitable barracks with gaols at Batoche and Duck Lake. Herchmer also came across as a tyrant, more interested in his own reputation than the well-being of his men. That seemed to be the case when several papers reported that part of Dickson's punishment was to dig "his comrade's grave." Herchmer issued a public denial, but the damage had been done.[12]

This infighting got the mounted police no closer to finding Almighty Voice. But it provided an outlet for their growing anxiety over their inability to capture Colebrook's murderer. The police had only a vague idea of where he might be. On 24 November, the coroner's inquest into the sergeant's death resumed in Prince Albert with testimony from scout François Dumont and Almighty Voice's companion Small Face. Neither witness knew where Almighty Voice was headed. The only clue was his parting remark to Small Face: "I will try to see you at the closed rock."[13] That was near the Saulteaux reserve at Nut Lake, the home of his paternal grandfather, Taytapisasung.

But the police knew from their pursuit of Almighty Voice that he fled north, instead of east, for the Fort à la Corne reserves–

James Smith (#100) and Cumberland (#100A)–on the south side of the Saskatchewan River. These two reserves were not far from where Almighty Voice shot Colebrook. He likely had ties there, too, in addition to Small Face's grandfather from James Smith. The Cumberland reserve included former members of the Chakastaypasin band, which once hunted bison with Almighty Voice's grandfather One Arrow. The two bands had also lived relatively close to one another after treaty and pursued subsistence activities in the Carrot River country.

The ice-choked Saskatchewan River hampered NWMP search efforts in November 1895. PRINCE ALBERT HISTORICAL SOCIETY, JAMES COLLECTION J-195

After the rebellion, the Indian Affairs department deposed Chief Chakastaypasin (Cikâstêpêsin or Shadow Falling/Lying on the Water) for disloyalty and broke up his band. Some Chakastaypasin members joined One Arrow, while other families moved to the Cumberland reserve in the late 1880s.[14] Almighty Voice was no stranger, then, to the people of the La Corne region, and in his desperation, he went there expecting to be shielded from the police. It was no coincidence that the police tracked him to that part of the Cumberland reserve where some of the Chakastaypasin Cree lived.

Finding refuge in the La Corne area proved elusive for Almighty Voice. Not only did the mounted police know he was hiding there, but they had tried to cut off any assistance by calling in the local Indians from their hunting grounds and confining them to their reserves. With the police watching and waiting, and small search parties out looking for him, Almighty Voice had to go elsewhere.

Sometime during the second week of November, he likely made his way southeast to the present-day Melfort-Tisdale district and the hunting territory of the Kinistin and Yellow Quill Saulteaux bands, among them, his paternal grandfather and other relatives. It was a perfect hiding place. While the northern prairies were on the cusp of a settlement boom, soon to be the home of tens of thousands of immigrant farmers, the rolling, bush-covered country reaching back south from the Saskatchewan River existed in isolation. There was little settlement here, nor the threat of any homesteading rush because of the rough, gravelly terrain, blanketed by a wall of aspen forest. Surveyor Thomas Fawcett, while conducting a topographical survey of the region in 1892, was forever being slowed by "a series of boggy marshes ... separated by narrow ridges covered with brûlé or timber ... intermixed with

The Almighty Voice search area was mostly rough, gravelly terrain, blanketed by scrub brush and aspen forest. PRINCE ALBERT HISTORICAL SOCIETY, JAMES COLLECTION J-145

thick scrub."[15] It was not until well into the twentieth century that the land would be cleared; apart from the predominance of sloughs, the landscape looks completely different today.

The local Saulteaux and Cree lived by the hunt, gathering and foraging, and trapping in the region. Their search for furs took them east to the western edge of the Pasquia Hills. And they were good at it. Their trade supported three competing posts at Stony Creek (Melfort) and another two at Nut Lake. As a skilled hunter, Almighty Voice would fit in, even thrive among these "wandering" bands as they were called.[16] He could travel in relative anonymity with small hunting groups and not worry about surviving or being found. Any outsider would be easily noticed. In fact, the police had to find a way to avoid detection as they searched for him, or failing that, find a way to drive him out into the open so that they had a better chance of taking him. Until the mounted police solved that conundrum, Almighty Voice would remain free.

NWMP Superintendent George Moffatt's answer was to send out no more police search parties from Prince Albert. It would make more sense, he told Commissioner Herchmer, to ask traders who worked in the region and knew the local Indians to quietly gather information about the whereabouts of the murderer during their winter rounds. They were dealing with a fugitive who had proven himself as "cunning [as] a wood wolf."[17] It was an apt description. Almighty Voice was reputed to be a spiritual shape shifter (ekweskimoot), able to assume animal form.[18]

Moffatt also reported that Almighty Voice was probably no longer on his own. Indian Agent Robert McKenzie's confiscation of the One Arrow guns had only strengthened the Willow Cree unwillingness to cooperate with government authorities. It was as if the entire band could not be trusted and was being punished for Almighty Voice's actions. "I think it was hardly politic," Indian Commissioner A. E. Forget derided the agent. "[I]t conveys ... the impression ... they [are] regarded with suspicion."[19] But that was exactly why McKenzie took away their weapons.

The confinement of the Fort à la Corne Indians to their reserves in early November had also not helped matters. By bringing them together under police surveillance, they all came to know the Almighty Voice story and how he had defied government and police authorities. And that was the mountie's worry. "He is no doubt," Superintendent Moffatt mused, "regarded as a hero."[20] At least two young men were now assumed to be with Almighty Voice. When the James Smith and Cumberland Indians were allowed to return to their hunting grounds in mid-November, Tee-ta-qua-petung (Wolverine Cap) and Kaquarain left their group and rode off on their own, seemingly intent to join the fugitive. The mounted police expected others to do the same, especially as his reputation grew with every day he eluded capture.

Commissioner Herchmer ignored Moffatt's assessment of the situation, apart from asking local traders to collect intelligence, and insisted that small police detachments be strategically placed in the five-thousand-square-mile search area. Almighty Voice had murdered a mountie, and the police had to be on hand to bring him to justice. Herchmer consequently ordered a small party of men to Nut Lake and directed Moffatt to place men in the field at Fort à la Corne and Stony Creek or Flett Springs. The groups were to conduct flying patrols through the region, sometimes deliberately going over the same ground, taking time to meet at prearranged locations to exchange news. The One Arrow reserve, meanwhile, was to be visited "frequently ... at night" in order to take the fugitive by surprise if he was ever foolhardy enough to return there. Herchmer also did not discount the possibility that Small Face, having just been released from custody, might lead the police to Almighty Voice, and asked that her whereabouts be closely monitored.[21]

These instructions did not sit well with Superintendent Moffatt. "There is the least use," he bluntly responded, "in our men attempting to invade the hunting grounds of the Indians with the idea of catching this man." That was the advice he was getting from people, such as Angus McKay of the Hudson's Bay Company, who knew the country and the Indians who lived there. "He is among friends," Moffatt reminded the commissioner, "who are now, & will be all winter, on the lookout, & in a land where secure hiding places are numberable [sic]."[22] Rather than being dissuaded, Herchmer was determined to flex his authority as commissioner, to show the doubters within the force that he was in charge. If necessary, he commanded Moffatt by telegram, his men were to camp out under canvas with stoves. They should also be supplied with snowshoes. "Keep the party moving," he exhorted. "Catch him if you can, if not, you can get information."[23]

This bickering over how best to continue the search ended when Almighty Voice was finally located—in more than one place! During the second week of December 1895, NWMP headquarters in Regina received dispatches that the fugitive had been spotted near Fort Pelly (on the east-central side of the future province of Saskatchewan) and at Green Lake (northwest of Prince Albert). These conflicting reports—the two sightings were several hundred miles apart—prompted long-serving NWMP comptroller Frederick White to ask whether Almighty Voice had ever been photographed, individually or as part of a group, and if so, to circulate copies to avoid future confusion about his identity. It was several decades, though, before Almighty Voice's studio portrait would become publicly known.

A more reliable report came from Willie Traill, a Hudson's Bay Company employee and son of Canadian author Catherine Parr Traill, who retired to Prince Albert in 1893 and bought a farm east of town in the Birch Hills area. While on a hunting trip during the first part of December 1895, Traill met some people who claimed to have come across the fugitive near Waterhen Lake. He followed up the story to confirm its accuracy and was convinced enough to inform the police.[24]

Another former HBC man, Reginald B. Beatty, heard similar stories and wanted to help as well. Beatty had settled with his family near the Stony Creek forks in 1883 and worked as an independent trapper and trader throughout the region that became the focus of the police manhunt. In early December, he offered his services to the NWMP for forty dollars per month, along with the promise that his visits to local Indian camps over the winter would not raise any suspicions about his true purpose. "If the culprit was anywhere in the vicinity," he vowed, "I would hear of it."[25] But the commissioner wanted his own men at the forefront of the search and would only pay Beatty for temporary lodging and stabling for mounties and their horses.

Almighty Voice returned to the One Arrow reserve
in late December 1895 to see his new son, Stanislaus
or Almighty Voice Jr. GLENBOW ARCHIVES NB-40-911

That Almighty Voice might be in the Birch Hills or around
Waterhen Lake led to speculation that the murderer was headed
back home. Superintendent Moffatt consequently ordered the
Duck Lake detachment to keep an even closer watch on the One
Arrow reserve and, if necessary, hire local Métis to help with
surveillance. The repeated police search of One Arrow homes
throughout December turned up nothing and only angered the
band. But Indian Affairs chose not to intervene and stop the police
harassment. All Indian Commissioner Forget did at the end of the
year was issue a statement that the government had "no intention
of providing for the defence of the murderer Almighty Voice,
should he be brought to trial."[26]

What the mounted police didn't realize, though, was why
Almighty Voice would risk capture by returning to the reserve.
His second wife (the daughter of Rock Child), pregnant at the time
of Colebrook's shooting, had given birth to a boy, named Stanislaus, or Almighty Voice Jr, on 28 December. The child's birth was

recorded in the Duck Luck agency register, but apparently Agent McKenzie never communicated this information to the police.[27]

The Traill report also necessitated another search of the Waterhen Lake area. That fell to NWMP Inspector J. B. Allan and a small mountie party that scoured the Fort à la Corne–Stony Creek district just before Christmas 1895. These were long, cold days in the saddle—the heart of the winter solstice—and it would have been especially demanding for Allan, now in his early fifties. But the inspector, nicknamed "Bronco Jack," relished the hunt. He looked upon Almighty Voice as another Wandering Spirit, the Cree war chief behind the 1885 Frog Lake massacres, and he wanted to ensure that Almighty Voice met the same fate at the end of a rope. Superintendent Moffatt trusted Allan's judgement and valued his experience, including past service in the Canadian militia as far back as the 1866 Fenian raids.

When not interviewing the handful of settlers and ranchers in the search area, Allan tried at several places to secure a local Métis guide, but no one would take the job, apparently out of fear of the fugitive. He also made surprise visits to Indian hunting camps, at one point sweeping into Dusty's camp in the hope that Almighty Voice was hiding out with Small Face's grandfather. But Allan found to his chagrin that "our movements are pretty well advertised in advance."[28]

Robert Ballendine, a HBC trader working out of Fort à la Corne that winter, had a similar experience. Asked to quietly seek out information for the police, Ballendine returned to the post in late December with "nothing fresh" about the fugitive.[29] A mountie patrol from Nut Lake had gone through his trading territory before his arrival and made the Saulteaux wary of any intruders, including Ballendine. As Allan summed up the situation at year's end, "the atmosphere is still tense."[30]

Commissioner Herchmer would not countenance defeat and insisted that men remain in the field throughout the winter if necessary. In late December, mounties Vickers and Carter were billeted with a settler named Scott in the present-day Morwick area, southeast of Flett Springs. Their job was to gather any information about the fugitive, noting the coming and going of people between Fort à la Corne and Nut Lake, while keeping their identity and purpose a secret. "You will be aided in observing the golden rule," Moffatt counselled in his letter of instructions, "of being a listener more than a suggester ... using other people for your information but giving none."[31] One wonders, though, how much they could learn in a fixed location and limited daylight hours.

Another three-man police detachment, under Corporal G. E. Pulham, continued to be based temporarily at Nut Lake, on the east side of the search area. Pulham was convinced that Almighty Voice's grandfather Taytapisasung and his two sons Tatartuck and The Cloud that Follows knew where their relative was hiding but were "on the guard all the time" and watch "every move that we make." In early January, two of the mounties, disguised as traders, left on separate trips with outfits headed to the northeast and northwest in the hope of "find[ing] out something." The ruse smacked of desperation, especially when, as Pulham acknowledged, the local Saulteaux were "fully aware that we are the police."[32]

Stories about Almighty Voice being in the Birch Hills continued to circulate into January 1896, prompting Superintendent Moffatt to suspect that the fugitive was actually holed up on the One Arrow reserve, "cached in [one] of the houses."[33] This time, the mounted police decided to set a trap. An elderly Métis, Jean-Baptiste Arcand, who claimed to be friends with Almighty Voice, was sent to the reserve to try to coax the Willow Cree man out of hiding. Arcand decided to host a dance, and while the band was distracted, the police would spring into action. Late in the evening of 11 January, while farm instructor Louis Marion kept watch at the reserve, a large party of mounties was secretly ferried into position, lying down in the bottom of the sleighs to avoid detection. Forming two groups, the mounties hurriedly went through every house but came up empty-handed. "The rumours ... going about," Moffatt conceded, "are very perplexing and the attempts ... to trace him ... fruitless."[34]

The normally cool-headed Inspector Allan, who had led the raid, was not so philosophical but became obsessed with finding the murderer. At the end of January, he set off again for the Stony Creek district, intent on checking out a new report that Almighty

NWMP Inspector J. B. Allan became obsessed with finding Almighty Voice and spent weeks in all kinds of weather chasing down any lead. RCMP HISTORICAL COLLECTIONS UNIT, REGINA SK

Voice had joined Pawānēns (Pawness or Little Dream/Vision) and his Saulteaux band. Searching for the Pawness camp proved just as frustrating as trying to find Almighty Voice. For the better part of a week, Allan and his party tramped around Basin and Lenore lakes, battling deep snow and extremely cold temperatures. On more than one occasion, interpreter and guide William Bruce, armed with binoculars, climbed by snowshoe to the highest ridge to survey the surrounding country.

When the Pawness camp was finally reached on 7 February, the Saulteaux expressed surprise that Allan and his group had made it through the heavily timbered hills. They also denied any relationship with Almighty Voice—had not seen or helped him—and said that he was "a bad Indian." Allan returned to Prince Albert

The search area today, having been cleared of brush and
trees for settlement in the first half of the twentieth century.
WOODLAND PHOTOS

The search for Almighty Voice was put on hold in the summer
months because of the wet boggy terrain and mosquitoes.
BILL WAISER

with little to report except that it had been a "rough" trip and that the hills offered a perfect sanctuary for the murderer—if he was out there.[35]

NWMP Commissioner Herchmer insisted that his men continue the search through the winter months—even if it meant living in tents.
GLENBOW ARCHIVES ND-44-3

By January 1896, more than three months after Sergeant Colebrook's shooting, a new story began making the rounds in the Métis communities near the Willow Cree reserves. It was rumoured that Almighty Voice had not committed any crime—that he had been originally "arrested on the report of a child"—and that he only ran away to be free. It was also said that he had killed Colebrook in self-defence only after warning him several times not to approach. When told about this version of events an incredulous police comptroller Fred White thundered that it was "too absurd for serious contemplation."[36] But the police on the ground in the Prince Albert district knew the story was generating sympathy for Almighty Voice. Inspector Allan even concluded that "we can look for no assistance outside of the Force to bring about his capture."[37]

The story also raised questions about the circumstances

surrounding the arrest of Almighty Voice, something that had not received much attention because of the focus on apprehending Colebrook's murderer. Superintendent Moffatt consequently asked Indian Agent McKenzie for a copy of the arrest warrant and any other supporting documentation. Allan also visited the agent at his Duck Lake office to discuss what evidence he had collected to lay the charge of cattle stealing. The police were uneasy that McKenzie had acted on the word of an informant and speculated whether the case would have been dismissed at trial. Even more troubling was a mid-March report that Almighty Voice had tried to set things right by compensating the rancher for the cow he had killed. "The Indian ... had gone to Parenteau, whose animal ... he had killed," Moffatt informed the commissioner, "and offered him a horse in settlement."[38]

The other more pressing concern was the continuing failure of the mounted police to bring Almighty Voice to justice. Former HBC postmaster and clerk James Hourston, with several years' experience in the Cumberland district, complained to Agent McKenzie that the police had bungled the search. Almighty Voice was a "desperate man" who "will never surrender" and "should be shot on sight." What complicated the matter, according to Hourston, was that "all the bad Indians in the Country are his friends, and none of the good ones will give him away."[39]

McKenzie dutifully forwarded Hourston's letter to Commissioner Forget, adding that "the search for the man should not be abandoned." Since Colebrook's murder, he noted, "there is a different manner to be noticed in the Indians, one of independence and defiance ... there would not appear to be much risk in shooting a white man."[40] McKenzie's comments were amplified in a hard-hitting editorial, "The Indian Murder," in the Prince Albert *Advocate* that called on the police to "shake off their lethargy." The newspaper warned that "the Indians are in an ugly mood" and "blood will be shed" if the murderer was not caught soon. If a reward were offered, then the culprit would soon be "behind ... bars, awaiting his well-earned dessert, the noose."[41]

Superintendent Moffatt tried to deflect the rebuke by claiming that "every effort which can be made, is being made."[42] But both the police commissioner and comptroller, who received copies

The NWMP were convinced that John Sounding Sky
was helping his son but never found the pair together.
GLENBOW ARCHIVES NA-1135-27

of all correspondence about the Almighty Voice search, were
disturbed by the censure. So, too, was Hayter Reed, now deputy
superintendent general of Indian Affairs in Ottawa. He did not
like to hear that his Indians were becoming insolent. Nor was the
demand for a reward going away. On 5 March 1896, the Regina
Leader warned that as long as the government failed to act, it
would "be held responsible for the murderer's non-capture, and
for any untoward event to which a circumstance may lead."[43]

The matter eventually found its way to the desk of Thomas
Mayne Daly, who served as both the minister of the Interior and
Indian Affairs in the Mackenzie Bowell Conservative government.
In a corner of the briefing document, Daly penned, "It astounds me
that a reward has not been previously offered." He was also "at a

NWMP Corporal G. E. Pulham disguised himself as an
itinerant trader to try to discover the whereabouts of
Almighty Voice, but the Nut Lake Saulteaux were not fooled.
RCMP HISTORICAL COLLECTIONS UNIT, REGINA SK, 1961.33.6

loss to understand" why he was not told about the fallout from
the Almighty Voice incident earlier.[44] Reed sheepishly replied that
he considered it a police matter once the Indian escaped custody.
Daly immediately asked Prime Minister Mackenzie Bowell
to approve a reward for the capture of the murderer—never
mentioned by name in the memorandum—to help bring about
"a better sense of security" in the West.[45] Sir Mackenzie replied
that he had already told police comptroller Fred White, who had
more influence over the force than the commissioner, to offer a
two-hundred-dollar reward "sometime ago."[46]

What White had done instead was prepare a handbill description of Almighty Voice and then distribute several hundred copies
to the various police divisions across the prairie west in early

Description of_____

"Almighty Voice,"

THE MURDER OF THE LATE SERGEANT COLEBRO

Height, about 5 feet 10 inches, slight build, rather good looking, sharp hooked nose with a remarkably flat _____ scar on left side of face about _____ inches long, running from near corner of mouth towards the ear. This scar cannot be noticed when his face is painted, but otherwise is plain. Skin is fair for an Indian.

Ottawa issued a handbill circular for Almighty Voice that was distributed to mounted police divisions across western Canada. RCMP HISTORICAL COLLECTIONS UNIT, REGINA SK

March. Daly's involvement now meant that a reward—in the sum of five hundred dollars—was formally sanctioned by the Department of Justice and issued in proclamation form, over the signature of Secretary of State Charles Tupper, on 20 April 1896. The poster described Almighty Voice: "About twenty-two years old, five feet ten inches in height, weight eleven stone, slightly built and erect, neat small feet and hands, complexion inclined to be fair, wavey dark hair to shoulders, large dark eyes, broad forehead, sharp features and parrot nose with flat tip, scar on left cheek running from mouth towards ear, feminine appearance."[47] It was too much to expect authorities to say he was handsome or even good-looking.

The offer of the reward made no difference to the ongoing police search for the fugitive. In mid-March, Inspector Allan had visited the three mounties who were stationed at Stony Creek and spent their days searching the hills to the north and east. They

NWMP comptroller Fred White consulted with Prime Minister Mackenzie Bowell about the offer of a reward for the capture of Almighty Voice. RCMP HISTORICAL COLLECTIONS UNIT, REGINA SK

had to start early each day to cross the hills and back "owing to the heavy underbrush," which exacted "wear and tear on the clothes." Allan had them move north towards Goose Hunting Creek, where they erected a small shanty in the timber as their new home. But the results would prove the same: "no trace of Almighty Voice."[48]

Corporal Pulham, based at Nut Lake, had fared no better. But he had been able to piece together Almighty Voice's movements after the Colebrook shooting. Šākanāhš (Chagoness or English), a member of the Kinistin band, told Pulham through his interpreter that Almighty Voice had indeed first sought refuge in the Fort à la Corne area before fleeing south to Wading Eagle Lake where he stayed with Yellow Snake Bird, a relative through marriage. Almighty Voice was rigged up with whatever ammunition and supplies could be spared and then set off west to find his grandfather, threatening to "kill the first man that tried to take him."

Chagoness also disclosed that Almighty Voice had visited his family at One Arrow before New Year's (probably around the time of his son's birth). When pressed for more details, he disclosed that Almighty Voice "would now and again take a run to his own Reserve ... to see his relations, and while there ... he would be kept in a cellar."[49]

That Almighty Voice was regularly under the nose of the mounted police seemed confirmed when Métis Philippe Gariépy and his son found a horse just south of the Minichinis Hills in the third week of March. When Gariépy took the animal to One Arrow to find its owner, several band members claimed that it once belonged to Almighty Voice, and he handed it over to his mother. Farm instructor Louis Marion reported what happened, and when the police came to investigate, Gariépy said that he had "seen other signs ... that Almighty Voice was in the Hills."[50]

One Arrow band member François Dumont, who had served as Colebrook's guide and been present at the sergeant's murder, certainly believed that Almighty Voice was about—and feared for his life. In the early spring, Dumont fled to the Qu'Appelle Valley and joined the Okanese reserve. He was not the first one to leave the area. Just a few weeks earlier, Indian Affairs employee Louis Couture suddenly abandoned his ranch. When a policeman queried whether he was afraid of Almighty Voice, Couture reported that the murderer's father had "threatened to get even" for sending him to prison for theft and that he would "not be safe" when Sounding Sky was released in April.[51]

Father and son were likely together later that spring and into the summer. One day on his way to the reserve, Louis Marion was "startled ... by seeing a strange Indian with painted face" that looked like Almighty Voice. Sounding Sky insisted, though, that it was his brother. Indian Agent McKenzie encountered the same two men the next day camped by the Batoche ferry and stopped to talk to them. "The young man appeared very excited when he saw me," McKenzie told the police later. "[T]he young man resemble[d] Almighty Voice yet I could not say ... as he was too much painted."[52]

Almighty Voice was also sighted in two other places that spring. In mid-May, "a very ragged and destitute" Indian, who bore a

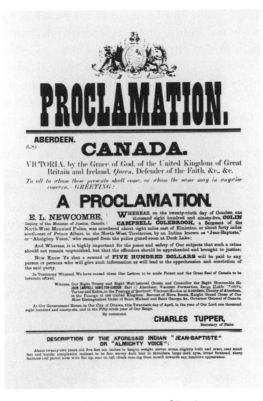

In April 1896, the Department of Justice announced
a five-hundred-dollar reward for Almighty Voice.

striking similarity to the murderer, tried to break into the HBC
store at Pine Creek, just east of Lake Winnipegosis in Manitoba.[53]
He had apparently been hiding in the Duck Mountain uplands.
That same week, Corporal T. A. Dickson, who was in Great Falls,
Montana, on mounted police business, heard that Almighty Voice
had been living at Horse Plains (now known as Plains) since the
previous fall. Montana newspapers later reported that the Kalispell
sheriff had apprehended the fugitive on the Flathead reservation.
Police in Canada shrugged off the news and simply added the
clippings, without comment, to the large and growing file on the
pursuit of Almighty Voice.

The summer months brought little news. On 21 June 1896,

Corporal Pulham, who had moved from Nut Lake to Kutawa, near the Touchwood station on the telegraph line, informed NWMP headquarters that Almighty Voice had taken up with the Pawness band—the Saulteaux group that earlier denied any association with the Willow Cree man. But Pulham could not check out the rumour because "it would be impossible to travel up in that country [Carrot River] as there is such a lot of water ... and the flies are very bad."[54]

The corporal was not heard from again until early September when he interviewed Pawness at Nut Lake and learned that Almighty Voice had been "staying at Batoche, his father looking after his wants" through the spring and into the summer. This information resulted in an intensive, and unsuccessful, three-day patrol of the One Arrow environs. "I searched every inch of the country within a radius of 20 miles," Corporal W. J. Bowdridge declared, "but I saw nothing unusual."[55] That apparently included the small bundles of food that some of the local people tied from tree branches for the fugitive.[56]

A month later, the police decided to comb the Minichinis Hills to the east, where Almighty Voice's horse had been found that spring. "It is very discouraging work," Inspector J. A. Wilson commented. "If a man was looking for a place to hide in he could not find a better place."[57] The Batoche detachment also continued to ride through the reserve unannounced and go through homes. A late-night visit on 17 October found no Almighty Voice, but his father "old John was very nervous." As the mountie in charge of this latest raid mused, "We can do nothing but keep on searching."[58]

But the question was where to keep searching? Inspector Wilson, now in charge of the Duck Lake detachment, believed that Almighty Voice had "found it too warm this fall" because of the constant patrolling of the One Arrow area and had once again taken refuge in the densely wooded hills that offered him shelter after Colebrook's shooting.[59] Yet, sending more search parties into that country for another winter offered no prospect of finding the fugitive, who had not been seen by another mounted policeman—except for the dead Colebrook—since he ran from the Duck Lake gaol. The only certainty was that more of the force's limited budget would be drained away, adding to the several thousand dollars already expended on the unsuccessful search over the past year.

Almighty Voice often hid in the Minichinas Hills immediately east of the One Arrow reserve. BILL WAISER

Nor could the police expect any help from the local bands who offered passive resistance at every turn. What had become painfully apparent over the past year was that the Cree and Saulteaux were not going to betray one of their own, even though he had killed a mountie. Even the sizeable reward had not led people to take justice into their own hands, as initially feared by the mounties. Some settlers, especially Métis, had stepped forward to serve as scouts, but many others continued to fear the fugitive and wanted no part of the search. The Batoche detachment knew, for example, that One Arrow farm instructor Louis Marion lived "in mortal terror of Almighty Voice" and what he might do to him.[60] The other complication was the flood of rumours about the murderer and his whereabouts. One of the most bizarre and unfounded was an October 1896 claim by the priest at the Duck Lake Indian school that Almighty Voice had committed suicide. Another was that Almighty Voice and his father were among a party of Indians "acting suspiciously" at Lesser Slave Lake, over a thousand miles away.[61]

The reputation of the force was also being challenged that fall by another Indian murderer. In late September 1896, Si'k-okskitsis (Charcoal), a Blood warrior and medicine man, shot his wife's lover when he found the pair together. That killing and the subsequent wounding of the farm instructor for the Blood reserve made Charcoal a wanted man. For more than a month, he remained on the run in present-day southern Alberta, eluding a police search party that numbered more than one hundred at one point. It was not until mid-November that Charcoal was finally captured, but not before killing a police sergeant.[62] The sorry episode led to more questioning of the mounted police's competence and highlighted that another police murderer was still at large, a full year after his cold-blooded deed.

The search for Almighty Voice over the winter of 1896–97 was dramatically scaled back in reach—a concession to the difficulties that past patrols had encountered and the growing cost of keeping several small detachments in the field. The plan was also based on the realization that, while police parties had been looking for the fugitive in isolated locations, Almighty Voice had ironically remained in contact with his family. Two small detachments were consequently stationed to the east and southeast of One Arrow—at Crooked (wâkâw) Lake and the Venne ranch, respectively—in order to intercept the murderer if and when he visited the reserve. A close watch would also be kept on Almighty Voice's father in the hope that his movements would betray his son to the police. NWMP Commissioner Herchmer inflated this new search strategy in his annual report for 1896, claiming the police were "still scouring the country [for Almighty Voice] in all directions." But he did not repeat his past promise that the murderer would be captured, but rather conceded, "we [are] unable to cover as much ground as formerly."[63]

Surviving police records are largely silent about these patrols. The urgency that had energized the previous winter's search had given way to a growing belief in mounted police circles that Almighty Voice might never be found. Other events had also pushed the story of the Indian murderer into the background. A new Liberal government, under Canada's first French Catholic prime minister, Wilfrid Laurier, had taken office in July 1896, while gold had been discovered in the Yukon a month later, setting off the Klondike Gold Rush and creating a renewed purpose for the mounted police.

Those policemen who were part of the search for Almighty Voice that winter quietly went about their business as if the posting had become routine, an unpopular assignment that had to be endured. Superintendent Moffatt did his best, though, to keep his men vigilant and ever wary of their quarry. When a new batch of mounties replaced those on patrol duty at the temporary Crooked Lake detachment in mid-January 1897, he insisted that the "work of searching for the fugitive [in the bluffs]" was not "to be done singly."[64] Little did Moffatt or any of the men involved in the manhunt realize how prescient this warning would turn out to be. Instead of fleeing from the region, Almighty Voice had chosen to remain close to family and friends. He was a reluctant fugitive who wanted to go home.

CHAPTER FOUR

Other Things to Do Besides Dancing

It was the big break that had eluded the North-West Mounted Police for more than a year-and-a-half. One of Canada's most wanted criminals was finally within reach. Late in the day, on Wednesday, 26 May 1897, David Venne rode from his father's Spring Valley ranch east to the Batoche police detachment to report an incident earlier that afternoon. While he and his brother Napoleon were rounding up cattle along the southeast edge of the Minichinas Hills, looking for strays from atop the Jungle Lake Hills, they spotted three Indians among their animals. The Venne brothers gave chase. Two of the pursued men rode into a nearby bluff, while the third was thrown from his horse. The Vennes captured the small red stallion and returned it to the fallen Indian after he had given them his name, Anihšināpēns (Little Saulteaux) from Nut Lake. They then asked about his friends, and it was only with great reluctance that Little Saulteaux identified one as Topean (Dublin), the son of Rock Child from One Arrow and brother-in-law of Almighty Voice. He wouldn't name the second man, but Napoleon thought he was riding a horse that belonged to Almighty Voice's father, John Sounding Sky. David Venne was suspicious—there had been stories circulating for the past year that Almighty Voice was hiding out with his family—and decided to take his concerns to the mounted police.[1] Could they have found Almighty Voice at last?

≈

The police were ready to admit defeat, or at least stop actively searching for the murderer Almighty Voice. For a month, starting 21 February 1897, the three-man Crooked Lake detachment had painstakingly explored by snowshoe the rolling, wooded country to the south, east, and north in search of "any place that would afford shelter to the fugitive." They suffered frigid temperatures that numbed hands and feet, wind gusts that nearly blew their tent away, bouts of the flu and snowblindness that kept them confined to camp, and dense thickets of brush that shredded their clothes. Upon their return, Constable Stanley Hildyard, leader of the party, glumly reported in late March, "I did not meet a single human being during the whole time I was out." Nor did he believe that other police patrols should follow in their wake. Almighty Voice might not even be hiding in the district. "I consider it utterly useless to continue the search," Hildyard concluded in his summary report, "and think the only chance remaining is that, having escaped detection so long, he might get bolder and ... endeavour to hold communication with his relations." For Hildyard, "the wisest plan [is] quietly wait and watch."[2]

This approach seemed the most sensible one as the second winter of Almighty Voice being on the run came to an end. The fugitive, the mounted police surmised, had to be getting help in order to evade capture for so long. And the most likely source of assistance was his father and family, including relatives among other bands. The Indian Affairs department concurred. It increasingly appeared that the surest route to finding Almighty Voice was through the careful monitoring of his father and his movements. When Sounding Sky, for example, left in the early spring for the Minichinas Hills, the police assumed he had other motives besides harvesting roots. They placed a careful watch over his camp.[3] The police also grew apprehensive when Almighty Voice's paternal grandfather, Taytapisasung, and some hunting companions passed through Beardy's reserve in early May on their way back to Nut Lake after spending the winter to the west in the Eagle Hills near Battleford.[4] Had his grandson been hiding with him over the winter months? Was that why police search parties had failed to find him? And was he now secretly returning to the area and rejoining his father?

Corporal W. J. Bowdridge, since assuming command of the Batoche detachment, had been relentless in his search for Almighty Voice on the One Arrow reserve and surrounding area. It had been a frustrating exercise, with nothing to show for his late-night rides through the reserve and nearby Indian hunting camps. When David Venne consequently turned up at the detachment, recounting how the fugitive and two teenaged companions tried to rustle one of his cattle, Bowdridge jumped at the news. He immediately telephoned Inspector J. A. Wilson at Duck Lake and asked for more men for a search party. He and Constable William Ferris then left shortly after midnight for the Venne ranch, anxious to locate the Indians hidden in the bluff before they slipped away.

The two mounties reached the Venne ranch about 3:30 a.m., on the morning of Thursday, 27 May, and after hiring Napoleon Venne as scout, set out to find Sounding Sky's camp. When they got to the site where the One Arrow people picked roots, several miles east of the reserve, they saw no one. Venne picked up their trail, and as they were riding south, they spotted a figure ahead on horseback but were unable to catch up. They found the Indian camp, east of Hoodoo Station, about 8 a.m.

Not wanting to cause any alarm, Bowdridge dismounted and then unsaddled and picketed his horse to graze. He spoke to Sounding Sky and some of the other men for a few minutes before instructing Constable Ferris to ride back and find the additional men being sent from Duck Lake. He also had a quiet word with Venne, but the scout did not see any of the men from the previous day in camp. Nor did the Indians seem to know where they were. When the mountie asked about the whereabouts of Topean and Little Saulteaux, no one answered.

Tired from his night's ride, Corporal Bowdridge sat down against a tent and made some entries in his notebook. He carefully took in his surroundings, drawing on his past experience in the Canadian militia, so that he was ready once the Duck Lake reinforcements arrived. When he checked on his horse, he discovered that Sounding Sky had moved to the far outer edge of camp. He also learned from Venne, who had been drinking tea in a small group, that Little Saulteaux had spent the night with Sounding Sky.

Around 11 a.m., the Indians began to strike camp. When Venne came over to talk to Bowdridge about their next move, he noticed two people a short distance away slipping behind some brush. Standing up on a cart to see better, he called to the corporal, "There are some Indians in the bluff ... as soon as they saw me

After Almighty Voice was sighted near a Willow
Cree camp east of the One Arrow reserve in late
May 1897, the mounted police detained his father,
John Sounding Sky. PROVINCIAL ARCHIVES OF
SASKATCHEWAN S-B11171

they lay down."[5] The mountie tried to remain calm, telling Venne
to "take things quietly."

Bowdridge saddled his horse and said he was going to get
water. Instead, he rode to the top of a hill, about 150 yards away,
where he could watch over the bluff with his rifle at the ready. An
unnerved Venne was supposed to follow but rode around the bluff
in a wide circle before joining Bowdridge. The mountie pointed
to a hill on the opposite side of the bluff and told Venne to take
up a position there. As the scout rode off, Bowdridge turned his
attention back to the camp to see that the teepees were almost
all down. That's when he heard three shots. Moments later, a

hunched-over rider raced towards him, yelling, "Indians, boy. They shoot." It was Venne, favouring his right side, bloody from shoulder to thigh. There was also a bullet hole through his hat.

Bowdridge took the scout down to the camp and dressed his wounded upper arm as best he could. He then asked one of the men to take Venne back to the ranch by cart. Only then did he think about his own situation—how the shooters were still out there and how they had been within striking distance during his time in camp. Feeling vulnerable, Bowdridge rode off in search of the reinforcements, keeping to the high ground to avoid being caught out in the open. But his anxiety got the better of him and he became lost in the hills. It was only with some luck that he found his way back to the Venne ranch, with his horse completely played out, by early afternoon.

The police reinforcements were not at the Venne ranch. Corporal Bowdridge hurriedly informed David about the circumstances behind the wounding of his brother and asked him to get a message to Inspector Wilson at the Duck Lake detachment. The policeman then galloped off on a fresh horse to find the mountie party. Bowdridge soon came across the Willow Cree camp, now on the move, and told the band members to return to their reserve. He found the reinforcements—four constables—back at the campsite with Ferris.

Taking two men with him, Bowdridge went in search of those who had done the shooting. It was late afternoon when they spied two people on foot to the north. The three mounties chased after and surrounded them, only to be confronted by Sounding Sky and one of his younger sons, carrying traps with a rabbit and gopher. Bowdridge cautiously ordered Sounding Sky to hand over his gun and then questioned him about the Venne shooting that morning. Almighty Voice's father had nothing to say. The corporal decided to take the pair back to camp. Sounding Sky was placed in irons and kept under guard all night, while sentries took turns on duty. They still didn't know who was behind the shooting, let alone how many.

At 6 a.m. the next morning, Friday, 28 May, Inspector Wilson with three more men arrived at the camp after a hard overnight ride from Duck Lake. They had hurriedly set out after David

Almighty Voice and two companions took refuge in a bluff
(left, middle) to evade capture by a NWMP patrol. CLIFF SPEER

Venne telephoned the detachment from Batoche, pleading for a
doctor because Napoleon had been "shot by Almighty Voice."[6]
It wasn't speculation, something that an overwrought David had
imagined on seeing his brother's injury. Someone from the Willow
Cree camp had taken the wounded Napoleon to his ranch, and
that person probably revealed to him during the cart trip who was
hiding in the bluff. That would explain why his brother David
not only blamed Almighty Voice for the ambush but identified
his companions as the same two young men he had chased from
his cattle herd.[7] When Inspector Wilson consequently set out for
the Minichinas Hills, he knew that the fugitive was out there,
no longer alone, but with two others armed and ready to defend
themselves. Whether he was still in the area was another matter.
Almighty Voice had had ample time to slip away.

Inspector Wilson immediately took command of the mounted
police encampment. He ordered Corporal Bowdridge and Constable Ferris to One Arrow to impound all the horses and secure a list
from farm instructor Louis Marion of those band members absent
from the reserve. The manhunt for Almighty Voice and his two
friends would also be continued, but now with more policemen.
But Wilson was looking in the wrong place.

That same morning, NWMP Inspector Jack Allan was leading

a fourteen-member police party towards the Venne ranch after crossing the South Saskatchewan River at 4 a.m. This heavily armed force had been dispatched from Prince Albert in response to news of Napoleon Venne's shooting, and Almighty Voice's involvement, and was to augment the search for the fugitive. As they rode south, past the eastern edge of the Bellevue settlement around 9 a.m., Constable Alfred Ascott, an advance outflanker, reported seeing three figures running through the underbrush towards a bluff, several hundred yards east of the trail.[8] On being questioned, Ascot couldn't decide whether they were actually deer. When Sergeant John Percy informed Allan what all the fuss was about, the inspector shouted for his men to surround the bluff; he knew from the information provided by David Venne that they were looking for three Indians.[9]

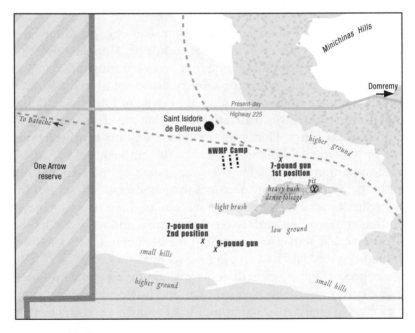

The bluff siege

The bluff was a sunken poplar island, oval in shape, about 140 yards long and sixty yards wide, situated in an open valley surrounded by small hills. The slumped ground, in places several feet below the surrounding land, was filled with trembling aspen and skirted by a dense tangle of willow, thick grasses, roots, and dead fall. Fire had recently licked the eastern edge, leaving that end more open with less foliage. The bluff still exists today at the southern edge of the Minichinas Hills, about three miles east of One Arrow and two miles south of Bellevue, on the southern side of the grid road (once a trail) leading to Domremy (northwest, section 31, township 43, range 27, west of the 2nd meridian). But it is decidedly smaller because the land has been cultivated for decades and the outer perimeter of the bluff has been steadily reduced by modern farm machinery. Finding the spot is not easy without detailed directions. Nor is the site marked in any way.

Once the bluff was surrounded, Inspector Allan ordered the men on the west and north to dismount, draw their sidearms, and enter the underbrush, while he urged his horse forward on the east side through an opening created by a recent fire. Almighty Voice and his two companions were to be forced south and into the open where they would be run down by a line of mounted policemen awaiting them. It was a foolhardy plan. If there was any lesson to be learned from the wounding of Napoleon Venne it was that the three Indians would not be captured without a fight. And by going into the bluff the mounties conceded any advantage they had in numbers and firepower to a concealed foe.

Allan, who had been doggedly pursuing Almighty Voice for more than a year-and-a-half, spending weeks in the saddle over the roughest terrain in all kinds of weather, did not take time to think through the possible consequences. He wanted to end it then and there. Nor was he afraid to go into battle if necessary. Before joining the police in 1885, Allan had been an underage soldier in the Crimean War (1853–56), served in a New York infantry regiment during the American Civil War (1861–65), been wounded three times during the Fenian Raids (1866–71), and been part of the Gordon Relief Expedition (1884–85) to Sudan.[10] Subduing three armed Indians, surrounded by a superior force, probably seemed a simple military exercise to him.

The shooting erupted as soon as the mounties entered the bluff. Inspector Allan, slowly picking his way on horseback through the underbrush, heard three rapid shots, followed by two shots in reply and then two more. Sergeant Charles Raven then shouted to Allan in a strained voice that the Indians were headed his way and that he had been shot in the upper leg. Allan moved to intercept them, watching for any movement in the brush, when one of the Indians on the run shot at him. He returned the fire with his pistol and shot at another, who immediately dove for cover.

NWMP Sergeant Charles Raven was wounded in a foolhardy attempt to flush Almighty Voice from the bluff. RCMP HISTORICAL COLLECTIONS UNIT, REGINA SK, 1934.22.43

Allan slowly wheeled his horse, from right to left, while he scanned the vegetation. As he came around to a patch of willows, there stood Almighty Voice, holding a Winchester rifle, with his two armed companions crouched on either side of him. It was the first time, since Colebrook's death, that a mounted policeman had come face-to-face with the Willow Cree fugitive. Allan instinctively tried to ride them down but was shot twice in the right arm and fell from his horse, breaking the same arm when he hit the ground. Desperate and in numbing pain, and without his revolver, the inspector frantically dragged himself towards shelter.

Almighty Voice slowly stepped forward with his rifle trained on the helpless mountie. The Irish-born Allan probably never thought he would die in a Saskatchewan bluff one early spring morning. But instead of shooting his defenseless adversary, in keeping with his public persona as a cold-blooded murderer, Almighty Voice pointed to the inspector's ammunition belt. He was about to bend down and try to take it from Allan's waist when Sergeant Raven and Constable William Hume, who had heard the shots, reached the east side of the bluff. Almighty Voice fled for cover with his two friends, while Hume emptied his revolver in their direction, not knowing if he hit anyone. Allan and Raven were then helped out of the bluff. Hume would be haunted by the shootout and later purchased his discharge from the force to get "away from those Indians."[11]

Despite his close call with death, Inspector Allan was ever the soldier. While his arm, with a bone protruding, was being bound in a handkerchief, he instructed his men to set fire to the bluff and be prepared for the Indians to try to escape under cover of the smoke. When that failed, he called on Corporal Charles Hockin, who had once served in the British army in India, to assume command of the party and get ready for a second rush on the bluff. For some inexplicable reason, Allan pictured the three Indians as "quite demoralized."[12] He also dispatched Constable Andrew O'Kelly, coincidentally one of the men on guard duty the night of the Almighty Voice escape, to ride to Batoche to report what had happened and ask for reinforcements.[13] Only then did Allan consent to his evacuation to McKenzie Crossing on the South Saskatchewan River, where a Prince Albert doctor was to be waiting to deal with his shattered arm, which he came close to losing. Sergeant Raven had been wounded between the inside of his thigh and his groin, but even though he remained on site, he was in no condition to participate in the siege.

Constable O'Kelly left for Batoche with the news that would be flashed across western Canada: the mounted police had Almighty Voice pinned down in a bluff. At One Arrow, he spoke to farm instructor Louis Marion, who headed for the site as soon as he could get away, but not before first calling in some Willow Cree gathering roots outside the reserve. Marion, in turn, relayed to Inspector Bowdridge that the Indians he was looking for had fought a second skirmish with the police earlier that morning south of Bellevue.

O'Kelly reached Batoche mid-morning but could not get a message by telephone through to Duck Lake. He consequently continued on to the detachment there and sent a telegram to Prince Albert divisional headquarters. He also spoke to Dr. A. B. Stewart and asked him to come out to the hills to attend to Raven.

Duck Lake postmaster Ernest Grundy (perched on fence) was one of several civilians who rushed to the bluff when it was learned that Almighty Voice had been surrounded. PROVINCIAL ARCHIVES OF SASKATCHEWAN S-B11151

By the time O'Kelly headed back, "the wildest excitement" had taken over Duck Lake. Several townspeople looked upon it as a chance to strike a blow against Colebrook's murderer, and possibly claim the reward. A handful arrived at the site with their guns throughout the afternoon. Among them was Ernest Grundy, the Duck Lake postmaster and father of four young daughters, who had served in the Prince Albert home guard during the 1885 North-West Rebellion. He was joined at the bluff by general store clerk William Pozer and station agent Charles Davidson. "The Police ... were not strong enough to take him," explained another civilian participant R. S. Cook, "so I thought I had better go and give a hand."[14]

Corporal Hockin spent the better part of Friday getting his men to secure the site and setting up a base camp, out of the line of fire, on a hill several hundred yards to the northeast of the bluff. Almighty Voice, his brother-in-law, and his cousin were busy, too. They were probably on their way to One Arrow, cautiously walking along the east-west trail that ran immediately north of the bluff, when they were spotted by the Allan mounted party. Being on foot left them no choice but to hide in the bluff. But it put them on the defensive with no way out but surrender. And they were without food.

After the morning shootout that left Allan and Raven wounded, the three Indians set out fortifying their position. With a butcher knife tied to a pole, they dug a pit in the densest part of the bush. They also cut runways through it to be better able to move about the bluff. Any attackers who tried to use these makeshift trails leading to the pit would find themselves exposed and vulnerable. The trio tried to find water by excavating a deep hole in a corner of the pit but, finding none, they were reduced to stripping bark from the aspen and sucking any available moisture. They also shot at birds passing overhead in their desperation to get something to eat.[15]

At 6 p.m., encouraged by the Duck Lake volunteers, Corporal Hockin decided to mount a second assault.[16] He was worried that the three Indians would steal away under the cover of darkness. Hockin led a small party of mounties and civilians down to the north side of the bluff, and after firing a few volleys, tried to set fire to the underbrush. Policemen on horseback waited at a safe distance on the south side, ready to pounce in the event that the Indians dashed out. This time, the bluff caught fire, but it soon died out, sending Hockin back up the hill to regroup and consider his next move.

Around 6:30 p.m., Hockin formed a line with seven men on the west side of the bluff, with himself in the centre, and slowly walked forward into the bush. The men encountered no resistance as they worked their way through to the east side. They then did a sweep of the northern part of the bluff—again, no Indians. As they began to search the south quadrant, Ernest Grundy, the Duck Lake postmaster, was shot through the abdomen. He staggered backwards, dropped to the ground, and called out in agony a few times before perishing. Constable O'Kelly returned fire and hit one of the Indians creeping through the bush. The man appeared to be seriously wounded, if not dead.

Farther ahead, another Indian peeked out over the top of the pit. O'Kelly tried to warn the others, but it was too late for Hockin. He was shot through the lungs. Three constables carried the mortally wounded corporal out of the bush, while the others directed their fire on the pit. Constable John Kerr got carried away in the excitement and failed to take cover. When he stopped shooting, because he ran out of ammunition, he was felled with a bullet to the heart. Davidson and Cook waited for relief, pinned to the ground, but after ten minutes, crawled out to safety. The bodies of Grundy and Kerr were left behind. It could have been worse. Davidson had the heel of his boot shot off. Cook had his coat sliced open by a bullet. Even the buckboard transporting the injured Hockin up to the police camp came under fire; one of the wheel spokes was splintered.

Police reinforcements, under Superintendent Sévère Gagnon, arrived from Prince Albert just as the failed attack on the bluff holdouts came to an end.[17] Gagnon, an original member of the NWMP and one of only a few francophone officers, had replaced George Moffatt as the officer commanding "F" Division and inherited the still-active Almighty Voice file. It was not the first time that Gagnon had tangled with a Cree murderer. While stationed at Fort Saskatchewan in 1879, the then captain Gagnon had investigated the suspicious death of a woman and her five children. Swift Runner claimed that his family had starved over the winter. But at the scene of the incident, Gagnon discovered to his horror that Swift Runner had killed and eaten them.[18]

Superintendent Gagnon had left for the battle site after he

NWMP Superintendent Sévère Gagnon led a Prince Albert police party to the bluff, only to arrive after two men had been killed and another mortally wounded. RCMP HISTORICAL COLLECTIONS UNIT, REGINA SK, 1934.19.7A

received the O'Kelly telegram about the early morning engagement with the Indians. The men at the barracks had just finished playing cricket when the alarm about Almighty Voice was sounded. Gagnon immediately placed sentries around the bluff, while refusing to countenance another assault, if only to retrieve the bodies of the dead. It would soon be dark, and the Indians were now better armed because of the rifles and ammunition that had fallen into their hands. It would be better to wait—despite the taunting, in Cree, coming from the bluff—until a cannon could be brought

The mounted police kept a constant watch on the bluff, from a safe distance, to prevent Almighty Voice and his two companions from slipping away. PROVINCIAL ARCHIVES OF SASKATCHEWAN R-A4522

to the site from Prince Albert. By midnight, both Inspectors Bowdridge and Wilson had arrived at the police camp with a few more men, bringing the size of the guard to about twenty. They were a dispirited group after the day's mauling, made worse by the death of Corporal Hockin.

During that day and into the night, Superintendent Gagnon had remained in contact with NWMP Commissioner L. W. Herchmer by telegraph. When he first wired that Almighty Voice was surrounded in a bluff in the Minichinas Hills and that he was headed there with every available man from the Prince Albert barracks, Herchmer offered to "send a party and horses from here [Regina] if required."[19] Gagnon's next message, received at the mounted police depot at 12:20 a.m., reported, "Constable Kerr and Mr. Grundy shot dead. Corporal Hockin dangerously wounded not expected to live."[20]

No sooner had this message been transcribed for delivery to the commissioner, than the telegraph machine started tapping out a second message from Duck Lake, this one from Dr. Stewart: "Just in from seat of trouble ... assistance with artillery should leave at once. Hard to say how many Indians are in the bluff ... Regular

The seven-pound cannon, last fired in the 1885 North-West
Rebellion, was brought from Prince Albert to the bluff. GLENBOW
ARCHIVES NA-2137-8

death trap. It is a prearranged location."[21] Where Stewart got
the idea that Almighty Voice had deliberately planned to ambush
the police was anybody's guess, or that there were more than
three Indians in the bluff. But the telegram spooked Herchmer. "I
determined to run no risks," he later told the police comptroller.
"If Almighty Voice got away again it might take months to catch
him, and ... entail loss of life ... it was quite possible that others
would join in."[22]

Clutching the telegrams, Herchmer headed to the hall where a
formal, send-off dance was being held for the policemen participating in Queen Victoria's upcoming diamond jubilee celebrations.
Holding up his hand to silence the band, he sternly announced:
"The police have other things to do besides dancing ... The rigs
will be at the door in a few minutes to take you to your homes."[23]
That Herchmer had made the right decision was confirmed by
yet another telegram from Gagnon: "Short handed. Send party
with gun."[24]

The next morning, Saturday, 29 May, a special Canadian
Pacific Railway train chugged north for Duck Lake. On board,
under the command of Assistant Commissioner J. H. McIllree,

an original member of the force and veteran of the rebellion, were twenty-four constables and non-commissioned officers, one inspector, fourteen horses—and a nine-pound cannon, mockingly dubbed by the men, "almighty voice."[25]

They weren't the only people headed to the police camp at the bluff. Superintendent Gagnon returned to Prince Albert with Hockin's body that morning, intent on returning as soon as possible with his own seven-pound brass cannon, even though it had been condemned for use. When he arrived at the barracks, he found a new message from the commissioner, directing him to "swear in as many good constables as you think necessary."[26] Gagnon quickly signed up thirty local men, thanks, in large part, to Crown prosecutor and future Saskatchewan appeals court judge James McKay, who had been busy raising a unit of volunteers to assist the police. Inspector Wilson, with help from C. E. Boucher, the local member of the territorial legislature, enlisted another thirty among the Batoche Métis, but many didn't turn up at the bluff as prearranged. It appears they didn't want to jeopardize their relationship with the local Indian population.[27] The official number of men squaring off against the three Indians —once the Regina contingent arrived—was ninety-one.

Commissioner Herchmer also planned to bring in more men if necessary. He asked all prairie divisions to be on standby. He also held back the queen's jubilee party to see if the men—along with a Maxim gun—would be needed. And he met with Indian Commissioner A. E. Forget early Saturday morning in Regina and reached an informal agreement to bring in fifty "scouts" from the Blackfoot tribes to deal with possible unrest on the Duck Lake reserves.

Herchmer was certainly overzealous in dealing with Almighty Voice and his two young companions, one of them presumably dead. But he was also afraid that the "excited" Willow Cree might turn the bluff showdown with Almighty Voice into a "general rising."[28] This fear, ironically, said more about the commissioner and his so-called understanding of the Indian character: that they were a primitive people, who could never be trusted since the rebellion, and whose savage tendencies were just below the surface. It also explains why the mounties couldn't simply wait out the Indians and starve them into submission; the bluff siege had to be ended quickly and decisively.

Superintendent Gagnon arrived back at the police camp early Saturday evening, and after being informed about a failed third attempt to set the bluff ablaze, he ordered the seven-pounder into action. The gun had last been fired in battle during the rebellion twelve years earlier. (The gun carriage had ironically been used to carry Sergeant Colebrook's body to the Prince Albert cemetery for burial in November 1895.) It took a few rounds to find the range before several fused case shells, filled with gunpowder and large iron balls, were lobbed into the bluff. The first explosion brought one of the Indians into the open to see the source of the bombardment, but he quickly withdrew back into the underbrush after firing a few times at the gunners.

No other movement was detected during the brief shelling. Nor did the police know whether the cannon had inflicted any damage. But Almighty Voice was grievously injured. The ball from one of the case shots had drilled with terrific force into his thigh just above the knee—"smashed the bones ... in a horrible manner."[29] He was fortunate that his femoral artery had not been ruptured. Using the lanyard from Constable Kerr's revolver, he tied a blanket around his knee to stem the bleeding. But he would have been in excruciating pain and able only to hobble about with superhuman effort.

McIllree arrived at the police camp about 9 p.m. on Saturday night followed by the nine-pound gun about an hour later. The assistant commissioner—described as "a conscientious but unimaginative officer"[30]—had taken an early dislike to Indian people. During the NWMP march west in 1874, he found them to be "very dirty" and "a nasty begging lot."[31] This view hardened with time. While posted at Calgary in 1883, McIllree had been sent to arrest the Sarcee leader Bull Head, who was protecting a band member who had broken into the reserve ration house. But several young men intervened, and McIlree was forced to withdraw while Bull Head pointed a rifle at him. The stand-off was peaceably resolved, but an unforgiving McIllree wanted the chief deposed.

McIllree could be expected to show Almighty Voice and his companions no mercy. But he was also on a short leash. Commissioner Herchmer was counting on him to put an end

NWMP Assistant Commissioner J. H. McIllree left
Regina on a special CPR train with police reinforcements
and a nine-pound cannon. RCMP HISTORICAL COLLECTIONS
UNIT, REGINA SK, 1987.127.7

to the Almighty Voice business, but not at the expense of any
more police or civilian casualties. The assistant commissioner was
consequently methodical and cautious to the point of overkill. His
patience would be tested, though.

Because the nine-pound gun wagon was wider than the trail,
its wheels did not fit into the ruts. It was only with great exertion
that the horses could slowly pull the cannon the seventeen miles
from the Duck Lake train station to the bluff. The trip was further
delayed because the Batoche ferry could carry only small loads
at one time across the South Saskatchewan. But McIllree had no
plans to shell the bluff that night. He was under strict orders to
delay any action until the next morning.[32]

Assuming command of the police operation from Gagnon,

McIllree strengthened the cordon to ensure that the remaining two Indians could not get away. He then settled into camp and waited for dawn. There would be no negotiation. Almighty Voice and his surviving friend were considered hostile and were not to be given any reprieve. This certainty—that death would be delivered in the morning—made for an uneasy camp. So, too, did the unusually cold, moonless night. The smoke from the campfires filled the hollow in which the bluff sat and shrouded the surrounding hills before the curtain was raised for the final act.

The frequent shouts of alarm, followed by the exchange of gunfire between the police guard and the occupants of the bluff, foreshadowed what was to come. The men on sentry duty claimed they prevented several escape attempts at different points around the bluff during the night. At one of these places, the mounties later found some blood, one of Almighty Voice's moccasins, and a crude crutch that he had fashioned.[33] It is more likely, though, that the occupants of the bluff were not trying to get away but determined to harass their besiegers through the night. Almighty Voice was ready to meet his fate. Around midnight, he called out in Cree to the police: "Brother, we've had a good fight today. I've worked hard and am hungry. You've plenty of food; send me in some. Tomorrow we'll finish the fight."[34] But there would be no act of chivalry for the doomed men.

At daybreak, the military operation got underway. Assistant Commissioner McIllree called in the sentries and posted men on horseback around the bluff at a safe distance. Gun crews also moved into position with the seven-pound cannon on the high ground north of the bluff and the nine-pounder on one of the small hills to the south. Constable Fred Smith, responsible for the battery, wanted to create an intersecting crossfire.[35] The remainder of the police force watched from the safety of the camp, along with a growing number of civilians, including several from Prince Albert, Duck Lake, and other nearby communities, drawn by the unfolding spectacle.

One of the recent arrivals was Indian Agent R. S. McKenzie, who had issued the arrest warrant for Almighty Voice in October 1895. He had been away on agency business and did not join farm instructor Marion at the bluff until early Sunday morning.

W. J. JAMES, PHOTO,
NISBET STREET, PRINCE ALBERT, SASK.

Men resting and eating in the makeshift bluff camp before
the Sunday morning cannon bombardment. RCMP HISTORICAL
COLLECTIONS UNIT, REGINA SK, 1988.25.3A

Neither McKenzie nor Marion mention in their official diaries
the presence of any other Indians at the site during the standoff.
Nor do the policemen in their official reports say anything about
the Willow Cree. It's a curious omission, but a telling one because
other eyewitness accounts report a small gathering of Indians,
including Almighty Voice's mother, on a nearby low hill. They
were there to bear witness. The sound of Spotted Calf's haunting
death chant—calling on her son to be brave—carried through
the valley below her.[36]

At 6 a.m., Sunday, 30 May, both guns opened fire on the bluff.
Prince Albert special constable Joe Walton had limited experience handling the seven-pound gun. And it showed. His first
shots sailed through the bluff or did not explode, probably to the
disappointment of those reduced to being bystanders. Walton
eventually found the range—after what amounted to target practice—and landed some double shells in the bluff. But the gun's

The shelling of the bluff lasted two hours. PROVINCIAL ARCHIVES OF
SASKATCHEWAN R-A4523

effectiveness, according to one mountie, was "not so good," and
it was taken out of action.[37]

Constable Smith, operating the nine-pound gun, had conferred
beforehand with Constable O'Kelly about the location of the pit
the Indians had excavated. He trained his first shot there but hit
the outer edge of the bluff. He adjusted the gun and sent four
common shells (high explosive) into the approximate area of the
pit, spewing fountains of dirt and debris into the air. Smith then
raked the length of the bluff with five shrapnel shells before pour-
ing another three common shells into the pit. He was convinced at
least one of the shots had struck home; shell fragments were later
found in the sides and bottom of the pit. Assistant Commissioner
McIllree called a halt to the bombardment after about an hour.

There was no response from Almighty Voice and his companions
to the shelling—no movement in the bluff, just silence. But were
they dead or just wounded? With McIllree's blessing, Constable

Smith moved the seven-pound gun to a hill to the south, near the nine-pounder, and began lobbing shells with time fuses—much like mortars—throughout the bluff. On the twenty-fifth shot, one of the carriage bolts broke and the brass cannon flew into the air backwards, turning completely over and landing several yards away. This freak accident brought the saturation shelling to an end.

McIllree was worried that the Indians might still be alive, and a threat. After consulting with James McKay, leader of the Prince Albert special constables, the assistant commissioner decided to dig a series of pits towards the bluff and gradually move men forward. There were no shovels or picks available, though, and the call went out to Duck Lake and Prince Albert for tools.

McIllree was prepared to wait all day and into the next before advancing into the bluff. But as the hours passed, the Prince Albert special constables grew increasingly restless and unruly. McKay could not hold them back for much longer. Nor could McIllree, who threatened to charge them with disobeying his orders. It also did not help that Indian Agent McKenzie apparently ridiculed the men—he would later deny it—and offered to send for some women to do their job.[38]

McIllree finally gave in at 2 p.m. "It struck me," he reported to the commissioner, "that it would be a ghastly joke on us if we guarded the bluff all night again, and ... find the Indians all dead."[39] He also did not want a protracted siege. The longer Almighty Voice was able to hold out, it was believed, the greater the likelihood of other Indians coming to join him.[40]

Once the men were armed and formed up on the north and east side, McIllree told them that on the word "go" they were to rush to the edge of the bluff, drop down, fire a volley, and then slowly move into the underbrush. His command, though, set off a foot race led by an impatient William Drain. Some men arrived at the bluff ahead of others, discharged their guns, and then ran on towards the pit shooting indiscriminately, only to come under fire by those behind them or on the other side. Some later claimed that the Indians had returned their fire during the charge. "There was pandemonium," the assistant commissioner recalled. "It was a great wonder someone was not shot."[41]

Once the shooting had subsided and some semblance of order established, McIllree proceeded to identify the dead and the circumstances of their death, with assistance from James McKay and Prince Albert doctor Hugh Bain. Constable Kerr was the first to be found, where he had been shot dead through the heart two days earlier. His skull had been bashed in by the butt of a rifle. He had also been shot in the head and right wrist during the wild rush on the bluff. Nearby was Almighty Voice's brother-in-law Topean. Constable O'Kelly thought he had killed him during an earlier battle. But he had been playing dead. Dr. Bain could find no wound on the body. What had killed Topean was a bullet that entered the left side of his forehead and blew out the back of his head. It was concluded that he had been shot during the skirmish with the sentries the night before.

Almighty Voice and his cousin Little Saulteaux were found together in the pit, perhaps both killed by the same shell. The top of Almighty Voice's skull had been blown off. It's not known where his skull fragment was found, and by whom, but it was later displayed in the RCMP museum in Regina, before being removed and placed in an envelope in a filing cabinet.[42] Almighty Voice

The gravestone of Duck Lake postmaster Ernest Grundy, who was mortally wounded in the stomach during a combined police-civilian sweep of the bluff. BILL WAISER

had also been hit in the foot, in addition to the dreadful wound to the thigh and knee he had sustained during the first shelling of the bluff on Friday evening. Little Saulteaux, with the side of his head broken open by a shell, lay on top of Almighty Voice. He had also been shot several times, again, during the final rush on the bluff.

NWMP Corporal Charles Hockin (left) and Constable John Kerr, both killed at the bluff, were buried within sight of the Colebrook grave (distant middle) in Prince Albert. BILL WAISER

The last to be identified, just beyond the pit, was Duck Lake postmaster Ernest Grundy, felled by a shot to the abdomen. His head had been smashed in, too. And he was riddled with bullets. "The sight was something horrible," reported Indian

Agent McKenzie, who walked through the bluff after it had been stormed.[43] He probably wanted to confirm with his own eyes that Almighty Voice was dead.

McIllree wished to move on from the sorry episode as soon as he could; he had the reputation of the force to uphold. He had the five dead men carried from the bluff and up to the police camp. There, he huddled with McKay and Bain about the necessity of holding an inquest, and the trio concluded it was not necessary. McIllree then went searching for Robert McKenzie but could not find him. The Indian agent had left. Not sure what to do, the assistant commissioner decided to turn the bodies of Almighty Voice, Topean, and Little Saulteaux over to farm instructor Marion for burial.[44]

Grundy's body was released to some friends and taken back to Duck Lake with a police escort. By mid-June, 103 members—almost half—of the House of Commons had signed a petition, urging the Laurier government to grant Grundy's widow, Mary Jane, and their four daughters a pension.[45] Constable Kerr and Corporal Hockin, hailed as heroes in Prince Albert, were buried at the foot of Sergeant Colebrook's grave in St. Mary's cemetery, bringing together in death the three mounties who had died in the pursuit of Almighty Voice. Their funeral was the largest in Prince Albert history. The procession was reportedly a mile long and watched by schoolchildren who had been given a half-day holiday. The hymns at the church service were sung, ironically, by a "native boys" choir.[46] The solemnity of the occasion contrasted sharply with the thunderous homecoming for the mountie "victors" in Regina. They arrived in the territorial capital just as the delayed jubilee contingent was about to board its train, and the station echoed with cheers for the two groups.[47]

Police and Indian Affairs officials spent early June tidying up a few outstanding issues. First, there was the matter of Almighty Voice's father, Sounding Sky, who had been detained after the wounding of Napoleon Venne. The police looked upon him as an accessory—but an accessory to what? While "Old John" was being held in the Prince Albert jail, waiting to be remanded, Inspector James Wilson "tried in every possible way to get something against him," including questioning members of the One

Hockin Avenue at the Regina RCMP training academy commemorates
Corporal Hockin, who led the second police charge on the bluff.
KNUCKLE, "IN THE LINE OF DUTY"

Arrow band.[48] When Wilson failed to secure any evidence of
wrongdoing, Sounding Sky was released.

The other nagging question was where Almighty Voice had
been hiding over the past few months. There were stories that
he had been living with his grandfather in Grizzly Bear coulee
in the Eagle Hills outside Battleford. It was also rumoured that
Almighty Voice had spent the winter on One Arrow—that "he had
a secret passage into the cellar" in one of the homes there.[49] The
police spoke to people on the Duck Lake and Battleford reserves,
assuring them that the matter was closed and there would be no
prosecutions for harbouring the fugitive. No one offered any
information about Almighty Voice's whereabouts.

Police and Indian officials were also worried about how bands
might react to the killing of Almighty Voice, afraid there might
be "further trouble."[50] That the Willow Cree people might be
mourning was never a consideration. Instead, the NWMP and
Indian commissioners worked together to ensure there would not
be another Almighty Voice episode.

Over the first week of June, mounted policemen visited reserves
throughout the Saskatchewan country to explain what had
happened and determine the mood. Special attention was paid to
the Nut Lake reserve, the home of Almighty Voice's grandfather

and cousin Little Saulteaux, one of the men killed at the bluff. If anyone was going to retaliate, the mounties believed, it would likely be Little Saulteaux's brother, considered "one of the worst Indians in the Territories."[51] The police also closely watched the Fort à la Corne bands in the belief that they had sympathized with the fugitive and surreptitiously helped him in the past. But everything was "very quiet." The only news was that Almighty Voice's companion Small Face was gravely ill and not expected to live.[52]

The biggest concern was the Duck Lake reserves and their apparent return to their rebel ways. In mid-June, there was a report that marauding Indians from One Arrow were raiding local ranchers' cattle. The story was found to be false, but not before mountie reinforcements were scrambled north from Regina. The Willow Cree people were indeed off reserve, but picking roots and, in the words of the agent, "appear peaceably inclined."[53] NWMP Commissioner Herchmer suggested that such alarms could be avoided if the One Arrow band was confined to its reserve and given supplementary rations until "any feeling of restlessness" had passed.[54] The Indian office readily embraced the plan without any concern about cost. Government authorities no longer trusted the Willow Cree—if they ever did.

Neither the mounted police nor Indian Affairs shone a light inward in the aftermath of the sorry incident. There would be no inquiry or investigation into what had gone wrong: why Almighty Voice had killed a cow, fled his trial, killed a policeman, and then eluded capture for more than nineteen months with the active assistance of family and relatives in local bands. It was simply assumed that Almighty Voice's bloodlust mirrored the worst qualities of his race and that he deserved to die before others joined him. "They sold their lives dearly" is how Indian Affairs summarized the bluff bombardment in the department annual report. "Thus the Indians learn that justice, although sometimes slow, is sure, and will be executed at whatever the cost."[55]

NWMP Commissioner Herchmer chose to focus on "the trouble that even one bad Indian can give ... to the peace and safety of the country," a view forcefully echoed by Edmonton Liberal MP Frank Oliver in the House of Commons in calling for a strengthened police force in the West to protect the settler population.

"In view of the circumstances that have occurred," Oliver said of the bluff showdown, "one or two or three Indians can make trouble for a whole settlement, a whole countryside, and require a large force to deal with them."[56] This statement represented quite a change from fifteen years earlier when Oliver, in his capacity as owner and editor of the Edmonton *Bulletin* published an excoriating editorial on federal Indian policy. "The Indians have become disgusted with the discrepancy between the promises and performances of the [Indian Affairs] department," he had warned then, "and unless a change takes place soon ... the prospects of an Indian war will be brighter than ever."[57] Sitting on the government side of the House of Commons apparently brought on amnesia.

If Almighty Voice was a ruthless murderer, then why did he not execute the helpless Inspector Allan in the bluff? And if the Cree were nothing more than primitive savages, then why were there not more violent incidents of this kind? Clearly, the police and Indian officials chose not to understand the treaty relationship and how the Cree had solemnly promised to remain peaceful. They had also become wilfully blind and deaf to how Indian "management" had made life absolutely miserable for the Cree to the point where a few, a very few, individuals like Almighty Voice might fight back. This management had already earned censure in 1885 from Presbyterian minister "Fighting Dan Gordon," chaplain to Winnipeg's 90th Battalion during the North-West Rebellion. Gordon proved his mettle while under fire during the battle of Batoche. But he found nothing heroic in his rebellion experience, just soul-searching doubt and pointed questioning about Canada's Indian policy. "It is a bitter mockery on the Christian name," he opened up to a fellow minister, "for us to apply it to ourselves as a people when we have treated the Indian in such a way." He then added, almost in anger, "If I were an Indian I would take all the risks of an uprising and have done with it."[58]

If and when it happened, as the sorry case of Almighty Voice demonstrated, the Canadian state would be ready to crush any Indian defiance—by violence if necessary. Government officials were determined to keep Indian peoples under their thumb and refused to accept any pushback. Almighty Voice was nothing more than a renegade. NWMP comptroller Fred White epitomized this

Almighty Voice (grave with leaning cross) and his two companions
were buried on the One Arrow reserve. FRANK ANDERSON

attitude when he complained in June 1897 that it was "unfortunate" that "so much fuss" was being made over the "Almighty
Voice affair." What bothered him even more was the "amount of
ridicule" he was getting in Ottawa circles over the use of cannon
to end the bluff siege. Sir Adolphe Caron, the former minister of
the Militia, bitingly suggested that "the Police will be taking out
their nine-pounder guns to shoot flies when the warm weather
comes."[59] But what happened to Almighty Voice was no joke.
Why he died was more important than how he died. That non-
Indigenous people would not see it that way was the real tragedy.
He was just a worthless Indian, best forgotten.

CHAPTER FIVE

The Worst of the Bad

The removal of Almighty Voice's lifeless body from the bluff did not end his story. In fact, the telling of what happened—how a young Willow Cree man chose a defiant death over surrender to the North-West Mounted Police—was just beginning. Newspapers scrambled to report on the armed showdown in the Minichinas Hills, relying on speculation and rumour in place of fact and analysis, especially when telegraph service went down for several critical hours during the siege. Even then, the only detail that mattered was that the mounted police had finally cornered one of Canada's most wanted fugitives after a nineteen-month flight from justice. Confident that Almighty Voice would soon meet his end, the local print media played up the unfolding drama and its climactic final act. There was no attempt to understand why the "Indian outlaw" openly challenged Canadian authority. Almighty Voice's actions were attributable to his race: Indians, in the words of the Qu'Appelle *Vidette*, were a "peculiarly excitable" people. "When one of them commits a crime and ... evad[es] prompt punishment," the newspaper gravely intoned, "he rapidly becomes a hero ... utterly reckless and ... can do an immensity of harm."[1] That's why Almighty Voice had to answer for the murder of NWMP Sergeant Colin Colebrook and the other men who lost their lives trying to flush him out of the bluff. The Willow Cree fugitive was a menace to white prairie society and had to be eradicated in the name of law and order. This theme dominated much of the early writing on the incident.

≈

"ON THE WARPATH." That's how the 29 May 1897 edition of the Prince Albert *Saskatchewan Times* portrayed the standoff between the mounted police and Almighty Voice and "other bad

Indians [number unknown] ensconced in a bluff" east of Batoche. Three days later, the paper gleefully announced that Almighty Voice "is now numbered among the class of Indians marked 'good.'" It also insinuated that the outlaw had been brazenly helped by his home reserve for the past few months and that his bluff "retreat" was a "prepared" hideout, meant to be "impregnable."[2]

The Prince Albert *Advocate* was equally sensational in its coverage, suggesting in bold headline that a "Gang of Indians, Headed by Almighty Voice" had launched "A SMALL REBELLION." But unlike its rival, the *Advocate* maintained that the Indians had hurriedly taken refuge in the nearest bluff to escape the police pursuit and "suffered much from wounds, hunger, and thirst." There would be no mercy, though. The police cannon saw to that. Almighty Voice's "career as a bad Indian" was ended "ingloriously" by a "death-dealing storm of lead and iron." Bringing him to justice, the paper regretted, had "cost the country ... valuable lives." And those certainly were not Indian ones.[3]

This blessing of Almighty Voice's "extermination" would be expected from the Prince Albert newspapers. After all, the community had known Sergeant Colebrook and been shaken by his murder. The NWMP "F" Division, based in Prince Albert, had also been vitally involved in the prolonged search for Almighty Voice and was determined to avenge the senseless killing of one of their own. But other prairie newspapers were just as pleased, if not enthusiastic, about the Willow Cree man's violent death at the hands of the mounted police. Nor did they shrink from printing half-truths or misinformation about the bluff siege.

The Regina *Leader* was filled with stories about "how the bad Indian died," thanks to a staff reporter named Trant who travelled north with the Regina mountie contingent on Saturday, 29 May, and witnessed the shelling and charge of the bluff the next day. But what was particularly noteworthy about the *Leader*'s coverage was how it first reported that "the trouble was wider than could be made by three Indians." Why else, the paper wondered, would such a large, heavily armed police force be dispatched by special train and the detachment for Queen Victoria's diamond jubilee celebrations be held back? The *Leader* even printed the rumour that Almighty Voice had the support of four hundred Indians from Nut Lake and that Cree Chief Piapot had left his reserve with armed warriors to join them.

In a later edition that same day, Trant provided a detailed, fairly accurate account of the scene at the bluff and how the cannons were used to bring the siege to an end. A feature editorial, "The Indian Tragedy," now downplayed the threat of an Indian uprising, insisting that Almighty Voice may have been "game to the finish," but he was not supported in his "murderous acts" except for his two "misguided" companions. "Acute trouble with North-West Indians is not to be feared," the paper counselled. "They did not raise a hand to save him, nor was the slightest demonstration made against the authorities." It was more important to take comfort in the fact that Almighty Voice was dead.[4]

That was the message—"Almighty Voice Stilled"—in the other Regina newspaper, the *Standard*. But it also argued that "a serious outbreak" had been avoided *only* because the bluff fight had been

AN INDIAN SPREADS DEATH

TRAGICAL ENDING OF THE CAREER OF "ALMIGHTY VOICE."

Resisting Capture, the Murderer of Colebrook Kills Three More Men, and Wounds Three Others—Driven to Bay, With an Army of 200 Men and Two Cannon Against Him, the Indian at the Least Died Gamely.

Regional newspaper coverage of the Almighty Voice incident dwelled on the Indian's murderous rampage and his deserved death at the hands of Canada's heralded North-West Mounted Police. REGINA "LEADER", 3 JUNE 1897 "speedily terminated." And that was reason enough, according to a *Standard* editorial, for not reducing the size of the mounted police force because of "the conditions that exist here."[5] Or as Winnipeg's *Nor'Wester* rhetorically asked, "If one Indian under such disadvantageous circumstances could hold such a large force at bay for so long, what could a band of Indians on the warpath do?"[6]

Other regional newspapers offered similar observations. The Qu'Appelle *Vidette*, in a piece cleverly titled, "Almighty Voice Hushed," expressed relief that the police murderer "has at last met with his death." It then stoutly defended the NWMP for "the time they took to finish the business" given the perils of rushing across open ground to reach the bluff.[7] The Moose Jaw *Times* also applauded the mounted police and civilian volunteers for putting an end to Almighty Voice's trail of "bloodthirstiness." "It does not detract," it maintained, "from the gallantry of the men in storming the bluff that there were no more formidable enemy than three dead Indians."[8]

The *Saskatchewan Herald*, meanwhile, used the incident to question whether Indians could ever be trusted, something that had been a constant refrain for the newspaper since the 1885 North-West Rebellion. It held that there could have been another uprising—"very serious trouble"—if not for the strong response from the police. The bluff showdown served to "show how easily the Indians can become excited and band themselves against the whites and ... bid defiance to the law."[9]

The Edmonton *Bulletin* shared these concerns. Owned and operated by Frank Oliver, the new Liberal MP for Edmonton and future Indian Affairs minister (appointed April 1905), the paper rarely had a kind word to say about Indigenous peoples. The bluff battle only reinforced these prejudices, with an error-riddled article suggesting that Almighty Voice had been deliberately "lying in ambush" for the police. "By dying," the *Bulletin* observed in an editorial, "Much from Little," the Indian outlaw "became much more useful than he could have ever been than living." Almighty Voice was not just standing up to the mounted police, but "all the white settlers of the west."[10] And that was the lesson here.

The story also made front page news in other parts of Canada and was even mentioned in some major world dailies.[11] The Winnipeg *Free Press* reproduced much of the same material that appeared in the North-West newspapers but added to the growing list of falsehoods by declaring that two Manitoba militia companies were being readied to tangle with five hundred Indians at the bluff.

In looking for a different angle on the story, the *Free Press* interviewed former mountie John Dickson, who had participated in the search for Almighty Voice and was supposedly "well acquainted" with the fugitive. He stated that the Willow Cree man had a "rather striking appearance," backed up by a weak or effeminate voice. He also said the Indian had made a criminal living "scour[ing] the country stealing cattle here and there" before he was finally apprehended at Duck Lake. His most remarkable statement, though, concerned Almighty Voice's companion Small Face and what she combatively told police interrogators after the Colebrook shooting. According to Dickson, Small Face warned that her partner had ten bullets: eight for the police; one for the reserve farm instructor he had a grudge against, and "the 10th marked with a cross for himself when his work of vengeance was complete."[12]

Another mountie, Odilon St. Denis, who had been part of the police cordon at the bluff, provided a similar tell-all story to the Ottawa *Journal* during a visit to the capital. He claimed that Almighty Voice was being tracked before he slipped into cover and that he had openly bragged that he would kill more policemen. "The reason we wanted so many men [at the bluff]," Denis explained, "was that we were pretty close to the Indian reserves and we were afraid that [other] Indians might take part."[13]

The Toronto *Globe* raised the spectre of a possible Indian war declaring that young men were deserting their reserves to join Almighty Voice. It also repeated the rumour that the bluff was a deliberate trap, perhaps one of many. But the mounties prevailed, and he was "Shot Dead in His Hole," like some cornered vermin.[14] The Toronto *World* offered more of the same in several articles, alternately calling Almighty Voice "dangerous," "a bad one," and finally "cunning." It could also not resist using the bluff showdown to poke fun at Nicholas Davin, the Conservative MP for Assiniboia West and the only territorial Tory at the time, in a front-page editorial cartoon, "At Bay." Derided for his verbosity—he would speak 1,023 times in the House of Commons, filling 250 pages of Hansard, in 1897—Davin or "Mighty Voice" is hunkered down in his grave, sporting feathers in his hat, reaching for fresh "charges agin' the govt" to reload his speech-smoking gun. Arrayed against him on a distant ridge are scores of government soldiers, armed with a cannon, in the "Grit Camp." The Irish-born Davin yells, "Bad scran [bad luck] till them, they'll not silence this Voice while there's a charge lift."[15]

This linking of Davin with Almighty Voice underscored how far newspapers were willing to go to exploit the Indian's death, especially the way he died. The press could not have asked for

CANADA.

(FROM OUR CORRESPONDENT.)
OTTAWA, MAY 31.

Almighty Voice, the Indian murderer whose arrest the North-West Mounted Police have been trying to effect, was shot dead yesterday with two companions. No losses beyond those already reported were suffered by the attacking party. There is no fear of further trouble.

The London *Times* offered a short, matter-of-fact account of the death of Almighty Voice. LONDON *TIMES*, 1 JUNE 1897

a better storyline—wanted murderer clashes with mounties in prairie showdown—in trying to reach out to more readers. But the articles were not shaping public opinion as much as reflecting it. Newspaper coverage of the Almighty Voice incident served to confirm and reinforce popular racist attitudes towards Indian peoples at the time.[16]

By the mid-1890s, the great agricultural promise of the "last best west" was finally being realized as tens of thousands of homesteaders began to pour into western Canada and to plough and cultivate land that Indians had continued to use for traditional activities after the signing of the treaties. These newcomers heralded a new beginning for the West, one that did not include Indian peoples. The Plains Cree and other western tribes had squandered that opportunity by failing to possess and improve the land, choosing instead to continue to hunt, trap, and gather. These were considered backward pursuits, especially when measured against farming and the larger march of progress. For many Canadians at the turn of the twentieth century, Indians were identified with a dark, pre-modern past, and the sooner they got out of the way—or simply disappeared—the better. Until then, they should be confined to their reserves, separate and apart from the growing white settler population, so that the agricultural development of the region and the realization of provincehood could proceed in an orderly and timely fashion. Otherwise, the region's potential might be compromised.[17]

That was the attitude of the new Wilfrid Laurier Liberal government that swept the tired Tories from office in 1896. Clifford Sifton, the new superintendent general of Indian Affairs (also minister of the Interior), lost little time dismissing his deputy Hayter Reed on the grounds that he wanted a reorganized, more efficient administration. But there would be no softening of the attitudes and policies of the Indian Affairs department. Had not the Canadian government expended considerable time and money since the late 1870s trying to uplift and civilize them with little to show for these efforts? Any glimmer of optimism that might have once been associated with federal Indian policies had been long extinguished, and, with it, any expectation that Indian peoples would ever change. The Laurier Liberals took office determined to limit Canada's responsibilities to Indian peoples, while dramatically reducing its Indian Affairs expenditures. One sure sign of the lowly place of Indian peoples under the new regime was the reduction in the size of several reserves in western Canada. The Laurier government confiscated parts of reserves—there was no better word for it—so that prime agricultural land would not be "wasted" by Indian bands.[18] "We may as well be frank," Clifford Sifton summed up the government's position in a House of Commons speech in 1904, "the Indian has not the physical, mental or moral get-up to enable him to compete. He cannot do it."[19]

This disdain, if not contempt, for western Canada's Indian

AT BAY.

MIGHTY VOICE: Bad scran till them, they'll not silence this Voice while there's a "charge" lift.

The editorial cartoon, "At Bay," used the Almighty Voice incident to mock territorial Conservative MP Nicholas Flood Davin ("Mighty Voice") for his verbosity in the House of Commons. TORONTO *WORLD*, 3 JUNE 1897

peoples saturated the media's depiction of Almighty Voice and his fate. The Indian fugitive might have been lauded by the Regina *Leader* for "his magnificent display of animal courage" during the bluff fight, but that same animal courage led to his murderous rampage. Almighty Voice's mother was equally bad. Instead of acknowledging her son's wrongdoing, the "sullen and defiant" Spotted Calf hissed at the police and vowed, "He will kill more of you first." The One Arrow people, meanwhile, were guilty of subverting law and order because they kept the fugitive "under their protection" instead of assisting the mounted police. Then, there was the "saucy" attitude of neighbouring reserves, ready to exploit the standoff and wreak trouble if given the opportunity.[20]

Add it all up, and the only conclusion was that Indians were standing in the way of progress and Anglo-Canadian civilization. That's why there was such opposition to the federal plan to reduce the NWMP presence on the prairies. As the Almighty Voice episode assuredly demonstrated, there was every reason to have a strong punitive force at the ready for any eventuality. "It was cheaper to pay for special trains," one newspaper justified the speedy dispatch of the mountie reinforcements from Regina, "than to risk lives."[21] It also explains why there was a spirited public meeting in Regina on 3 June, four days after Almighty Voice's death, to protest the relocation of the federal Indian offices. A closer watch was needed over the unpredictable Indian population and that could not be done if Commissioner A. E. Forget and a much smaller Indian Affairs staff were headquartered in Winnipeg.

The bluff siege also had religious overtones. When the mounted police put out the call for civilian help, "a body of brave men" in nearby communities readily volunteered—much like crusaders—to do "their duty nobly." They answered a higher calling by "plac[ing] themselves in peril ... in maintaining the laws of the land."[22] Several other newspapers also noted how the final assault on the bluff had taken place on the Sabbath. Much like the ringing of church bells, "the booming of the guns and the exploding shells" called forth the police and civilians on that lovely Sunday spring morning to smite the pagan enemy in the form of Almighty Voice.[23] And when the rush was over, there were prayers of thanks that no one else had been hurt. Christian forces had triumphed over a savage, depraved foe.

Only one newspaper editorial sympathized with Almighty Voice's situation. "A.V. was the champion of a race that is up against it in civilization," bluntly observed the Toronto *Telegram*. "The wonder is that not an occasional brave cuts loose, but that all braves do not prefer the sudden death to the slow extinction of their race." These were tough words; clearly, there were larger questions at play here. But the editorial then went on to simply denounce the Liberal government's handling of Indian Affairs.

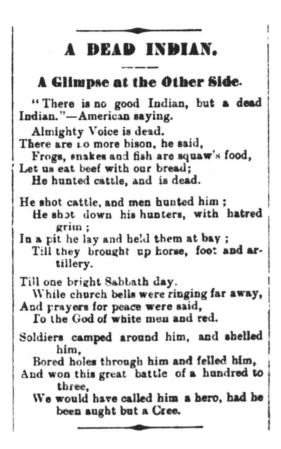

A DEAD INDIAN.

A Glimpse at the Other Side.

"There is no good Indian, but a dead Indian."—American saying.

Almighty Voice is dead.
There are no more bison, he said,
  Frogs, snakes and fish are squaw's food,
Let us eat beef with our bread;
  He hunted cattle, and is dead.

He shot cattle, and men hunted him;
  He shot down his hunters, with hatred grim;
In a pit he lay and held them at bay;
  Till they brought up horse, foot and artillery.

Till one bright Sabbath day.
  While church bells were ringing far away,
And prayers for peace were said,
  To the God of white men and red.

Soldiers camped around him, and shelled him,
  Bored holes through him and felled him,
And won this great battle of a hundred to three,
  We would have called him a hero, had he been aught but a Cree.

The poem, "A Dead Indian," attempted to offer "a glimpse at the other side." REGINA STANDARD, 24 JUNE 1897

Even then, there was no analysis of why federal Indian policy was failing or, more important, why someone like Almighty Voice chose to "be shot ... [rather] than starved to death."[24] Nor was there any attempt to understand the trauma that the One Arrow community had experienced during the bluff siege, especially the repeated shelling of the fugitive's hideout while band members gloomily looked on. That the Willow Cree might be despondent—might be grieving for their own loss—did not matter.

The only other newspaper item that offered "A Glimpse at the

Other Side" was an anonymous poem in the Regina *Standard* in late June. "A Dead Indian" was a clumsily rhyming attempt to place hunger as the driving force behind the incident. The poem also singled out race as a roadblock to understanding Almighty Voice's bravery in the end. "We would have called him a hero," it concluded, "had he been aught but a Cree."[25] It was an isolated opinion. Although many newspapers acknowledged, in the words of the *Nor'Wester*, that "there was real grit in the Redskin," Almighty Voice was still a cold-blooded murderer, regardless of his race. He may have "won notoriety" with his "daring," but he found that his "glory [led] but to the grave."[26]

There were no follow-up stories in the press that offered an in-depth look at what happened or why. Almighty Voice was dead, no longer a threat to white society, and that was that. On reflection, though, some western newspapers expressed concern that the image of the region as a peaceful, orderly place had been defamed by the lurid coverage of the bluff standoff. In an editorial, "From Molehill to Mountain," the Winnipeg *Free Press* charged that immigration and settlement would be harmed if such negative stories continued to be published. The Regina *Leader* also chimed in, righteously declaring that exaggeration of the recent event was

Western Canadians looked upon Indians (like this group near Saskatoon in 1908) as standing in the way of the region's great future. BROCK SILVERSIDES COLLECTION

irresponsible, unwarranted, and potentially damaging.[27]

Maybe Britain's London *Times* got it right in its only comment on the affair the day after Almighty Voice died. "There is no fear of an Indian rising," it calmly observed. "It is simply a case of ... evading arrest."[28] But such a measured response, in comparison to western Canadian reporting, was not possible given the general public unease about the Indian population. Exaggerated articles matched the Canadian mindset.

Western newspapers also did not correct the questionable statements they had made during the tense days of the bluff showdown, except to assure readers there was no Indian rising, either because of the speedy response of the mounted police or because there never was one in the making. The papers simply published new information as it became available, sometimes contradicting what had already been reported or generally adding to the misinformation. But that did not matter. Most things written about Indians, no matter how callous or sordid, were accepted at face value.

The Prince Albert *Advocate* did, however, repudiate a "cock-and-bull" story by J. C. Birch, formerly of Prince Albert. In a Calgary *Herald* interview in early July, Birch claimed that Almighty Voice had "come out in full view" at the bluff, "undressed one of the policemen he had killed ... and intended to cook and eat" him. He also said the Duck Lake Indians "had been trading horses for ammunition south of the line" in preparation for "a future showdown" with Canadian authorities. The *Advocate* rightly dismissed the Birch interview as "nonsense," but the fact that it was printed gave it credibility and an audience.[29]

"Nonsense" also applied to other stories about Almighty Voice in the western press. It was said, for example, that Almighty Voice had "ambushed" NWMP Sergeant Colebrook before the mountie had a chance to re-arrest him in October 1895 and that he had prepared a similar trap for the police at the bluff. Another report had Almighty Voice's father, Sounding Sky, lurking near the bluff with ammunition. Newspapers also had the mounties setting off from Regina with both a Maxim gun and Gatling gun to do battle with the Indians. One of the other widely circulated stories was that Almighty Voice had placed the body of one of his dead companions up against a tree along the edge of the bluff to confuse the police.

The most contested detail, though, was how Almighty Voice died. The Winnipeg *Free Press* stated that the Indians had fired three shots when police rushed the bluff after the Sunday morning shelling and that Almighty Voice had been shot in the head by the return fire. He was "literally riddled with rifle bullets" when the mounties removed his body from the bluff. The Toronto *Globe*, on the other hand, suggested that Almighty Voice perished two ways—in the same edition. He was seen alive after the shelling and died "instantly" when shot while in the pit, but not before the top of his head had been blown off by a shell. The Edmonton *Bulletin* further muddied the story by alleging the fugitive was already dead by his own hand before the shelling. Almighty Voice had tried to escape from the bluff Saturday night, and when he could not get away, he committed suicide. The head wound from the shell was inflicted after he shot himself.[30]

These rumours and falsehoods, when combined with conflicting accounts, blurred the line between fact and fiction. Critical aspects, including background context, were also excluded, downplayed, or ignored so that the telling of the Almighty Voice story aligned with the values associated with Anglo-Canadian civilization. What emerged, then, in the months and years following Almighty Voice's death was essentially a one-sided, one-dimensional story that ignored the Indian perspective in favour of extolling the mounted police and how they would "not let up until they have got their man."[31]

That was certainly the case when the first article about Almighty Voice appeared two years later in July 1899. Journalist William A. Fraser, a regular contributor to *McClure's Magazine*, included the incident in a feature story on mounted police methods, "Soldier Police of the Canadian Northwest." How was it, Fraser wondered at the outset, that a force of less than one thousand men could "guard half a continent, peopled by warlike Indians, so well" that a lone and unarmed white man felt safer than in New York City? The answer: a combination of "prestige and determination." The mountie not only embodied law and order but upheld the right to law and order, a fact not lost on those who came up against the police and backed down. Almighty Voice, according to Fraser, broke that understanding by murdering a policeman "handicapped by his order to arrest and not kill." And it fell to his comrades to apprehend the Indian outlaw so "that the peace ... might be made whole again."

"'If he advances I'll kill him,' answered Almighty Voice." FRASER, *SOLDIER POLICE OF THE CANADIAN NORTHWEST*

Fraser's account—complete with black-and-white illustrations—opened with a "hungry" Almighty Voice, committing a "little irregularity" by killing a cow that belonged to someone else. Thereafter, the focus was on the mounted police and how the Indian openly defied their authority. Sergeant Colebrook and his scout François Dumont had set off to fetch Almighty Voice—no mention was made of his escape from the Duck Lake goal—when they chanced upon him and not one, but two women ("squaws").

"They scoured the land far and wide." FRASER, *SOLDIER POLICE OF THE CANADIAN NORTHWEST*

Fraser's description of the confrontation was remarkably accurate except for the imagined dialogue. He must have relied on someone inside the force who had access to the inquest testimony. Colebrook calmly rode forward, calling on Almighty Voice to lay down his gun and surrender. Almighty Voice replied, through Dumont, that he wanted to be left alone and that he would kill the sergeant if he kept advancing. But Colebrook was duty-bound. "The sergeant, according to his code, had no choice," Fraser explained. "He could not retire; he had no authority to shoot the Indian; his orders were simply to arrest him, even if it cost him his life—and it did." The Indian guide Dumont, by contrast, had no such honour. "He could retire," Fraser sarcastically noted, "and he did, very fast."

Fraser briefly mentioned how Almighty Voice, now a wanted fugitive, eluded capture "for many moons." It was not the fault of the police. Rather, the outlaw was "shielded" by the Duck Lake Indians. Then, one day, a "half-breed scout" (Napoleon Venne) captured an Indian horse thief and was leading him through a clump of trees when Almighty Voice appeared out of nowhere and gave chase. Frantically riding for his life, with Almighty Voice "making savage clutches at the swishing tail" of the horse, the scout barely got away, but not before being shot in the back.

"Bending low along with his horse's neck, the scout rode with reeling pain." FRASER, *SOLDIER POLICE OF THE CANADIAN NORTHWEST*

"Three constables ... crept in through the thick,
dangerous undergrowth of the bluff." FRASER,
SOLDIER POLICE OF THE CANADIAN NORTHWEST

News of the encounter raised the alarm in Prince Albert, and
a police party rode through the night—an improbable eighty
miles—to track down the murderer. Fraser claimed that Almighty
Voice "had two other killings to attend to"—presumably the
Indian agent and farm instructor—when he was intercepted and
forced to take refuge in the bluff. The repeated police assaults
on the "dangerous" bluff are cast as a story of good versus evil.
When the seriously wounded Inspector Allan, for example, falls
from his horse and finds himself helplessly staring down the barrel
of Almighty Voice's gun, he is said to shout, "Never," instead of
giving up his cartridge belt. That Almighty Voice could have shot
the "brave trooper" was never considered. And when Corporal
O'Kelly stumbled upon the Indians in the pit, he held his ground
against their withering gunfire and sent "a bullet ... crashing
through [one of] the redskins' brains." That his shot missed his
"dark" adversary was also never mentioned.

Fraser did admit that Almighty Voice bravely met his end. His mother, Spotted Calf, on the other hand, comes across as a contemptible creature during the bluff siege. The old woman alternatively "crooned a weird death song," while "cheer[ing] her son to fight to the death" and "slay many more" police. But, as Fraser noted, "his end was drawing near" once the field guns arrived on the scene. It took only "a few shells" before "it was 'all quiet along the Saskatchewan' once more."[32]

"A hawk-eyed Indian with a leveled rifle." FRASER, *SOLDIER POLICE OF THE CANADIAN NORTHWEST*

Fraser's article would become the standard telling of the Almighty Voice story in the early twentieth century and serve as the template for future police accounts. In 1906, Ernest J. Chambers, a former journalist and gentleman usher of the black rod for Parliament, borrowed heavily from Fraser's rendition in his official 1906 history of the now "Royal" North-West Mounted Police. The words and sentences may have been paraphrased, but the thrust and sentiment were the same. Here was a police force, built on the pillars of strength, courage, and discipline, that enjoyed relatively good relations with the Indian population except for a few incorrigible individuals. "The death of Colebrook," Chambers solemnly pronounced, "was … clearly a case of self-sacrifice on the altar of stern, manly duty … A bold bearing … is always shown by the Mounted Police in their dealings with the Indians, [and] has brought them, as if by miraculous intervention, safely out of many a tight hole." But as Chambers sombrely noted, "There was no such intervention in poor Colebrook's case, and he paid the penalty."

What followed was a rehash of the Fraser article with some additional observations. Almighty Voice, for example, may have been a "really bad Indian," but he repeatedly warned Colebrook not to advance because he "hesitated about taking the life of so chivalrous a man." That Almighty Voice really did not want to shoot the mountie—if only he had been left alone—was never a consideration. Chambers also devoted more attention to the search for Almighty Voice, insisting that "the work of scouring the country in all directions was never for a moment relaxed." And the triumphant conclusion of the bluff siege meant that "Colebrook's death had been avenged and the supremacy of the law in the North-West once more asserted." That conclusion, moreover, could not have come soon enough for "had the swaggering outlaw remained much longer at liberty, it would undoubtedly have unsettled all the Indians in the country."[30]

The Riders of the Plains, published four years later, offered a similar treatment of the incident. In a chapter entitled, "Almighty Voice, Bad Indian," author A. L. Haydon opened the story by suggesting that Almighty Voice "little dreamed of what a coil of trouble would arise" from the killing of a cow that did not belong to him. "He was in great need of fresh meat," Haydon wrote. "The cow offered a tempting mark, and the moment seemed propitious; so he brought his gun to his shoulder, fired, and became a criminal." The rest of the chapter, based largely on published materials, including annual police reports, documented Almighty Voice's evil career as a wanted fugitive and police murderer up until the moment he was killed at the bluff. And even though Haydon acknowledged that the incident was "an exceptional act of outlawry," he issued a warning that the "spirit of unrest" among Indian peoples "though apparently dormant, is by no means dead." The Indians of the region "requir[ed] careful police supervision at all times."[34]

The Almighty Voice incident was featured in the mounted police magazine *Scarlet and Gold*. SCARLET AND GOLD, 1922

After the Great War, the RNWMP Veterans' Association launched *Scarlet and Gold* magazine to commemorate the activities and personnel of the mounted police force since 1873. For the "second annual" (1920), W. B. Cameron contributed a feature article on "Almighty Voice—Outlaw" that set out to correct the

historical record. Cameron had never read "any authentic …
story … printed" about Almighty Voice. "Things written about
him," he complained, "are chiefly fiction." What made his account
different—apparently accurate—was that he had served as a clerk
in the Duck Lake Indian agency office in the early 1890s "and
saw Almighty Voice often." In fact, Cameron claimed to know
the inside story of "one of the old Saskatchewan Indian wars."
Almighty Voice was "a redman of spirit" with "an ambition … to
be great." But his "longing for distinction" was based on the "ideals
… of the North American savage." And that was his undoing.

Cameron presented Almighty Voice as a "wilful" young man
who would rather hunt than farm, rather take several wives than
one. This attitude led to quarrelling with the Indian agent. The ille-
gal killing of a cow only made things worse. Cameron maintained
that Almighty Voice's arrest would have resulted in a warning and
that he would have been let go. But his run from gaol made him
a fugitive. The remainder of the article provided a detailed and
accurate account of Colebrook's killing, the police search, and
finally the bluff standoff, all apparently gathered from internal
police documents and interviews with police participants.

What held Cameron's account together, though, was Almighty
Voice's misguided ambition and how it led to several deaths and
his eventual downfall. The story reads like a tragedy, divided into
three chapters or acts, with the shelling of the bluff serving as the
climax. "It was dawn on the morning of May 26, 1897 [actually
May 30], and the angel of peace seemed to brood over all the
virgin loveliness of the Saskatchewan," Cameron effused. "But
suddenly, the roar of the cannon broke the Sabbath stillness." It
was all over in a matter of minutes. The firing of the field guns
"ended Almighty Voice's war … With it ended, too, the ambition
of Almighty Voice, exactly where the ambition of other men,
sooner or later, end—in a hole."[35]

If there was a tinge of bitterness and spite to the article, it was
because Cameron was the lone white survivor of the Frog Lake
massacre during the 1885 North-West Rebellion and loathed
Indians like Almighty Voice. He had also been involved in a nasty
dispute with Indian Agent Robert McKenzie, who had accused
his clerk in 1892 of drunkenness and immorality in the perfor-

mance of his duties for the Duck Lake agency. Cameron laid countercharges against McKenzie. In the department investigation, several witnesses exonerated McKenzie, while Cameron admitted that he had been sleeping with an Indian woman and may have fathered her child.[36]

The "Almighty Voice" bluff was a popular local attraction—even in winter—in the early twentieth century. PROVINCIAL ARCHIVES OF SASKATCHEWAN S-B267

Several other police accounts of the incident appeared in the interwar period. In *Policing the Plains* (1921), a book that was more propaganda than history, R. G MacBeth deliberately focused on the "gallant young" Colebrook and his tragic death at the hands of the "notorious" Almighty Voice. "It was the price he paid for his devotion to orders," MacBeth eulogized, "but it maintained the Police tradition."[37] Morris Longstreth took the opposite approach in *The Silent Force*, choosing to dwell on the challenges the police faced in subduing "a wild young buck ... whose blood fermented with unease."[38] Curiously, Cecil Denny, an original member of the force, did not mention the incident in his memoirs, published posthumously as *The Law Marches West* in 1939.[39]

Mounted policemen J. B. Allan and Charles Raven, who had both been seriously wounded trying to flush the three Indians from the bluff, shared their memories with the *Scarlet and Gold*. It was a nasty firefight, fraught with tension and confusion because of the thick undergrowth. Inspector Allan derided Almighty Voice as "unworthy to be classed with white men," while Corporal Raven never forgot the "most blood-curdling shrieks ... hideous noise" coming from the Indians. Raven also repeated the police explanation that "a display of force" at the bluff had prevented "another Indian uprising."[40]

William Parker, a member of Prince Albert's "F" Division, also wrote about the incident, as part of his memoirs, more than half a century later. Parker led the reinforcement detail that helped guard the bluff. The veteran mountie criticized Sergeant Colebrook's decision to advance on Almighty Voice instead of trying to talk with him. It was a "grave error," Parker suggested. "With a good explanation, Almighty Voice probably would have surrendered." The rest of the chapter described the police picketing of the bluff. Parker brought along his dog, "Ike," an Irish setter "who hated Indians." The dog would accompany Parker during his review of the sentries and constantly growled in the direction of the bluff. Almighty Voice once called out, in response, that the police had brought dogs to help them fight. Parker also took part in the final rush after the shelling spree and, on reaching the pit, apparently found Almighty Voice still alive: "his body quivering as if he had just been killed."[41]

Indian Affairs employees also commented on the incident. In his memoirs, "Fifty Years on the Saskatchewan," published by the Canadian North-West History Society in 1929, Robert Jefferson, the former farm instructor for the Poundmaker Reserve, said that Almighty Voice was well known to the NWMP—"a positively friendly feeling"—because he worked for them during his youth. One day, Almighty Voice asked the One Arrow Indian agent for permission to slaughter one of his own cattle to feed his sick wife, and when denied he still went ahead. That led to his immediate arrest and escape from custody. This explanation for Almighty Voice's actions, especially the need to feed someone ill, would be repeated in later accounts. Jefferson also argued that Almighty Voice could easily have disappeared but "was determined to fight it out at home." And when he was found dead in the bluff, according to Jefferson, he had used "his last cartridge [to blow] the top of his head off."[42]

William Graham, who served as Indian commissioner from 1920 to 1932, discussed the affair—"the most outstanding trouble" since the rebellion—in his reflections on Indian life. His source was guide François Dumont who joined the Files Hills reserves shortly after Colebrook's shooting and regularly chatted with Graham, the local Indian agent at the time. Graham maintained the outcome would not have been the same if Almighty Voice's arrest had been handled differently. He also learned from Dumont that Almighty Voice had no intention of surrendering to Colebrook and, if necessary, would have shot them both. Nor did Dumont get over the murder but continued to fear for his life even after he had left One Arrow.[43]

Local people involved in the search for Almighty Voice contributed to the telling of the story. On the tenth anniversary of Almighty Voice's death, the Saskatchewan *Times* sought out those who had been at the bluff, excluding people from One Arrow. By this time, the spot where he had died had become something of a curiosity, and families from Prince Albert and other nearby communities regularly picnicked there. N. H. Russell, who had been one of the citizen volunteers, made a special trip to the bluff in May 1907 and returned with a poplar limb "with grape shot firmly embedded in the wood." Russell took the memento to the *Times* office and proudly identified himself as one of the men—one of apparently many—who had pulled the lifeless body of Almighty Voice out of the pit.

Prince Albert Mayor Richard Cook, another bluff fighter, also shared his memories of the incident. He told the *Times* that Almighty Voice had a sick child and when the Indian agent refused to help, the Indian killed a government cow. Almighty Voice fled before the warrant for his arrest could be served—he was never held at Duck Lake—and shot Colebrook when the sergeant tracked him down. Cook also claimed that he had wounded Almighty Voice in the knee during one of the early firefights in the bluff. These statements were at best false, at their worst an attempt by Cook to put himself at the centre of the story. He did not stop there.[44]

In 1907, Mae Harris Anson, an American newspaper correspondent and magazine writer, published the "Last Stand of

Claiming to be a good friend of Almighty Voice, Prince Albert Mayor Richard Cook provided one of the most bogus accounts of the incident. PRINCE ALBERT HISTORICAL SOCIETY H588

Almighty Voice," in the Chicago *Record Herald*. It was a sympathetic treatment, but one that was largely fabricated. Her source was Richard Cook, a self-described authority on the ways of the Cree and the incident in particular. When Anson asked what Almighty Voice had done to start "all the trouble," Cook scoffed, "He didn't do anything. They said he killed a calf."

The Prince Albert mayor then recounted how until 1895 Almighty Voice was the fastest runner and best shot at the annual summer field day, something that is not supported by the Prince Albert newspaper record for those years.[45] He was also, in Cook's words, a "commendable citizen," welcomed and respected throughout Prince Albert.

Then, it all went sour when a boy from One Arrow accused

Almighty Voice of killing a calf. Even though "Prince Albert to its last man refused to believe in his guilt," a posse was sent to bring him in and found him "peacefully ploughing" on the reserve. Almighty Voice steadfastly maintained his innocence, but when handcuffed "a thoroughly good Indian was changed into the worst of the bad." The prisoner was paraded down Prince Albert's River Street, greeted by "a silence as profound as it was full of pity." While his jailer slept that night, Almighty Voice slipped the key from his pocket and fled. He was brought back the next day—in shackles—but escaped again when a "respected" white citizen of Prince Albert crept into his cell and filed off his chains.

For the next nine months, the fugitive "broke every law of God" before word reached Prince Albert in the fall of 1895 that he was hiding near Duck Lake. Sergeant Colebrook was dispatched to arrest him. "[The mountie] must face danger unarmed without flinching and with a smile," Anson affirmed. But Almighty Voice refused to give himself up and "without apparently taking aim shot him [Colebrook] through the heart."

Almighty Voice eluded capture for another eighteen months before the police learned that he was hiding in the Minichinas Hills; there is no mention in the article of the wounding of Venne. When a patrol happened upon Almighty Voice and two companions in the open (not the bluff), two policemen were killed (not wounded). At this point Cook, hearing the gunshots, arrived at the scene and immediately urged the police to rush the bush where the three Indians had taken refuge. But the assault resulted in three more deaths when the search party was ambushed by "their prey stealthily creeping along in their rear."

Cook claimed that he came face-to-face with Almighty Voice during this encounter and wounded him during an exchange of gunfire. He also claimed that he crawled down from the sleeping police camp to the edge of the bluff during the night, and as "a friend," called on Almighty Voice to surrender. There was no answer, just "a chant, weird and strident—a death chant that turned Richard Cook cold." Cook returned to camp, knowing that Almighty Voice had chosen death and that the field guns would soon be called into play. Even though "Canada's fine-grained sense of law and order had been appeased" Cook wondered "if that single heifer was worth it."[46]

That question had hung over the affair since Colebrook's death. But the article itself was little more than bullshit, dressed up as the real story. It was part and parcel of Cook's modus operandi. He once predicted that Prince Albert would become a major manufacturing centre for western Canada by it harnessing the power of the North Saskatchewan River. He also proclaimed that the limit of wheat production was several hundred miles north of Prince Albert in the shield country along the Churchill River.[47] Mayor Cook died in office in 1908, but his published interview continued to influence future writers.[48]

Almighty Voice also made an appearance at the fictional "Flying U" ranch—ironically, as a steer! The popular western series, authored by B. M. Bower (a pseudonym for Bertha Muzzy Sinclair), revolved around the adventures of Chip and the Happy family on the Flying U ranch in northern Montana in the early

In another far-fetched story, Almighty Voice was said to have killed one of his wives and her lover with one shot. D'EASUM, *THE KILLING OF ALMIGHTY VOICE*

1900s. One morning, after a fierce blizzard, Chip found a stray, gaunt steer, marked with a Canadian brand, in the coulee occupied by the ranch buildings. The Happy family took pity on the animal and gave him a few generous forkfuls of hay. That was a mistake because the steer expected to be fed daily. And when he was chased away, back into the hills, he would return at night and bellow for hours behind the bunkhouse. "Did yuh hear him knock the top off high G last night about midnight?" one of the ranch hands asked in amazement. Because of "the depth and volume" of his singing, the steer was named Almighty Voice "in dishonour of a notorious Cree."[49]

An even more bizarre treatment, "The Killing of Almighty Voice," appeared in the August 1899 edition of *The Quaker*. The article was completely divorced from reality, but one that exploited the popular belief in the "primal savagery of an Indian's nature." Author Basil D'Easum imagined Almighty Voice as a great Cree brave with many followers. He tolerated newcomers and tried to learn their ways, but in his heart, he despised them "as a nation of squaws, poor hunters, blind on the trail, and full of empty words." On trading day, Almighty Voice and his two wives Prairie Chicken and Big Moccasin visited the local Hudson's Bay Company with a bundle of furs, including muskox and caribou skins. Percy Bradley, a young clerk fresh from Aberdeen, was smitten by Prairie Chicken and paid several clandestine visits to her teepee. Almighty Voice caught them together and killed both with a single shot from his rifle. "And this was the way," D'Easum explained, "Almighty Voice became ... a 'bad Indian.'"

Almighty Voice then "turned attention to even greater crimes: he stole cattle." It was one thing, according to D'Easum, for the cuckolded Cree, in a moment of blind rage, to end the tryst between his promiscuous wife and a foolish white clerk. But rustling cattle was "an unforgivable sin" and ranchers went looking for him. The mounted police eventually tracked Almighty Voice and two companions to a camp on "Kinni Kinck" creek in the "Cottonwood" Hills and drove them into a nearby clump of willows. After a few shells were lobbed into the Indians' refuge, Almighty Voice stood up and mockingly told the police they had to improve their aim. That they did with the next few volleys, and, when the police stormed the bluff, they found a dead Almighty Voice, his head torn open by a shell. A search of his body turned up some of the murdered HBC clerk's personal belongings.[50]

Other popular treatments of the Almighty Voice story in the early twentieth century never strayed much from the standard version, but there were some foolish mistakes. Author and women's rights activist Emily Murphy, writing as Janey Canuck, argued that the selfless death of "the firm-jawed man in the scarlet coat" represented "another stone [in] the foundation whereupon our Western Empire is laid four-square." But the real tragedy, according to Murphy, was that the trouble had been set in motion by the theft of "a sheep."[51]

Saskatchewan educator N. F. Black raised the incident as a rare instance of police "mismanagement" and then repeated the Cook

Almighty Voice's son Stanislaus and his twin sons, Edward and Ernest. UNIVERSITY OF SASKATCHEWAN, UNIVERSITY ARCHIVES AND SPECIAL COLLECTIONS, A.S. MORTON MG 437, C565-2-11.6-p.1

version of the story that Almighty Voice was a widely respected member of the Prince Albert district who had been driven to a life of crime because of a false accusation. That the bogus account appeared in Black's semi-official *History of Saskatchewan and the Old North West* (1913) gave it credence. He also got the date wrong: it supposedly happened in 1905, the same year Saskatchewan entered confederation as a province.[52]

The most intriguing early account—signalling a shift in the telling of the Almighty Voice story—was published in 1924 by John Hawkes, Saskatchewan's first legislative librarian. In the first part of a chapter devoted to Almighty Voice, Hawkes included lengthy excerpts from the W. B. Cameron article in *Scarlet and Gold*. He ended the section by stating: "what we have written above is an accepted version, and we will let it stand as it is."

Hawkes then turned to what he called, the "inside light on the tragedy." He informed the reader that Almighty Voice's parents were still alive and finally speaking out about their son and what had happened. And what they had to say cast a completely different light on the story. Sounding Sky and Spotted Calf reported that "the whole tragedy was occasioned by ... trying to 'throw a scare' into him [Almighty Voice] by telling him the Mounted Police would hang him." That is why Almighty Voice fled from custody and remained on the run for nineteen months. "He carried with him the full conviction," they said, "that if the police got hold of him they would hang him without process of law."[53] It was an explosive allegation. The telling of the Almighty Voice story would never be the same again.

CHAPTER SIX

On the Warpath

A new version of the Almighty Voice story emerged in the 1920s. For the past quarter century, the incident had been told from the non-Indigenous perspective. There was no attempt to understand, let alone explain, why the Willow Cree man murdered a mounted policeman on his way to becoming one of the most wanted fugitives in Canada in the late nineteenth century. He was simply a bad Indian. The story became a much different one when Almighty Voice's parents, Sounding Sky and Spotted Calf, were interviewed in the summer of 1923. Almighty Voice had apparently escaped from the Duck Lake gaol when one of his mountie guards had jokingly told him that he would be hanged for killing the cow. In other words, Almighty Voice believed he was running for his life, believed the hangman's noose was waiting for him if he allowed Sergeant Colebrook to take him into custody. This new information, though, was the work of one writer's overactive imagination, someone who deliberately twisted what he had been told by the One Arrow couple. Many things that were now introduced into the Almighty Voice story did not actually happen but made for good drama. This new telling of the incident would never be challenged for its accuracy given the supposed source of the information. Instead, it was widely accepted, and repeated, as other authors added more made-up bits and pieces, somehow believing they had the creative licence to do so. These new accounts widened the gap between fact and fiction, bringing the Canadian public no closer to understanding what had happened and why. The historical Almighty Voice, in the process, gave way to an invented one: who he might have been was less important than who he became. It could even be argued that he was missing again.

≈

In May 1923, Chief Buffalo Child Long Lance, a journalist with the Winnipeg *Tribune*, visited Duck Lake to do some background research for two articles: one on the 1885 North-West Rebellion,[1] the other on Almighty Voice. Long Lance had a growing reputation as a chronicler of Indian stories, something that came naturally because of his Indigenous background. He appeared to have the unique ability to bridge the Indian and white worlds. But he was not the person he claimed to be.

Chief Buffalo Long Lance, who claimed to be a Blackfoot Indian from Alberta, was actually Sylvester Long, a mixed-descent black American from North Carolina. MANLIUS OLD BOYS ASSOCIATION

Long Lance was born Sylvester Clark Long in the Winston-Salem area of North Carolina in 1890. The mixed-descent son of "non-white" parents (white, Indian, and black), he grew up black in the rigidly segregated south, with no hope of advancement or opportunity. Long played up his Native heritage—he claimed he was half Cherokee—to secure entrance to the Carlisle Indian Residential School. He then attended a military academy but discontinued his studies to travel to Montreal and enlist in the Canadian Expeditionary Force. When he returned from the First World War, he settled in Calgary, Alberta, and became a freelancer for the *Herald* newspaper. This work took him to nearby reserves and triggered his transformation into the son of a Blood Indian chief, namely, Chief Buffalo Child Long Lance. Much of what he later claimed about his past, including the stories and memories, came from his Indian informants.[2]

When Long Lance visited Almighty Voice's parents, he was an imposter, not above using his contrived identity to secure material for a good story. Nor was he constrained by the facts, often bending the truth, or just making things up, to suit his purposes. Sounding Sky and Spotted Calf would not have known much about their visitor, just that he was from the Blackfoot tribe and wanted to meet and talk about their son. Unaware of his true identity or purpose, they probably welcomed him because he had made a special trip to One Arrow.

Long Lance's interview transcript can be found today at Calgary's Glenbow Archives.[3] The notes in pencil in a stenographer's notepad are no more than hurried jottings; the entries are short, staccato-like, with only a few words on each line. Prosper John, Almighty Voice's younger brother, likely served as translator for his parents although his role is never credited in the transcript. Long Lance did not know Cree—or Blackfoot, for that matter—but would never have admitted it. The story is also somewhat disjointed and convoluted. Sounding Sky (misidentified as Clear Sky) and Spotted Calf, then in their seventies, talk interchangeably, sometimes going forwards and backwards in time, about the rebellion, life on the reserve, and, of course, their son's fate. Other voices complicate the story. Two sections in the transcript are attributed to other informants.

In the interview, Sounding Sky said that the killing of the cow happened in May while he was away digging Seneca root, that Almighty Voice was hungry and slaughtered a stray animal "by mistake." François Coyote [Dumont] later reported the matter to the agent and that was how his son came to be arrested in October and taken to Duck Lake for his hearing. Almighty Voice, according to his father, had already been sentenced and awaiting transfer to the Prince Albert gaol when he slipped away after being left unattended. The trial, though, was actually scheduled for the next morning, after the escape. Even more significant, however, was what was not said. Neither Sounding Sky nor Spotted Calf stated that their son had been threatened with hanging while in custody.

Following his escape, Almighty Voice stayed only one night with his mother at One Arrow before leaving with Small Face for the Fort à la Corne area reserves. He warned Sergeant Colebrook and Dumont "not to come forward" after he had been tracked down, but the mountie was determined to arrest him. Colebrook was said to have had a gun; maybe that was the revolver he was holding in his left hand inside his coat. Almighty Voice "at last fired" and then fled with Small Face. Nothing was said in the interview about the nineteen-month manhunt except that Almighty Voice often came back to the reserve. On one of his visits home he went to Prince Albert to speak to his father being held there in gaol.

Almighty Voice eventually tired of running and spent more and more time around One Arrow. One crucial section of the interview transcript reads:

Stayed around
All Spring. After
saw father didn't
want to hide any
more. Going to
have show down.
Did not want to hang.

This excerpt likely refers to the spring of 1897 before the standoff at the bluff—and nearly a year-and-a-half after he shot Sergeant Colebrook. Almighty Voice feared hanging for killing a mountie, not for killing any stray cow, and was prepared to meet his fate, just not at the end of a noose.

The showdown started when Almighty Voice's cousin Little Saulteaux fired at Napoleon Venne at the Indian camp. The Métis scout was lucky he was only wounded. "If Almighty Voice/shot him would/have got him," Sounding Sky proudly recounted. "That fellow kills/every time he shoots." Following the skirmish,

Almighty Voice and his two companions took refuge in the bluff. The pit was later found with "holes as far as arm could reach, dug/with knife" in their desperate search for water. Spotted Calf made several trips to the bluff by wagon. She was turned back each time by the police or farm instructor but persisted. She "had nothing eat or/drink 2 days." Sounding Sky, meanwhile, was taken into custody by the mounted police at the start of the siege and held at Batoche.

Topean was the first of the three to be killed when he came to the edge of the bluff to harass the police sentries on Saturday evening. That was the "same day Almighty/Voice wounded" by the shelling from the seven-pound cannon. When the bluff was overrun the next day, Almighty Voice was found "killed by bullet in the temple." That the top piece of his skull was once displayed in the old Royal Canadian Mounted Police Museum in Regina suggested a different death. Regardless of how Almighty Voice met his fate, just talking about it was still hard on the family. At one point, Long Lance noted that "Old Mother [Spotted Calf] went out/and cried while we sat/and talked./Began crying/over grave."

Henry Smith, a Métis from nearby St. Louis who reportedly "brought AV out of/Hole," also spoke to Long Lance about what happened at the bluff. He maintained there were "about thousand people/here. About 500 police." This exaggerated claim was matched by another: that Little Saulteaux had been found alive in the pit with Almighty Voice and a mounted policeman had administered the coup de grâce.

Long Lance's other informant was Father Henri Delmas, a Roman Catholic priest and principal of St. Michael's Indian boarding school, who served as Long Lance's Duck Lake host. Delmas didn't take up his duties at the school until after Almighty Voice's death, but that didn't stop him from talking as if he had personally known the Willow Cree Indian. He said that "young Almighty Voice/Movements like a/Tiger." He also blamed the boy's behaviour on his parents and suggested that "nobody ever/ understand young/Almighty Voice … no man to be crossed." Delmas also had bluff stories, little more than baseless rumours that had been told and retold over the years. He informed Long

Lance that Almighty Voice "got out that night and/through pickets/found dead man's/moccasin." And when the siege was over, a memorial to the three braves was found, carved in Cree, in one of the trees.

Long Lance photographed Spotted Calf and Sounding Sky during his visit to One Arrow in May 1923. GLENBOW ARCHIVES NA-1811-24

In preparing his article on Almighty Voice, Long Lance put together some summary notes at the end of the steno pad, listing the people involved, key dates and locations, and general observations. He had already started to embellish the story: "Police in charge had/told AV that he would/be hanged." This allegation was not part of the interview transcript. It was never mentioned nor implied. And it can't be explained away by suggesting that it was a simple mistake, that Long Lance either misunderstood what he was told by Almighty Voice's parents or was confused about the timeline. It was a deliberate falsity, the first of many fabrications that Long Lance sprinkled throughout the story. Nor were Almighty Voice and the facts the only victims. So, too, were Spotted Calf and Sounding Sky, taken advantage of by an unscrupulous writer out to make a name for himself and cash in on what happened to their son. They even posed for a picture, looking melancholy but resolute, as Long Lance clicked the shutter.

Long Lance's version of the Almighty Voice story appeared as a feature piece in the Sunday edition of the Winnipeg *Tribune* on 6 January 1924. It was also picked up by several other North American newspapers (such as the El Paso *Times*).[4] In an introductory note, the editor heralded the article as the first telling of the incident from the Indian perspective. "Through conversations with Sounding Sky ... and Spotted Calf," Long Lance had "gained a full recital of the circumstances ... and here presents them ... still infused with the Indian spirit."[5] An accompanying photograph of Long Lance, in ceremonial dress astride a horse, confirmed his credentials as "'Big Boss' of the Plains Indians, all tribes of whom ... are said to look up to him as leader."

The story headline read, "INDIAN HOLDS 1,000 AT BAY" (more than ten times the actual number of people at the bluff in 1897). Then, in italics, a short opening passage claimed that the words, "Here died three braves," could still be seen carved in Cree syllabics in a tree trunk at the spot where Chief Almighty Voice killed his last three victims. With this hook, Long Lance began his saga: how the young Cree man, arrested for killing a government steer, had secured his release by taking a key from a sleeping guard and unlocking his chains. That was another fabrication that would become woven into the story; the prisoner was never secured to a ball and chain. Perhaps because Long Lance was himself an invention, he saw nothing wrong with inventing large parts of the Almighty Voice story, including dialogue.

Almighty Voice ran, he told his mother, because the mounted police planned to hang him for killing the steer. "But they will never put a rope around my neck," he proclaimed. "I will die fighting them." A mountie later confessed, Long Lance explained, that the hanging threat was only a joke and that the usual penalty was one month's imprisonment, something Almighty Voice never knew. That joke, though, led to the Almighty Voice vow never to be taken, led to what Long Lance claimed was "the greatest single-handed stand in the history of the North American West."

Spotted Calf hid her son under a pile of blankets in their teepee. The police searched everywhere on the One Arrow reserve, but apparently stayed away from the blankets out of fear of what might happen. Almighty Voice fled the next day with Small Face but was soon found by NWMP Sergeant Colebrook and his Métis guide. Colebrook was armed—"his gun was pointing at Almighty Voice"—and called on the fugitive to surrender. But Almighty Voice warned the mountie to stop and only shot him when he continued to ride forward.

Almighty Voice was said to have "dropped into mysterious oblivion" for almost two years after Colebrook's murder, but Long Lance revealed how he spent much of his time in and around One Arrow. When he was finally discovered in the area in May 1897, his reappearance struck fear into local settlers. "They knew that he was on the warpath," Long Lance solemnly declared. "He had assumed the offensive and ... with an Indian, this means that he intends to get as many as he can before he is gotten." This portrayal of Almighty Voice as a calculating "killer," a creature of his "primitive ... environment," were not the words of someone who claimed to speak for Canada's Indian peoples and their mistreatment. But Long Lance was really more concerned with infusing the story with escalating drama and gripping tension. The bluff showdown was perfect for these purposes. Before slipping into the thicket, Almighty Voice and his two companions had "stripped for battle" in preparation for their "final stand against the mounties."

The two failed assaults on the bluff led to the call for reinforcements and a field gun from Regina. Long Lance used the siege to bring the story to its climax. As the growing camp of police and volunteers, numbering in the hundreds, watched and waited through Saturday night, an eerie stillness descended over the scene. It was broken only by the occasional exchange of gunfire, the yip, yipping of coyotes who could smell the dead bodies [Kerr and Grundy] in the bluff, and the death chant of Spotted Calf. "I wanted to go into that bluff," she told Long Lance about being repeatedly turned away, "and take my son in my arms and protect him." Almighty Voice, in turn, responded to her singing. "Presently, a deep-tone echo … came rumbling out of the bluff," Long Lance reported. "That was the last time his voice was ever heard." Curiously, no one at the bluff reported hearing him. But they all remembered his mother's plaintive cry.

Long Lance's account of the Almighty Voice incident, in which he claimed that the Willow Cree man held one thousand pursuers at bay, appeared in North American newspapers in January 1924. *EL PASO TIMES*, 6 JANUARY 1924

Almighty Voice was found dead in the pit after the Sunday morning bombardment of the bluff. He had been killed by a shell; his head split open. Long Lance got that right. But he was not done with his melodramatic makeover of the incident. He maintained that Almighty Voice's cousin was still alive in the pit and that a mounted policeman "put a finishing bullet" through his head. He also insisted that Almighty Voice, bleeding from a badly injured knee, had crawled one hundred yards beyond the heavy police cordon—demonstrated he could have got away—but returned to the bluff. And he described how Almighty Voice, facing imminent death, had carved, "Here died three braves" as a "commemorative tribute" to the "Redcoats" who died during the second assault on the bluff. It was all pure fiction.

Long Lance closed the story with a visit to the bluff with Spotted Calf and two of her sons. If it did happen, it was never mentioned in the interview transcript, nor what was said during the tour of the site. It was apparently Spotted Calf's first return to the site in twenty-six years. Long Lance knew that this imagined scene would make the perfect ending to his article. "With a sleeping grandchild strapped over her back," Spotted Calf stood a little way back from the pit "soaking her tears in the corner of a crimson and yellow blanket." He would never forget how she met his gaze. "Her head was bent," Long Lance tenderly recalled, "as though she were ashamed of the emotions which she could not control."

The story found a receptive audience, all the more so because it supposedly came directly from Almighty Voice's parents. Here, finally, was an "authentic" explanation for why Almighty Voice fled custody, killed Sergeant Colebrook, and then defiantly fought it out to the death against the police. John Hawkes, Saskatchewan's legislative librarian, was certainly fooled and was probably the first to reprint excerpts in his 1924 book, *The Story of Saskatchewan and its People.* "Personally," Hawkes wrote, "we accept its truthfulness without hesitation."[6]

But Long Lance was not done recreating the incident. Under contract to the American Cosmopolitan Book Corporation to write his life story, especially his boyhood days in southern Alberta, he published *Long Lance: The Autobiography of a Blackfoot Indian Chief* in 1928. The book enjoyed immediate success, catapulting its Native author to international acclaim. Indeed, in the dedication, Long Lance credited his personal advancement in moving beyond his Indian beginnings and "tak[ing] a place in civilization" to Canadian Indian officials. He also lauded the mounted police as "the best friends, brothers, and protectors that the Indians ... ever had" and blamed any conflicts on "individual Indians."[7]

The Almighty Voice incident was one of the chapters ("Outlaw") in the new Long Lance book. The chapter also appeared in *Maclean's* magazine under the title, "The Last Stand of Almighty Voice."[8] It was essentially a rehash of what he had written several years earlier, but with some new—bogus—details. Long Lance now held that Spotted Calf was his adopted mother, a claim he repeated in the chapter as if to give his account some special imprimatur.[9] Sounding Sky, on the other hand, was "the most dangerous Indian in that part of the North-West" and had been imprisoned before his son's arrest to prevent "an Indian uprising." Almighty Voice was likened to a superman: "he was dauntless, resourceful, physically powerful, and enduring."[10] At the Duck Lake gaol, he picked up his "heavy iron ball" restraint as if it was an annoyance and tiptoed quietly over to the sleeping guard to retrieve the keys. When he was free, he bolted across the barracks yard and "with a mighty leap cleared the high fence without touching it."[11] That there was no fence apparently did not lessen the feat.

Other new fabrications included the wounding of the Métis scout who helped Sergeant Colebrook track down the fugitive. Almighty Voice shot François Dumont in the elbow as a warning to leave the district; he was never seen again. Small Face also remained at Almighty Voice's side during his months in hiding. Once, when they came "in from the depths of the wild, she ... carried ... a tiny brown baby ... born to them in the wilderness."[12] Perhaps the most stunning suggestion was that some Indian tribes wanted to use the Almighty Voice showdown "to rebel and try to drive the white man off the plains." This baseless assertion had been voiced in the days and weeks after the bluff showdown. Long Lance gave it new life. "It will surprise many," he revealed, "to learn just what hair's-breath the North-West escaped what would have been the most terrible massacre in the history of America."[13] It was exactly the kind of venomous statement that would have been expressed by police and Indian officials at the time of the incident.

Long Lance's autobiography was reprinted in 1929, the same

MacLean's Magazine, February 1, 1929

The Last Stand
of Almighty Voice

*A thrilling description of one of the most poignantly
dramatic episodes in the history of the
Canadian Northwest*

By CHIEF BUFFALO CHILD LONG LANCE

Long Lance published another, more embellished version of the
Almighty Voice story in conjunction with the release of his fictional
autobiography. MACLEAN'S, 1 FEBRUARY 1929.

year he embarked on a film career. His growing fame was soon
dogged by nagging questions about his Blackfoot background,
and, by extension, his true identity. An investigation confirmed
his black heritage. Exposed as a fraud and deserted by many of his
friends, Long Lance committed suicide in 1932. But his account
of the Almighty Voice incident lived on. It could not be taken
back as if it were never written, never published, never read. As
sometimes said in the courtroom, it was not possible to "unring
the bell."[14] Long Lance may have been an imposter, but he was
the first writer to interview Almighty Voice's parents and that was
all that mattered. No one knew how he used—or more correctly,
abused—what he had been told. His version was simply accepted
as the real story behind the sorry episode, even though it was a
gross distortion of what happened, and, more important, obscured
the real reason for Almighty Voice's flight from the Duck Lake
barracks.

American anthropologist David Mandelbaum learned first-
hand about the power and reach of the Long Lance story in the
1930s. On 17 July 1934, Mandelbaum interviewed Sounding Sky
at Duck Lake as part of his field work on the Plains Cree. The old
Willow Cree man, now in his eighties, said little about his son

Almighty Voice during this meeting, certainly nothing about any hanging threat. That information was happily provided by the hotel keeper where Mandelbaum was staying. The man offered a garbled account of the incident that drew largely upon the Long Lance version. Mandelbaum also found that the story was "being exploited by the tourist brochures."[15]

Something similar happened two decades later. In 1956, RCMP Inspector J. J. Atherton visited One Arrow and talked to Almighty Voice's younger brother, Prosper John, eight at the time of the incident, about what he could remember.[16] (In 1936, Prosper John became the first chief since One Arrow's death fifty years earlier; he was succeeded by Almighty Voice's son Stanislaus.) Prosper John revealed that his brother spent more and more of his time as a fugitive at his parents' home. He took Atherton to the spot on the reserve where the family home once stood and pointed out two depressions in the ground connected by a shallow trench. Almighty Voice would enter the root cellar via a trap door in the floor and then crawl along the trench into the second dugout. Prosper John also recalled travelling to Prince Albert with Almighty Voice and his mother, Spotted Calf, and how they secretly spoke to his father, Sounding Sky, as he was cleaning out the barracks stables as part of his gaol sentence. Sounding Sky counselled Almighty Voice not to do anything rash, but his son was tired of running and hiding.

Atherton forwarded his typed notes to his Prince Albert friend, retired Hudson's Bay Company trader H. S. M. Kemp, who wanted the information for his article, "Almighty Voice–Public Enemy No. 1," in the *RCMP Quarterly*. At no point in the interview did Prosper John say that his brother had been threatened with hanging in gaol. Perhaps he didn't want to raise it because he was talking to the police. But Prosper John was very forthcoming, vividly describing how, as a young boy, he saw the big gun being taken to the bluff and hearing the boom of the cannon the next day. Near the beginning of his article, though, Kemp felt compelled to write, "Legend has it that the Indian was told, following his arrest and merely in a joking manner, that he would hang for his crime."[17]

The telling of the Almighty Voice story was consequently never the same after Long Lance published his fictionalized account. There were still a few authors who continued to stick to the standard mountie police script that Sergeant Colebrook "tried hard to avoid bloodshed" and that he had an unquestioning duty "to do or die" in trying to arrest Almighty Voice.[18] Generally, though, writers now put their own spin on what happened. They continued to use the basic incident structure but introduced new features and details that came out of nowhere, except their imaginations. Many of these new iterations also borrowed freely from earlier accounts, and the repeating of these story fragments, many of them false, gave them an acceptance and authority. Much of the mid-twentieth century writing about Almighty Voice, then, was a creative exercise, while the Willow Cree man himself became something of a legendary figure, imbued with qualities that may never have been part of his character or personality.

In *This is Saskatchewan* (1953), provincial legislative reporter Robert Moon blamed the incident—the "final outburst of [Indian] rebellious spirit"—on Almighty Voice's primal ambition "to be a warrior." But instead of killing a cow, the Willow Cree man knocked down a settler's fence to build a fire. That got him arrested and led to escape "through his cell window" after he had been sentenced to thirty days in gaol. Almighty Voice then "stole a squaw from another Indian ... an act which laid the pattern for subsequent events." Sergeant Colebrook, with Gabriel Dumont (former Métis leader Louis Riel's redoubtable general) serving as his guide, set off to bring him in. The rest of the account is riddled with similar errors, but there is no mistaking Moon's interpretation. Once Almighty Voice was dead, Saskatchewan "became a peaceful farmland."[19]

Al Cooper took a similar tack in "The Brave They Fought with Cannons" in the Dominion Day edition (1 July 1953) of *Maclean's* magazine. Whereas Long Lance had instilled the fugitive Indian with noble qualities, Cooper's Almighty Voice was a hot-blooded warrior who "set out on his own private warpath" to make a name for himself. The young Willow Cree man was angry and confused by the momentous changes that had taken place around him, and not knowing how to respond, blindly lashed out against "the hated whites" in the form of the mounted police.

"The Brave They Fought with Cannons" suggested that Almighty
Voice was rebelling against the changes brought by white settlement.
MACLEAN'S, 1 JULY 1953

British author John Prebble's Almighty Voice character
wanted to recapture the glory days of the Cree. NORMAN
THELWELL, *LILLIPUT*, JANUARY 1957

Cooper, like Moon, attributed the start of the trouble to
Almighty Voice chopping down part of a settler's fence to start
a fire. But when ordered off the land—land he still regarded as
Cree land—Almighty Voice shot the settler's cow. These simple
acts of defiance provoked a running war with the mounties and
ultimately led to the bluff showdown, dubbed "the grove of
death." In Cooper's story, with the cannon in position and ready,
the police repeatedly called on Almighty Voice to surrender. But
that would have robbed him of "the glory that his savage heart
demanded."[20]

A more accurate treatment might have been expected from celebrated British journalist and author John Prebble, probably best
remembered for his screenplay for the 1964 film *Zulu*. Prebble had a
Saskatchewan connection. In 1921, at age six, he emigrated with his

family to Canada to live with an uncle in Sutherland, a former rail-
road community and now a Saskatoon neighbourhood. Although
they stayed only six years before returning to England, the prairie
experience left quite an impression on young John. Prebble was
fascinated by Indian tales, especially the one a Métis school friend
told about Almighty Voice. He later claimed to have seen Sounding
Sky and Spotted Calf when the Duck Lake Cree participated in the
Saskatoon rodeo and dreamed what it would have been like, if by
"some miracle," Almighty Voice had ridden with them.[21]

In January 1957, by then an accomplished author, Prebble
published a short story about Almighty Voice in the small-format
British monthly magazine *Lilliput*. It was included the following

In John Prebble's account, the Willow Cree man lies prone
on his back, manacled to a heavy iron ball in a stone cell.
NORMAN THELWELL, *LILLIPUT*, JANUARY 1957

Spotted Calf sang a death chant for her son Almighty
Voice at the bluff. NORMAN THELWELL, *LILLIPUT*, JANUARY 1957

year in his collection *My Great-Aunt Appearing Day, and Other Stories*.[22] Prebble had undoubtedly read the Long Lance and Cooper articles on Almighty Voice, because his story was largely an amalgam of what they had written about the man and incident, with a few minor additions. During his nineteen-month run from the police, for example, Almighty Voice was said to have sought refuge along the Churchill River. The story was also accompanied by simple sketches, including one of Almighty Voice lying prone on his back and manacled to a heavy iron ball in a stone cell.

The only thing missing in the short story was a reference to Welsh poet Dylan Thomas's 1951 poem "Do not go gentle into that good night"; especially the line, "rage, rage, against the dying of the light." That was exactly how Prebble depicted Almighty Voice and his "last Indian battle," as someone raging against the changes that had engulfed Cree peoples in the late nineteenth century. "He was born into the evening of his race," Prebble explained, when "the greatness" of his people had passed. "There was a restlessness about him," he observed, and when he reached maturity, that restlessness gave way to a "bitter[ness] against the white man" that ate away at him until he could take it no more and killed a government cow.[23]

This interpretation—that Almighty Voice yearned for the days when the Cree freely roamed the plains hunting great herds of bison—also shaped and informed Manitoba author Nan Shipley's 1967 booklet, *Almighty Voice and the Redcoats*, in the Canadian Vignettes series. The text largely repeated earlier accounts, apart from the addition of new dialogue. But Shipley also suggested that Almighty Voice was following in the footsteps of his maternal grandfather, Chief One Arrow, and his father, Sounding Sky, who had joined the 1885 North-West Rebellion to protest their treatment under treaty. "Indians had paid dearly for their part in it [rebellion]," Shipley recounted. That included the largest mass hanging in Canadian history when eight Indian warriors were executed at Battleford in November 1885. "Almighty Voice shuddered whenever he thought of death by hanging," she noted, "the most ignoble end of all."

Shipley was one of the few writers to raise Indian policy as a contributing factor to the Almighty Voice incident. But she only poked around the edges: the young Willow Cree had broken a department rule when he killed a government cow, even if the animal was supposedly for Indian use. There was no other discussion of how the Canadian state had failed the Cree people in the 1890s. Nor did the mounted police come under much scrutiny. Rather, it was "the story of a tragic misunderstanding." Because

THE SCARLET TRAIL OF ALMIGHTY VOICE

Murder lay in the wake of the rebellious Cree brave who defied the law imposed by the White Man even against 100-1 odds and cannon

By Philip H. Godsell

"The Scarlet Trail of Almighty Voice" told the story in red and white terms: a rebellious Cree versus the white man as represented by the mounted police. FURY, JANUARY 1949

of the hanging threat by his mountie guard, Almighty Voice had been "tricked into killing" Sergeant Colebrook. And now that he was a father, with a child born in the wild, he was tired of running and "wanted a better life" for his wife and son. But he could not surrender—that would mean certain hanging—and chose to "fight this out" with the police. "I am on the warpath," he announced to his friends and family. "There is no return."[24]

Almighty Voice also found his way into men's pulp fiction magazines after the Second World War. It was a perfect tale for a male audience, but even more so with melodramatic touches. "The Scarlet Trail of Almighty Voice" appeared in the January 1949 edition of *Fury: Exciting True Adventures for Men*. Other articles in the issue included "The Sin of Teen-age Sex Clubs" and "The G-String Buccaneer." Author Philip H. Godsell, a former HBC man, painted the incident in stark red and white terms: a rebellious Cree versus the white man as represented by the mounted police. Almighty Voice was an ill-tempered, randy "wayward young buck" who refused to do "squaws' work" on the reserve but preferred to go hunting. That got him into trouble when he killed a settler's cow and taunted the Indian agent that the white man's law could not stop him. Godsell also reduced Indian peoples to stereotypes, especially their physical appearance. Sounding Sky had "mahogany features [that] convulsed with savage anger," while the police were "surrounded by a sea of hawk-like faces and eyes glinting with hate" when they searched One Arrow for the fugitive.

Godsell made silly mistakes, such as calling the mounted police "Long Knives," a term used by Indians for the American cavalry.

Many popular accounts focused on Almighty Voice's cold-blooded murder of Sergeant Colebrook. HAROLD VON SCHMIDT, *TRUE*, MARCH 1954

He also played loose with the facts. Almighty Voice escaped the Duck Lake gaol with his brother-in-law "Young Dust." The pair eventually ended up in the pit together during the bluff standoff. But Almighty Voice was forced to shoot Young Dust in the head when he put on a dead mountie's uniform and quietly tried to slip away. Godsell also insisted that the "here died three braves" tree carving had nothing to do with honouring the three fallen white men but was Almighty Voice's "last defiant gesture... and his epitaph."[25]

True: The Man's Magazine offered a competing version of the incident—"the warpath of Almighty Voice"—in the March 1954 issue. Despite the title, writer Howard O'Hagan delivered a more sympathetic portrait, likening Almighty Voice to famous American Indians Sitting Bull, Crazy Horse, and Geronimo. "He was that kind of Indian," O'Hagan mused. "The mistake the white men made was in not recognizing him at once for the Indian he was."

The first part of the article, illustrated with full-page sketches, closely followed Long Lance's interpretation, something the author readily admitted. Long Lance apparently had inside knowledge of the incident because Sounding Sky and Spotted Calf had saved the Blackfoot writer as a baby and raised him as Almighty Voice's brother. That ridiculous claim was followed by others as O'Hagan ploughed new ground in the story. After escaping from the Duck Lake gaol, Almighty Voice visited the home of Métis trapper Dumont and left with his wife for the barren lands—yes, the barren lands to the north. And after he killed Colebrook, Almighty Voice sought refuge in the United States where he fell under the influence of the Ghost Dance, a new Indian religious movement that sought to drive the white man from tribal ancestral lands. Almighty Voice returned to Canada as a "menacing" preacher who barnstormed reserves across western Canada in a call to arms. The "troublemaker" had to be silenced, according to O'Hagan, and that meant driving him to ground in the bluff. There, with his two "disciples," Almighty Voice met his fate as a martyr, while hundreds of white witnesses looked on.[26] It was certainly a novel interpretation.

The Almighty Voice story continued to receive media coverage into the mid-twentieth century. On the sixtieth anniversary of

In a 1954 *True* magazine article, Almighty Voice (shown crouching in the bluff) is said to have been a religious prophet who tried to inspire an Indian rebellion against the white man. HAROLD VON SCHMIDT, *TRUE*, MARCH 1954

the bluff siege, Saskatchewan newspapers carried a retrospective piece that reproduced John Hawkes' chapter in *The Story of Saskatchewan and its People*. The editorial setup to the excerpt called the incident "the most tragic and yet remarkable criminal case in the annals of the old West." And it began simply because of "Almighty Voice's insatiable appetite for female company and ... a dispute over the ownership of a steer."[27]

The story also surfaced whenever there was a mounted police manhunt. Albert Johnson, better known as the "Mad Trapper," was compared to Almighty Voice during the month-long police pursuit through the western Northwest Territories and Yukon in

1932. "Both cases," an editorial counselled, "show the extent of the resistance which can be made by one desperate man."[28] The *Minot Daily News* also did a feature piece on Almighty Voice in October 1970 in response to the search for the killer of two mounties who were slain responding to a family dispute at a rural property south of Prince Albert.[29]

There was also a growing fascination—if not need—to identify sites, as well as secure and preserve artefacts, associated with the incident, especially given its continuing notoriety. In February 1948, Roy Lobb of Willow Lane Farm in Beatty, Saskatchewan, contacted the RCMP Depot Division in Regina and asked about placing a cairn at the spot where Sergeant Colebrook had been killed in October 1895. Lobb had homesteaded in the area in 1905 and became friends with E. B. Cay, one of the two Métis settlers who had assisted the police constable stationed at nearby Flett Springs in retrieving Colebrook's body. Lobb even provided the legal description for the site (in the centre of SW, section 29, township 45, range 20, west of 2nd meridian) and recommended that the provincial Department of Highways put up a marker near

Roy Lobb of Beatty, Saskatchewan, standing near the spot where Almighty Voice killed Sergeant Colebrook, wanted a marker placed there. PROVINCIAL ARCHIVES OF SASKATCHEWAN R-A2622

"where Colebrook gave his life in the service of his country."[30] The bluff in the Minichinas Hills, meanwhile, remained a better-known site and was frequently visited by people interested in seeing where Almighty Voice made his stand. It, too, lacked any signage at the time.

Almighty Voice was also featured in the RCMP Depot Division museum in Regina; or to be more precise, the upper part of his skull plate was held there as a kind of war trophy. Other items were added after the Second World War. In 1958, the museum curator acquired the iron ring in the floor of the old Duck Lake

Dr. A. B. Stewart took Almighty Voice's rifle as a souvenir of the bluff fight and displayed it in his office.
GLENBOW ARCHIVES NA-1811-26

barracks that he believed had been used to secure Almighty Voice in place. The ring had been bolted to a log under the floorboard and removed only with great difficulty. That the floor ring had not been used to manacle Almighty Voice the night of his escape did not matter. It was put on display as part of a new Almighty Voice exhibit.

The museum curator also added photographs of some of the people and places involved in the story but was unable to find a picture of Almighty Voice. He did, however, get a copy of the April 1896 proclamation offering a five-hundred-dollar reward and providing a physical description of the wanted man. Then, in 1961, a parcel containing a NWMP riding crop arrived at the depot. An accompanying note said that the crop had been given to Dr. A. B. Stewart while attending to the wounded from the bluff fighting—probably Inspector J. B. Allan—and passed to a family friend who thought the "relic" should be on exhibit.[31] Dr. Stewart had also taken Almighty Voice's rifle, a 1866 Winchester carbine, from the pit and proudly displayed it in his office for years thereafter.[32]

This local interest in the Almighty Voice story was matched by international attention. In April 1957, R. van Vleuten from The Hague, Netherlands, contacted the superintendent of the Duck Lake Indian Agency for information about Almighty Voice's surviving descendants, in particular his son Almighty Voice Jr and his twin boys. The Leiden University student was president of the three-year-old Kake Manitou Wayo (Almighty Voice) society, whose growing membership had an "admiration for and a sincere interest in the red race."[33]

A similar request for information—this time, a letter to the editor—appeared in the Regina *Leader-Post* in February 1964. Dennis Stone of Derby, England, was toying with the idea of writing a book about the Almighty Voice incident but needed help. The curator of the RCMP museum saw the letter and sent Stone a copy of the Kemp article, "Almighty Voice–Public Enemy No. 1." Stone responded by contacting the Duck Lake Indian Agency and asking to be put in touch with Almighty Voice's relatives, as well as someone who could provide some history about the band and the reserve.[34]

Almighty Voice's sister Angelique (left), mother Spotted Calf, and son Stanislaus at the bluff, circa 1928. GLENBOW ARCHIVES NA-1811-25

Despite all the articles about Almighty Voice in circulation, it was not until late 1953 that radio finally picked up on the story. Dick Mayson, a Prince Albert historian, devoted three segments of his weekly CKBI *Pioneer Trails* program to the incident: Almighty Voice's escape; the showdown with Sergeant Colebrook; and the bluff siege. Mayson's radio scripts offered nothing new to the story but simply repeated what others had said. He opened the first segment by extolling "the bravery shown by the Mounted Police" but concluded in the end that the "tragedy [should] never have occurred had he [Almighty Voice] not been irresponsibly told that he would receive an undeserved hanging."[35]

The three radio episodes were also instructive for what was not covered: Almighty Voice's nineteen months as a fugitive from the law. Mayson was not the only one to exclude this part of the story. Most authors did. Maybe it was just assumed an Indian should be able to survive in the wild and there was no real story to tell. Then again, it was easier than believing that other bands would have actively helped Almighty Voice and shielded him from the law. After all, there was supposed to be only one bad Indian.

The obvious next step was a visual presentation of the story. There was clearly material for a documentary, even a movie or play. John Hart Wilson, manager of the Imperial Bank of Canada in Prince Albert and one-time president of the local board of trade, had been thinking along these lines for years. His wife was the daughter of the NWMP surgeon who performed the Colebrook autopsy, and he was living in Prince Albert at the time of the incident. Wilson liked to give an after-dinner speech on Almighty Voice, telling his audience, "Want to make you *SEE* my story. *VISUALIZE.*"[36] He then went through a series of points—like scenes on a storyboard—about how this true western story could be told. Many years later, in 1971, a copy of Wilson's speaking notes were deposited with the Public Archives of Canada (now Library and Archives Canada). Call it a coincidence, but the same decade would see the performance of an Almighty Voice play and the release of a feature film.

CHAPTER SEVEN

Spectator Sport

Almighty Voice stormed onto the national stage in the 1970s. Up until then, his story had been largely a Saskatchewan one, known mostly to people who lived in the Prince Albert area or to those with an interest in mounted police history. Magazine and book coverage had generated some outside interest in the incident, but the Canadian public would have been hard pressed to explain when and where it happened, let alone who or what an "almighty voice" was. That changed in 1970 when Toronto's Young People's Theatre staged *Almighty Voice*, a one-act play for young audiences. Four years later, in February 1974, Onyx Films of Montreal released the feature film *Alien Thunder*. That the story now appeared in these formats was not surprising, maybe even overdue. The many phases of the incident—from the Willow Cree man's arrest in October 1895 to his violent death in May 1897—were perfect fodder for dramatic treatment. But what made the play and movie different from past coverage of the story was their sympathetic portrayal of Almighty Voice and Indigenous peoples in general. He was not simply a bad Indian, sprung from an inferior race, who went on a murderous rampage. There was another, more nuanced, side to the story that helped explain Almighty Voice's motives and actions, and of those who passively resisted North-West Mounted Police attempts to get their man. Getting at the truth, though, was muddied by past distortions of the story and the need to weave creative elements into the play and movie that would appeal to and hold an audience.

≈

One of the most simplistic, and seductive, explanations for the tensions between Indians peoples and the Canadian state in the late nineteenth century was cultural inferiority. Confronted by a "superior civilization" in the form of the British empire, and not knowing how to respond to the momentous and bewildering changes going on around them, the Cree of western Canada challenged, resisted, and even lashed out at the federal policies that "well-intentioned" government officials had put in place to help them.[1] This Indigenous pushback did not surprise settler society at the time but was expected, even feared. Even though the Department of Indian Affairs was understood to be genuinely interested in the welfare of Indian peoples and actively pursued positive change,[2] it was dealing with a "heathen" race that had no system of government or set of laws, no concept of land ownership or property rights, and no great thinkers, scientists, or artists. That's why Canada's generous Indian policies were not appreciated. The Cree were generally incapable of improvement, blindly determined to maintain old ways and traditions by whatever means necessary.

This clash between "primitive" and "more advanced" peoples was the key to explaining why Almighty Voice killed a cow that did not belong to him, shot the mounted policeman who tried to re-arrest him, and then chose a defiant death rather than surrender to Canadian justice. Several authors had used this "clash of cultures" template to tell the Almighty Voice story because it seemed to make sense that he was trying to relive the nomadic, glory days of the Cree before treaty and reserve life. This interpretation cast a long shadow over much of the twentieth-century writing on Native-newcomer relations in western Canada. In his 1910 history of the force, *The Riders of the Plains*, for example, mounted police historian A. L. Haydon argued that Indians were captive to "outlets of energy so dear to the primitive mind. These instincts are hard to eradicate."[3]

After the Second World War, Canadians began to reconsider their relationship with Indigenous peoples. Part of the explanation was the growing worldwide decolonization movement. Canada may not have controlled an empire, but its treatment of its Indian population smacked of colonialism. And its policies were decidedly not working. Surveys of living conditions on and off reserve in the early 1960s painted a grim picture of an impoverished and disadvantaged people. As one Indigenous leader sarcastically quipped, "we were discovered" that decade.[4] Change was urgently needed at the time, but there was no clear path forward to bring about an end to Indian marginalization and the attendant social and economic problems.

Cree children at Beauval Indian residential school in September 1949. Canada's assimilationist Indian policies were increasingly questioned after the Second World War. PROVINCIAL ARCHIVES OF SASKATCHEWAN R-B5860

Starting in the late 1960s, scholars also began to rethink and re-examine the history of Native-newcomer relations in Canada. There was a gradual movement away from the popular image of Indians as simple "stick-like" figures, as if they were fixed in time and helpless in dealing with newcomers and the challenges they represented. Instead, the rereading of traditional sources, through different lenses, suggested they were motivated by their own interests and needs and were both resourceful and resilient. This historical revisionism did not take the profession by storm but slowly gathered support as more researchers took up the sub-discipline. In the process, there was some tough questioning of Canada's so-called honourable and just treatment of Indian peoples. Maybe Canada was an unreliable treaty partner who had consistently evaded its obligations and responsibilities. Maybe Indians found federal policy objectionable because it denied them an active and meaningful role in their own affairs. Maybe Indians had limited opportunities because they were confined to reserves and lacked access to land and resources. And maybe Indians were a disadvantaged group because of systemic racism.

It was against this background—this Canadian self-reflection about Indians and their place and role in society—that celebrated playwright Leonard Peterson wrote his Almighty Voice play. The telling of the story for the Toronto-based Young People's Theatre was something of a personal journey for Peterson. Born in Regina in 1917, Peterson lived the first nineteen years of his life in the Queen City before completing his undergraduate education in the United States, serving in the Canadian army during the Second World War, and then embarking on a long and distinguished career as a writer for radio, documentary film, and the stage. Peterson's work often revolved around the human struggle, especially individuals against bigger or more powerful forces and groups. The Almighty Voice incident clearly fit here. But there was more to it than that.

In the 1974 introduction to the Book Society of Canada publication of the children's play, Peterson offered something of a confession. His public schooling in Regina was steeped in British imperialism, or his tongue-in-cheek term, "Our World of God's Select." He learned to recite the rulers of England as if speaking aloud their names imparted some special power. He was also taught that "British blood was the best blood" and that other ethnic groups were little better than riff-raff. "The more we learned of great men and great happenings elsewhere," he recalled, "the less regard we had for ourselves. We were nobodies."

This insistence that "history ... is elsewhere" did not sit well with the young Peterson. Growing up on the outskirts of Regina, playing outdoors with friends in all weather, he often noticed Indians camping there for a few days before moving on. He also heard stories from old-timers about the territorial days and how the Métis rebel leader Louis Riel had been hanged in the mounted police barracks not far from Peterson's home. This history, in his own backyard, fascinated him. But whenever he wanted to talk about this Indigenous past, especially in school, he was told that "their world was not worth much ... something to be swept aside." And even though he lived "smack in the middle of Prairie Indian country … we didn't see them, talk to them, play with them or study with them."

Years later, Peterson reflected on this experience in preparing his Almighty Voice play script. "These were questions we couldn't walk around or away from," he admitted. "They wouldn't go away." What he came to realize was that settlers may have shared the same geography as Indians—were shaped by it—but not the same history. "Whiteskins," as Peterson called them, looked only to the future. They were more intent, more focused, on transforming the landscape and erasing the Indian past, including taking away their land. "We've come on to the prairie," he observed, "and left our souls behind."

The remedy, for Peterson, was to admit that Indian history mattered, that "[Indian] history is our history," while also "making amends for our trickery and injustices" towards Indian peoples. "[We need] to roll about in [it]," he urged. "We begin there. At one with our Indian past … Building on that … we may cease floundering, fretting, and warring in our geography and history and flourish in them." That included coming to terms with Almighty Voice. At the time of the incident, he was looking for "justice" in what had become a foreign world. "He found no big answers," Peterson mused. "He left that to us. Our agony."[5]

These were heady words. The challenge for Peterson was getting this message into a script. He began with some field research. He visited the One Arrow reserve and spent hours tramping the land and talking with Prosper John, Almighty Voice's younger brother, now in his late seventies. Their stops included the old Duck Lake barracks, where Almighty Voice had been held, and the bluff in the Minichinas Hills, where the fugitive had been shelled to death. Peterson also consulted several popular sources that clearly influenced his telling of the story. He came to believe that Almighty Voice had been "taunted by his Mountie guard … that he would be hanged for his crime"; that he was following in the footsteps of his rebel father and grandfather who fought alongside the Métis during the 1885 North-West Rebellion; and that he had deliberately lured the police to his bluff "hideaway" to make his last stand. This reading—backstopped by his own

Promotional poster for
Leonard Peterson's *Almighty
Voice*. NATIONAL ARTS CENTRE,
DESIGN INTEGRATED GRAPHICS

thinking about the need to learn from Indian history—convinced Peterson that the incident had a larger significance. In a background statement about the play, he declared, "Almighty Voice's importance lies in his being the last defiant expression of the Canadian prairie Indian spirit." It was this "spirit" that Peterson ought to capture in the play, even though "some necessary dramatic license has been taken with incidental fact."[6]

Peterson's other challenge was writing for a young audience. Almighty Voice was specifically commissioned by Toronto's Young People's Theatre, founded in 1965 by actress and producer Susan Rubeš to introduce live theatre to school-aged children. Peterson readily appreciated that the play not only had to capture kids' attention but get them involved in the performance. "The kids like to participate," he jotted down at one of the play's first rehearsals. "Hate sitting still." He also worked with limited props because Young People's Theatre took its productions into schools. Peterson's solution was to have four main characters play multiple speaking parts: Actor A, Almighty Voice and a Cree man; Actor B, Sergeant Colebrook and other mounties; Actor C, Spotted Calf and a Cree woman; and Actor D, a settler, mountie, and Indian. Interestingly, Spotted Calf was a commanding force in the play, her role just as important as that of her son Almighty Voice. The children in the audience also had constantly shifting roles, depending on the scene, and served in places as a chorus. The only stage feature was a painted box that served as a platform for the four actors; holes in the platform allowed for the alternating placement of poles to represent a teepee, flagpole, or bluff of trees. The audience sat on the floor, around the box, but separated by a passageway to allow for actor movement. This seating focused the children's attention on the central box. It also suggested that Almighty Voice was surrounded. In his rehearsal notes, Peterson scribbled, "A.V. - get in the centre! + stay in the centre!"[7]

The play opened with the actors inviting the children to become settlers—break the prairie wilderness into farmland as good loyal citizens of Queen Victoria. But the "settler" was confronted by an "Indian woman" who insisted that the Cree did not understand the treaties and that the land belonged to all. The woman then called on the children to become Indians, chanting, "Our Way," to the beat of a drum, while she talked about the glory days of the Cree. The settler interrupted her, insisting that the old ways were "savage ways" and that the One Arrow band was "a treacherous lot!" This exchange prompted the aside: "There you have it: not too good a feeling between the settlers and the Indians."[8]

Almighty Voice enthralling a young school audience during a Young People's Theatre performance. JULIEN LEBOURDAIS

A bugle blast announced the arrival of a mountie, who set a flagpole in the platform and asked for recruits "to keep the Indians from going on the warpath." After the children were sworn into service and started drilling in formation, a gunshot was heard. A settler rushed up to Sergeant Colebrook, screaming that Almighty Voice had shot one of his cows. At this point, Almighty Voice leapt onto the platform, boldly proclaiming, "Yes, shot by Almighty Voice!" Spotted Calf added, "We are starving." Colebrook remained unmoved by their plight, authoritatively stating, "Cattle are not wandering buffalo." As Almighty Voice was taken into custody, Spotted Calf softly told the audience, "How quietly my son goes with the policemen. How quietly we do so much these days."[9]

Colebrook handed Almighty Voice over to Corporal Dickson, who chained the Indian to a floor ring and then casually remarked that there would be "one less Indian" once he was hanged. Spotted

Calf, watching from nearby, turned to the audience, "The Corporal thinks he is having fun. But to my son, after a while, it sounds too real." She continued, "Hang an Indian for a dead cow? Why not?"[10] When Dickson nodded off to sleep, Almighty Voice grabbed the keys and made his escape to One Arrow.

The mood darkened at this point of the play. Seething with anger, Almighty Voice told his mother, "I'm done with reservations, no more asking any white man if I may do this or that!" He would take up the stand that his father and grandfather had taken against the government ten years earlier. Sergeant Colebrook was consequently already doomed when he chanced upon Almighty Voice hiding in the nearby hills. The fugitive threatened, "I want no meeting with a white man ... You want me to hang like a dog." When Colebrook persisted, Almighty Voice gave one last warning and then shot the mountie. Dickson is heard to say offstage, "Was I so dumb, seeing the murderer in him before he murdered?"[11]

Peterson captured the tension during the nineteen-month police search for Almighty Voice by having postmaster Ernest Grundy (who died during one of the rushes on the bluff) and Spotted Calf talk over one another. When Grundy claimed, "All the prairie Indians are rallying around Almighty Voice," Spotted Calf replied, "Must we go empty-handed among these white men? Empty-eyed, empty-mouthed, empty-souled?" And when he insisted, "The Indian must stop being Indians and be like us," she answered, "Almighty Voice has made some of us brave again." The audience played a supporting role: some children, as settlers, shouted, "God Save Queen Victoria!," while others, as Indians, chanted, "Our Way!"[12]

The closing scene featured the bluff siege. Almighty Voice has come out of hiding, ready to "stand and fight alone." When Spotted Calf questioned what he was seeking in death, he asserted, "Feeling! That alive ... Indian feeling! ... Let me find the courage we all once had. Long ago. Let me choose my battleground." Inspector Allan, representing the police, called on Almighty Voice to surrender, "In the name of the Queen! In the name of the Law!" Almighty Voice defiantly responded, "Go from this land, you White Man! ... We welcome you as brothers, but you leave us nothing!" While the two men stared at one another, Spotted Calf announced that the One Arrow band was ready to join her son in his fight—something that never actually happened. This news prompted Allan to summon reinforcements and gave Almighty Voice time to slip out of the bluff to see his mother, and demonstrate that he could have run away instead of meeting his fate. That fate was delivered by the sound of a cannon bombardment, while Spotted Calf sang her death chant and slowly beat a drum. "An Indian has been an Indian for the last time," Spotted Calf complained. "He can only be white and sad, sad." But then, with the drum stirring back to life, she exclaimed, "No! One day the whites will be Indians! Content with the earth. Too wise to change it much! ... Happy even with Almighty Voice! My son."[13]

Kids were invited to serve as mounties and in other roles in the Young People's Theatre Almighty Voice play. JULIEN LEBOURDAIS

Almighty Voice enjoyed a highly acclaimed run, first in Toronto-area schools and then throughout Ontario. It was even filmed during one of the gymnasium performances and adapted for a half-hour time slot on CBC television in November 1975. Kids loved the play. They jumped at the opportunity to join the action, to become a part of Canadian history as a settler, Indian, or mountie. They also revelled in the protest message and watched with rapt attention as Almighty Voice fought back against white mistreatment of Indians. "A slice of strong truth," said one reviewer. But the play created the impression that Almighty Voice was yet another rebellious Indian, one in a long line going back to the rebellion, trying to drive the white man from the region. It was as if the Cree knew only one way to respond: with violence. "Somehow I found myself," another review began, "caught in an Indian uprising the other day."[14] Equally unfortunate was the conflation of the bluff fight into the last stand of the Indian people. At the play's end, the Cree were a defeated people. "Dying in that bush was us, all of us," Spotted Calf had solemnly announced upon her son's death. "Dying: dead."[15]

That was the same empty feeling that the movie *Alien Thunder* left with viewers. Getting there, though, had been something of a circuitous route for Quebec director Claude Fournier and producer Marie-José Raymond of Onyx Films. In preparation for the NWMP centennial in 1973, Jean-Pierre Goyer, the solicitor general of Canada, asked Fournier in 1970 to direct a movie about the force. The request came with a $250,000 government investment in the film, the use of period uniforms, and the availability of the world-famous musical ride. Before Fournier found a story that would serve as the basis for the film script, he went in search of someone with box office power and convinced American movie legend John Wayne to play the lead role on the understanding that he would be a "good" mountie. But they still needed a script proposal. Day after fruitless day of research in Ottawa turned up nothing suitable. Then, a mounted police archivist quietly took Fournier and Raymond into his office and nervously handed over a bundle of photocopied documents and articles about the Almighty Voice incident, saying that the police did not like the story but that it had to be told. Fournier had found his dramatic western. But it meant the loss of Wayne even before he had read a script.[16] In his place, Fournier recruited Canadian Donald Sutherland, who had stormed to international stardom in the 1970 hit movie *Mash*. The other big signing was Chief Dan George of the Tsleil-Waututh (Salish) Nation, best known at the time for his role in *Little Big Man*, a revisionist 1970 American western about a white boy raised by the Cheyenne nation.

Writing the script fell to literary legend W. O. Mitchell, a Canadian icon because of his unparalleled distillation of small-town prairie life in the early twentieth century, most notably in

Who Has Seen the Wind (1947). Fournier sought out Mitchell because of his ability to develop character and capture personality through dialogue. And the Saskatchewan-born author was enthusiastic about the project—even more so because the story was new to him—and read all he could about Almighty Voice, including the archival materials that had been secretly supplied. Working up a script, though, proved a challenge. Fournier and Raymond spent months at the Mitchells' Calgary home in 1971, struggling over the movie's narrative arc and theme development with the author and sometimes his wife, Myrna.[17]

This brainstorming about the Almighty Voice movie was not constrained nor limited in any way by the facts. At one point during the story development sessions, all recorded on eleven tapes, Mitchell asserted, "We aren't the first people to come along and try and take liberties with actualities." Fournier agreed, "We will have to take liberties." He then proclaimed, "I'm a showman, that's my job. You'll be the thinker ('I'm a showman, too,' interrupted Mitchell) and I'll try to show what you are thinking."[18]

Mitchell maintained that "the initial flick or lever that starts this tragedy of fate" was Almighty Voice's escape from the Duck Lake gaol. "Everything else is inevitable." A yet-unnamed police sergeant, to be played by Donald Sutherland, would be consumed by a "dreadful responsibility and accountability" when his good friend Sergeant Colebrook was murdered by the fugitive.[19] Raymond added that the Sutherland character should also be ashamed to face Colebrook's widow, who for some inexplicable reason, was to be a sophisticated French woman.

Mitchell had also ruminated on the naming of Almighty Voice and how it could serve as an "important thread" in the story. He imagined Almighty Voice being born during a prairie thunderstorm, and that when he later took on the police, Chief Dan George, portraying his father, Sounding Sky, would tell him, "When you were born, there was thunder in the sky … and I had a vision, when you die, there will be thunder." That second thunder, for Mitchell, would be the "goddamn" cannon at the bluff, hence the title, "*Alien Thunder.*" He also argued that if this linking of "the two kinds of thunder" was used, then it had to be Sounding Sky, not Spotted Calf, who sang the death chant before the bombardment.[20]

Theatre placards for the *Alien Thunder* movie.

Theatre placards for the *Alien Thunder* movie.

Other topics included Sutherland's character: how he had to have "that touch of irreverence" and "cannot be the ideal mountie." Or how it might be effective to have kids look through the window of the Duck Lake barracks and tease the imprisoned Almighty Voice that he was going to hang. Mitchell refused to believe the police documents that Almighty Voice had not been chained the night of his escape or that one of his guards had left him alone. It was "too goddam cliché," he declared. It was also decided that Chief Dan George should have "a mystic quality," but they continually worried about replicating his role in *Little Big Man*. This concern carried over into their discussion of Almighty Voice's wives and whether they could find a suitable Indigenous actress to represent his young partner, Small Face.[21]

The bluff siege at the end of the film also elicited much debate. Mitchell visualized the death of Almighty Voice as a "spectator sport ... the Roman circus thing." Settlers and their families would head to the bluff with picnic lunches and expect to be entertained. The Indians would be on another hill, dignified and restrained in contrast to the party atmosphere among the whites. But it was "most important," Raymond interjected, that the bluff scene not be too "contrived." Settlers and police still feared the Indians after the rebellion and were prepared to crush any resistance, like that posed by Almighty Voice. Fournier wanted Sutherland to undergo some kind of conversion at the bluff, where he realized that "white civilization has screwed up everything for everyone." Mitchell picked up on the idea, suggesting that Sutherland should be overcome with the "realization that he and Almighty Voice have been pawns in this terrible, the inevitable tragedy" and that he leaves the force at the end of the movie. "He's got a new guilt," Mitchell argued, "and this demon of Almighty Voice ... is a worse demon than the one he's exorcised [the death of Colebrook]. I love that."[22]

These discussions formed the basis for a sixty-page booklet, complete with archival photographs, used in early 1972 to interest investors and potential distributors in the feature film *Alien Thunder*. "History, action, romance," the first sentence promised," will be the main fare of [this] unusual western." The prospectus also promoted that it would be the first movie about the world-famous mounted police "written and directed by Canadians." What followed offered a taste of the "inherent dramatic qualities" of the story. The year 1874 was a "double birth" summer, that of Almighty Voice and the arrival of the first mounted police contingent on the prairies. Then, there was the "hunter-hunted relationship" that stitched Sutherland and Almighty Voice together in a dance that could only end in a poplar bluff. The remainder of the booklet profiled the main characters and the general filming sequence for the story—all enlivened by snippets of Mitchell's dialogue. Sutherland, for example, said that his commanding officer is "so goddamn stubborn that if he drowned you'd find his body upstream."[23]

The film synopsis created considerable buzz in Los Angeles. But talk of Oscar material was one thing, a film script another. Mitchell still had to deliver. And when he did, after several months of cajoling and prodding, the script was more than three hundred pages. It meant the running time could be twice as long as the planned one hour, forty-five minutes. Without consulting Mitchell, Fournier asked Dalton Trumbo, widely regarded as one of the top American screen writers (including Academy award winner *Roman Holiday*), to look over the *Alien Thunder* script. Trumbo recommended cutting scenes that did not advance the action. Mitchell was furious when he found out and almost threw

Actor Donald Sutherland played Sergeant Dan Candy, a mountie obsessed with finding Almighty Voice. DENNIS FISHER

Fournier out of his Calgary home when he came to talk about revisions to the script. That's when New York writer George Malko became involved. He was asked to make the changes that Mitchell refused to do. Malko produced a revised screenplay that kept the rich dialogue whenever possible and came in at slightly more than 150 pages. The script went through five versions. Mitchell, meanwhile, distanced himself from the project and eventually asked that his name be removed from the credits.

Shooting got underway around Duck Lake in the fall of 1972. The budget was $1.5 million dollars, the largest for a Canadian film to that time, thanks to Paul Desmerais of the Montreal-based Power Corporation, who funded the entire project. Set designer Anne Pritchard and her team built a replica village, mostly false storefronts, as it might have looked in the 1890s, about two miles southwest of Duck Lake. Little did they realize that the site on rented land had once been a slough and subject to flooding. Some six miles of temporary track was laid for a period train. Horses were purchased and held in a nearby corral. Donald Sutherland had to learn to ride. Many of the cast and crew stayed in motels in Rosthern or Saskatoon, or on-site in a trailer in the case of Sutherland with his dog and motorcycle. They also set up a dining room, managed by the former maître d' of Chez Son Père of Montreal. Dozens of extras were recruited, mostly in Saskatoon, and bussed to central shooting locations—either the Big Hat or Goose Creek—depending on the daily schedule. The Federation of Saskatchewan Indians, a supporter of the movie, probably helped secure the Indigenous actors (in addition to Chief Dan George). Mohawk August Schellenberg, well known for his theatrical work, had originally been cast as Almighty Voice. But he was replaced by Gordon Tootoosis, a giant of a man from Poundmaker First Nation who would go on to an illustrious acting career, especially in Canadian television. Almighty Voice was his first role—and big break. Ernestine Gamble from the Beardy's & Okemasis reserve, just outside Duck Lake, played the part of Small Face.

Director Claude Fournier doubled as cinematographer. He loved shooting in Saskatchewan's prairie parkland, especially at dawn, when the early morning mist gave the landscape a surreal effect. But the relative isolation of the region presented challenges

Men and women from local First Nations bands were cast as extras in *Alien Thunder*. DENNIS FISHER

for the film crew, made worse when the fields got wet and mucky. Fournier also shot a lot of film, which made editing difficult. One extra, Bud Sillinger, who played the minister, claimed there was enough footage for three movies.[24] The film consequently did not closely follow the script. Nor did the script, for that matter, closely follow the historical documents about the incident. Names were changed (for example, Colebrook to Grant), events streamlined or altered, and new people introduced. The best that could be said about *Alien Thunder* was that it was loosely based on a true story.

The movie opened with Almighty Voice and a companion quietly slipping away on horseback from their village at sunrise. Their destination: the reserve cattle herd. Almighty Voice stealthily ran among the animals, forced one to the ground, and slit its throat. Both men then proceeded to skin and butcher the cow. The action then switched to Sergeant Dan Candy of the North-West Mounted Police (Donald Sutherland), in red serge and with a heavy moustache, playfully adjusting his Stetson before a mirror, while chatting with Métis Napoleon Royal (Sarain Stump) about the harsh spring. These two scenes at the outset of the film seem intended to introduce the hunted (Almighty Voice) and the hunter (Candy).

Sergeant Candy next appeared alongside Sergeant Malcolm Grant (Kevin McCarthy) in the office of the local NWMP inspector

(Jean Duceppe). An example had to be made of Almighty Voice for killing a government cow—his father, Sounding Sky, was a bad influence (in actuality, Sounding Sky was in prison at the time of his son's arrest). The two mounties were dispatched to the One Arrow reserve to bring in Almighty Voice. As they crossed the South Saskatchewan River on the ferry, Candy belittled the assignment, telling Grant that the orders did not make "any coon-shit sense" and that "bringing in one Cree boy is about as dangerous as picking a crocus."[25] At One Arrow, the mounties and the Indians argued over the supposed crime: that permission was needed to kill the animal even if they were hungry. When Grant claimed that the herd were the Queen's cattle, Sounding Sky retorted that "Queen Victoria forgot to burn her brand crown and scepter on that one." Candy cuffed Almighty Voice's hands behind his back and took him away in a wagon.

Director Claude Fournier doubled as cinematographer for *Alien Thunder*. DENNIS FISHER

Back at the dinner table at the Grant home in Duck Lake that evening, Emilie Grant (Francine Racette) complained to her husband and Candy that Almighty Voice had good reason for killing a cow. "Such a cruel country," she lamented. Candy then went upstairs to tuck the Grant son, Edouard, into bed. He told the incredulous boy about a buffalo stampede and how when the animals went over a cliff to a slough below, the dust mixed with the water to produce a mud blizzard. The tale was straight out of W. O. Mitchell's *Jake and the Kid*.[26] This storybook scene contrasted sharply with the next one at the police barracks, in which a loud, tipsy Candy had the chains removed from Almighty Voice and then told him he was to be hanged. In the morning, Candy learned that Almighty Voice had escaped, and that Grant and Royal had gone after him. "Stupid, goddamn Indian," he muttered twice to himself before riding after them. Candy came across Grant, lying dead in the grass, felled by a gunshot blast. He looked around him, his face full of shock and then anger, and as the sun started to set to the sound of melodramatic music, shouted repeatedly, "You red son-of-a-bitch, I'm gonna get you!"

Grant's Duck Lake funeral was interspersed with scenes of the sergeant's confrontation with Almighty Voice: how he repeatedly called on the fugitive to put down his gun and surrender. But in the movie, while Royal looked on, Grant suddenly pulled his service revolver and Almighty Voice reflexively shot him. As the "Last Post" was played at the end of Grant's funeral, Candy spied Sounding Sky, watching from horseback nearby, doffing his hat in salute to the fallen mountie. Candy grabbed the horse's reins and threatened Sounding Sky that he was going to bring in Almighty Voice, that he was going to die at the end of a rope, and that he was going to be at his funeral. An amused Sounding Sky answered, "Maybe not."

Some six miles of temporary track was laid for a period train in *Alien Thunder*. DENNIS FISHER

A mounted policeman on picket duty at the bluff in *Alien Thunder*.
DENNIS FISHER

At this point, the focus of the movie shifted to Candy's tormented search for Almighty Voice. Not only was the mountie a changed man because he felt responsible for Grant's death, but his character dominated the story for much of the rest of the film. Instead of being dismissed from the force for his actions, Candy convinced the police inspector that, in true mountie fashion, he was going to get his man and nothing would prevent him from discharging his duty. He patrolled the One Arrow reserve at all hours, at one point dashing into Sounding Sky's tent with his gun drawn. No sooner did he leave one evening than Almighty Voice reached under the side of the tent and touched his partner, Small Face, on her cheek.

When the police inspector announced that the search would be scaled back, an obsessed Candy took leave of the force to continue the search on his own. "I'm gonna be out there," he said with shining eyes, "an' he'll know it ... an' I want him to smell me—see me—know I'm there for good." In the next few sequences, now wearing a fringed buckskin jacket instead of his uniform, Candy was filmed riding along ridges, lying in wait on horseback in the snow, never at rest but always on the hunt. Once, a drunken Candy confronted Sounding Sky at the reserve, only to be mocked

by the old man, "You've become a hunter with nothing to hunt."
Almighty Voice, for his part, remained in the area, camping with
Small Face along the riverbank. When Candy discovered their
hiding place, the men shot wildly at each other. The posting of a
reward for the fugitive only made Candy more desperate. "My
hunt, it's my hunt," he blindly insisted to the inspector. He even
took over a locomotive at gunpoint when the engineer informed
Candy that he had seen Almighty Voice, and forced the train to
go backwards.

The mounted police did not come across favourably in *Alien
Thunder*. DENNIS FISHER

Candy's erratic behaviour in the film was set in contrast to the
gentle, almost idyllic, nature of life on One Arrow. People were
sitting quietly around campfires, chatting amicably in Cree and
sharing food. Their clothing was mostly European, and remarkably clean. It's hard to imagine the Cree in the movie as a starving
people. Viewer sympathy for the band was reinforced by Small
Face giving birth, with the help of several elderly women, while
Almighty Voice kept guard, rifle at the ready, over the group. That
it never happened was irrelevant. What was more important to
the action was that a menacing Candy was riding nearby when
the baby was delivered, disturbing the joyous moment. Almighty
Voice got his revenge. Candy had holed up in an abandoned cabin,

where he had crudely drawn the search area on one of the walls. Almighty Voice tried to flush him out one night by dropping a grass bundle down the chimney and causing the stove to fill the cabin with smoke. Candy got away in the ensuing firefight.

The film's climax began with Candy and Métis guide Royal riding hard, trying to pick up any sign of Almighty Voice. "Today we didn't start anywhere, we didn't get anywhere," complained Royal. "Then we ain't losin' any ground," interjected Candy, "are we?" "But my horse is very confused," Royal explained. "He thinks we been ridin' too long without restin.'" "Get a smarter horse," Candy growled. As the two men bickered, three Indians on horseback—Almighty Voice, Many Birds (Vincent Daniels), and Rolling Grass (Lenny George)—dismounted and hid in a large bluff. Their faces were painted and they were heavily armed. Candy sensed they were there as he rode by and went into the other end of the bluff with a reluctant Royal. It was soon dark, and the two sides moved warily about the brush trying to outmanoeuvre one another. In a twist of the actual story, where the three Indians were initially assumed from a distance to be deer, Almighty Voice and his two companions sported branches as antlers and crept towards Candy. The mountie, though, was not fooled by the ruse. Royal used the moment to disappear.

Early the next morning, Candy rode madly towards a group of

Only a few cannon shells were fired in the movie—unlike the actual saturation bombing of the bluff in May 1897. DENNIS FISHER

mounties and civilians coming over the hill, screaming at them to "stay back, stay back, you bastards, he's mine." He then turned his rage on Royal for getting help, before pleading wide-eyed to the inspector, "I'm bringing him in, I'm bringing him in." All Candy could do, though, was watch helplessly as several mounties on foot ran towards the bluff, only to be mowed down in a hail of bullets. Their red serge against the yellow fields made them easy targets. In the next scene, police reinforcements arrived by train in Duck Lake—with not one, but two field guns—under the command of a stiff, white-helmeted, English-accented officer who was little more than a caricature. As the column marched towards the bluff to the sound of a brass band, dozens of spectators joined in, many of them families enjoying the carnival-like atmosphere. Candy called on Almighty Voice to surrender—he was surrounded with no chance of escape—but the three men went about fortifying their position by digging a pit.

The police now formed into two riding columns and, after being photographed, galloped towards the grove with their guns firing indiscriminately. The Indians picked off the riders as if it were a shooting gallery. The mountie commander, walking rigidly forward with his head high and his sabre drawn, was wounded, as was Almighty Voice, who was shot in the knee and hobbled back into the bush. A second mounted charge, with the men circling the bluff, was just as futile—and bloody.

That night, as the three men in the bluff smoked a pipe and prayed, singing could be heard from the One Arrow Indians on a nearby hill. When the commander announced that the field cannon would be used the next morning, Candy sought out Sounding Sky, calling on him to get Almighty Voice out of the bluff. Sounding Sky answered back, "So that you can hang him." An infuriated Candy, glared at the old man, angrily spitting the words, "Bastard, you goddamn red bastard." Sounding Sky started to sing, in a low guttural tone, looking plaintively around, waiting for an answer. Almighty Voice responded, in a higher pitched cry, while his two companions stood stoically by his side. The camera then switched to Small Face, watching from the hill and listening, with a gurgling baby on her back.

The suspense was broken by the commander's bark to fire

Chief Dan George, who played Almighty Voice's father, Sounding
Sky, being interviewed on the set. DENNIS FISHER

the cannon. Only a few shells hit the bluff—not like the actual
saturation bombing in May 1897—but the explosions killed
Almighty Voice and Rolling Grass, sprawled lifeless outside the
pit. A frantic Many Birds ran through the smoke and darted from
the bluff. A settler calmly raised his rifle, took aim, and fired at
the fleeing Indian, who seemed frozen mid-step before he dropped
dead. The message could not have been blunter: there would be
no escape from the white man's revenge. The movie ended with
close-ups of people who were witness to Almighty Voice's final
moments, while flute music played in the background. There was
no cheering, no frenzied rush of the bluff by the citizen volunteers,
just an empty silence. There was the jaded Candy, the smiling
commander, an expressionless Cree boy, a tight-lipped mountie.
All seemed lost in their thoughts, trying to make sense of what had
happened. The final few frames dwelled on a distraught Spotted
Calf, dressed in black, seemingly trying to blink away the scene
before her. The screen then went black and the credits started to
roll. It was exactly the kind of ending that W. O. Mitchell had
railed against during the story development session. "You don't
end with passivity," he warned. "The only thing we know about
human beings is that they keep on going."[27]

Critics panned the film. So, too, did audiences. Despite its
compassionate portrayal of Indian peoples, *Alien Thunder* failed

to capture the broken treaty relationship between the Willow Cree and the Crown: how the One Arrow people lived an impoverished life under Canadian government control. Almighty Voice may have told mounties Grant and Candy at the time of his arrest that he killed the cow because the band was hungry, but life on the reserve in the movie was anything but bleak. *Alien Thunder* also downplayed the deep-seated white settler mistrust, if not outright fear, of the local Cree population—made worse by the cold-blooded murder of a policeman. This tension was missing from the film, never ratcheted up and, consequently, it was never understood why Almighty Voice was one of the most wanted fugitives in Canada at the time. One reviewer brutally observed, "There isn't much of a movie here … [it] does not ask any original questions and … has nothing new to say." Another claimed that the "whole movie [was] botched."[28]

Donald Sutherland interviewed on set by Saskatoon CFQC's Denny Carr (left) and Wally Stambuck. DENNIS FISHER

Alien Thunder's greatest failing was that it was never really about Almighty Voice, but mounted policeman Dan Candy. Maybe that's why the movie was released in the United States as *Dan Candy's Law* (1974). Even then, Sutherland's character (like all the characters in the movie) was underdeveloped and lacked complexity. One critic summed up his performance as "incredibly, unbelievably terrible."[29] Even his swearing was largely restricted to "bastard." Almighty Voice, on the other hand, remained an elusive figure—in more than one sense—in the film. He was reduced to a supporting role, largely floating around the edges, in a movie that was supposed to be about him.

Before the public release of *Alien Thunder*, Onyx Films arranged a special screening for RCMP Commissioner W. L. Higgitt and several senior mounties. It's not known what the mounted police expected—probably only that the movie was originally to be part of the NWMP centennial celebrations. Director Claude Fournier watched Higgitt view the film and noticed that the commissioner's face became as red as his uniform jacket. His reaction was understandable. The force did not come across favourably in the movie, especially in the bluff scene at the end. Their assault on the entrenched Indians could be kindly described as chaotic. Higgitt stormed out at the end of the screening, stating through his teeth, "I hope this film is never shown."[30] The movie's star, Donald Sutherland, provided an equally damning assessment. During his time in Saskatchewan during the shooting, Sutherland had dinner one evening with *Saskatoon Star-Phoenix* journalist Ned Powers, who wrote a movie column for the paper. A few years later, Powers encountered Sutherland in Toronto and reminded him about his work in *Alien Thunder*. Sutherland cut him short, "The worst movie I ever made."[31]

CHAPTER EIGHT

Can't Put the Wind in Prison

For the past half-century, the search for Almighty Voice and the telling of his story have come under greater scrutiny. That didn't mean, though, that the Willow Cree man ceased being portrayed as a renegade Indian, someone who defied Canadian authority at the cost of his own life and several others in his senseless quest for fame and glory. This theme continued to run through popular literature, including mounted police histories. Almighty Voice also found a steady home in collections about western Canadian outlaws and other disreputable characters. But the story lens was also opened up to shed more light on the Indigenous perspective. In the process, the focus shifted from what he did to *why* he did it. Or put another way, Almighty Voice's world view was more important than the simple facts of the incident. Seeing the world through his eyes—how he struggled to survive on the One Arrow reserve in the mid–1890s, and more generally, how Indigenous peoples were viewed and treated at the time—gave his story new meaning, if not greater significance. Almighty Voice refused to live a hungry, impoverished, restricted existence, as if, metaphorically, he had a rope about his neck. That's why he engaged in a spirited and uncompromising battle with authorities, first Indian Affairs officials and then the North-West Mounted Police. Almighty Voice was not an aberration—a rare case of an Indian stepping out of line—but an expression of all that was wrong with Canada's treatment of the Cree people. As one Indian Affairs official gravely warned at the time of the incident, continuing disgruntlement on reserves might "swell the catalogue of Almighty Voice."[1]

≈

"The problem is to make the story."[2] That's how award-winning Canadian novelist Rudy Wiebe opened his provocative 1971 short essay, "Where is the Voice Coming From?" Wiebe wanted to engage with the Almighty Voice incident and get to the root of the story, not simply watch from the sidelines like a spectator. But engagement was hard because "all the parts of the story are … available only in bits and pieces." Wiebe also found that published accounts were never the same, but often contradictory. "An affair seventy-five years old," he remarked, "should acquire some of the shiny transparency of an old man's skin. It should."

Wiebe tried reciting the names of the people involved, especially the Indigenous ones, as if saying them aloud would connect him to the story. It wasn't enough, he admitted. Viewing surviving artefacts also did not help. Wiebe had travelled to Depot Division in Regina to inspect the Almighty Voice display in the RCMP museum: the seven-pound gun used at the bluff, the 1866 model Winchester rifle found in the pit, and the most gruesome exhibit of all, the top of Almighty Voice's shiny skull in a glass showcase. He also poked around inside the old NWMP log barracks in Duck Lake, as well as stood before the headstones of Almighty Voice's three police victims in St. Mary's cemetery in Prince Albert. Wiebe couldn't find the burial place of Almighty Voice and his two companions on the One Arrow reserve. But as he observed, "A gravestone is always less evidence than a triangular piece of skull."

The top of Almighty Voice's skull was once displayed in the RCMP museum in Regina. PROVINCIAL ARCHIVES OF SASKATCHEWAN R-B9654

Then, there was the photographic record. Wiebe found the "supposed" picture of Sounding Sky and Spotted Calf that Chief Buffalo Long Lance had taken during his 1923 interview. The look on the face of Almighty Voice's mother, according to the narrator, "can only be called a quizzical expression ... [as if] she does not understand what is happening." Wiebe also wondered about the "purported" photograph of Almighty Voice that he found next to the skull fragment in the RCMP museum. "It must be assumed," he said, "that a police force with a world-wide reputation would not label such evidence incorrectly." What was troubling, though, was that the "supposed official description" of the fugitive did not match the "supposed official picture."

Wiebe's attempt to know and understand Almighty Voice through existing sources was an abysmal failure. "The elements of the story have now run me aground," he confessed. Writing about the man and the incident had either little to do with Almighty Voice or were told from the dominant white settler perspective. Either way, Wiebe was no closer to knowing Almighty Voice, hearing his story. There were clues, though. At the Duck Lake guardhouse, Wiebe imagined he heard "the sound of Constable Dickson's voice," threatening the young man in custody:
hey injun you'll get
hung
for stealing that steer
hey injun for killing that government
cow you'll get three
weeks on the woodpile hey injun

And just as these words were still to be heard, so was "the unmoving tableau of the three-day siege" in the Minichinas Hills still "there to be seen."

It was at the bluff, imagining Almighty Voice's final hours, that Wiebe found his story. There were the repeated assaults to dislodge the three Indians, including the attempted burning of the green brush, followed by the placement of the two field guns for the deadly Sunday morning bombardment. Throughout these actions, "nothing moves" inside the bluff, a phrase repeatedly used by Wiebe to stress that the mounted police and civilian

The "Almighty Voice Jailhouse" in Duck Lake has been designated a Saskatchewan municipal heritage property. PROVINCIAL ARCHIVES OF SASKATCHEWAN S-B11138

volunteers were the aggressors. Then, "there is a voice ... an incredible voice that rises from among the young poplars ripped of their spring bark." What Wiebe realized was that other accounts had effectively silenced Almighty Voice—never allowed him to speak—and this recognition allowed him to hear "a voice so high and clear, so unbelievably high and strong in its unending wordless cry." It was Almighty Voice's death chant. But even though Wiebe could hear it, it was a "wordless cry" because he could not understand Cree. And he was not going to impose meaning, as others had done, because "that is the way it sounds to me."

Wiebe's essay was a call to hear the other: to get beyond traditional, one-sided accounts of the incident. Ironically, he still included the hanging threat in the story even though he acknowledged that "it has never been recorded in an official report." He evidently believed that it was the kind of stupid thing a mountie would say, joke or no joke. What also troubled Wiebe was the prominent display of Almighty Voice's skull fragment as if it were a war trophy. Others were upset, too. In November 1972, Peter Frank of Oakville, Ontario, complained to the *Western Producer* magazine about his startling discovery during a visit to the Regina home of the mounties. "It is beyond comprehension," he charged, "how the RCMP Museum can display a skull fragment, with attached hair ... claiming this gruesome object to be part of the Force's history as they see it ... The Mounties got their man, and his scalp."[3] The skull fragment has since been removed from exhibit and is at present held in the secure artefact storage area at the new RCMP Heritage Centre.[4]

Wiebe also questioned the authenticity of the Almighty Voice photograph in the RCMP museum display. It was not the same

Stanislaus (left) standing before the grave of his father, Almighty Voice, with his son Edward and his wife, Ernestine. PROVINCIAL ARCHIVES OF SASKATCHEWAN S-B8547

man on display at Duck Lake. This second photograph appeared to be a studio portrait, probably taken some time before the incident. It was never available at the time of the incident—never

mentioned in any of the mounted police or Indian Affairs correspondence or used on the wanted poster—but surfaced decades
later. Fred Anderson of the Duck Lake Museum Society provided
the Glenbow-Alberta Institute with a copy in 1971. How he came
to possess the photo is not known, but he served as museum
curator and local historian and would have had access to local
collections and artefacts. In 1973, the Glenbow sought to confirm
the identity of the person in the photograph and contacted Métis
elder Sam Boyer of Duck Lake. "As far as I can remember," he
scrawled at the bottom of the letter seeking his help, "this is the
picture of Almighty Voice who was killed in 1897."[5]

There was also pushback over how the Almighty Voice story
was presented in the Grade Five school reader *Under Canadian
Skies* (1962). In Unit Four, "Long Arm of the Law," Nell MacVicar
claimed that Almighty Voice was not really a bad Indian. "He just
wanted his own way," she explained, "and didn't want to obey
laws." He was also a braggart who "wanted to show them what
'a heap big Indian' he was." The rest of the story dealt with the
killing of the stray cow and all the trouble that Almighty Voice
subsequently brought upon himself. "Poor mistaken Almighty
Voice!" MacVicar reminded her young readers. "He fought and
killed ... the men appointed to see that the law was kept by everyone." At the annual meeting of the Union of BC Indian Chiefs in
November 1971, one delegate condemned the textbook story for
"belittling our culture." The following June, the BC Association
of Non-Status Indians demanded the removal of the story from
the Grade Five curriculum because of its use of derogatory terms,
like "squaw." Education Director Brian Maracle pointedly asked,
"Who knows how many thousands of kids' minds have been
poisoned by this type of thing?" This criticism did not stop the
textbook from being used in Canadian schools. In 1974, when
Mary Thomas, principal of Toronto's Earl Beatty public school
and a consultant to the book, was asked whether children should
be reading the Almighty Voice story in classrooms, she offered no
comment—not once, but four times—in response to a journalist's
questions.[6]

First Nations' accounts of the incident also appeared in the
1970s, introducing a new version of the story: that Almighty

"Almighty Voice" was the lead story in the unit "Long Arm of the Law" in the Grade 5 reader *Under Canadian Skies*.
UNDER CANADIAN SKIES

Voice was a reserve farmer with his own cattle. In 1972, one year before his death at ninety-eight, Dan Kennedy of the Carry-the-Kettle Nakoda Nation published his handwritten manuscript, "Recollections of an Assinboine Chief." In his story about "Shu-Kew-weetam" (accompanied by an explanatory note by editor James R. Steven of Confederation College in Thunder Bay), Kennedy said that Almighty Voice had asked the Indian agent for permission to kill one of his own cows to feed his brother's sick child. When Almighty Voice was told no, he went ahead anyway and landed in gaol for trying to help his family. From his cell, Almighty Voice could see men building the frame of what the guard told him was a scaffold—he was to be "hanged in the morning." When the guard fell asleep, Almighty Voice crawled out the window to freedom. Kennedy insisted that government bureaucracy was to blame for the tragedy. Almighty Voice had more cattle than he needed and was justified in killing one of them.[7]

Joseph F. Dion of the Kehewin Cree band also talked about the Almighty Voice incident in his book, *My Tribe, the Crees*, prepared in the 1950s but not published posthumously until 1979. Dion also insisted that Almighty Voice had sought approval to kill one of his animals, but the meat was to be used to nourish his sick wife. This claim had been made half a century earlier by Indian Affairs official Robert Jefferson in his booklet "Fifty Years on the Saskatchewan" (1929). In reading the Dion text, it becomes painfully apparent that he had relied heavily on Jefferson, reproducing phrases and sometimes sentences verbatim. Parts of the two stories line up almost perfectly. But Dion added an important new wrinkle. Because Almighty Voice and Sergeant Colin Colebrook knew one another well ("two friends who had no quarrel between them"), the mountie believed he could use their friendship to convince the fugitive to surrender. But when Almighty Voice refused to give up, Colebrook pushed too hard, at the cost of being shot.[8]

The real test of whether the Almighty Voice story would undergo critical re-examination and rethinking was how it was handled in the popular literature. Acclaimed journalist-turned-author Pierre Berton seemed prepared to consider a different approach in "The legend of Almighty Voice," a chapter in his 1979 collection *The Wild Frontier: More Tales from the Remarkable Past*.[9] Berton, like Rudy Wiebe, had tried to wade through the existing literature, only to conclude that "the sorry, garbled story of Almighty Voice ... has long since assumed the proportions of a legend." He then began to interrogate the "accepted" or common telling of the story by going back to the Indian Affairs department records and NWMP files. It could be argued—and that's certainly the case here—that these official documents were biased, prepared and written for the dominant settler society. But they remain one of the few comprehensive sources on the incident, and they can provide an alternative perspective if read differently.

Berton found that the cow in question did not belong to the government but was a stray, belonging to a settler named Parenteau, and that "Almighty Voice's action was anything but planned." He also took issue with Constable Dickson being "cast as the villain" because of his apparent threat that Almighty Voice would hang for his crime. "Only a moron ... would have believed such a trumped-up tale," Berton maintained. "Reckless he [Almighty Voice] certainly was, and impulsive, but not stupid. Nor was he ignorant of the law." The more reasonable explanation was that Almighty Voice ran away from the police barracks because the key was on the table and the guard absent. His two companions chose to stay and were released the next day with a warning. Berton also slammed Long Lance's narrative for being "studded with so many errors ... that it is not possible to give credence to his account." What he found "astonishing," though, was that "Long Lance's tale ... should be believed. And other writers have embellished it."

Berton, for his part, had no patience with myth-making and even less sympathy or understanding for Almighty Voice. He regarded the Willow Cree as nothing more than a ruthless young "punk." "If he had been born a white kid from the city slums," Berton asserted, "he would have gone down in history as a mad-dog killer" for causing the deaths of three mounties, one civilian, and his two adolescent companions. His violent death was "pathetically unromantic." What followed was a dressed-up rehash of the standard fare. Almighty Voice had the "misfortune to be born when the frontier was undergoing a fundamental change." He had a "consuming but transitory interest in young girls." And finally, "Almighty Voice was the last of his kind."

Berton did, however, add some "new" detail to the story. He said that the brother of Almighty Voice's first wife had tipped off the police about the killing of the cow because he wanted to get back at Almighty Voice for jilting his sister. Where this information came from is uncertain. Berton also suggested that "a man of Almighty Voice's temperament" could not surrender to Sergeant Colebrook while Small Face looked on. He chooses to ignore the history of Almighty Voice's family with the law—how he likely equated a return to custody with the loss of freedom and perhaps sickness and death.

Berton used the showdown between Almighty Voice and Colebrook to play up larger frontier issues. Here were "two men who seemed perfectly cast by fate for their roles … both were captives of history." Back of Colebrook's raised hand, as he slowly rode forward, were "all the other policemen who by the magic of the scarlet uniform had worked their will on armed braves." Nor was Almighty Voice alone that day. Behind him "hovered the ghosts … of the old days when his people freely roamed the plains." Neither could back down. So much for not wanting to cast the story in symbolic terms.

Other popular literature on the incident continued to be both melodramatic and exaggerated. In *Portraits from the Plains* (1971), writer Grant MacEwan, serving as Alberta's lieutenant governor at the time, presented Almighty Voice as "one of the last Indians to stand defiantly against the great tide of invading white men."[10] This interpretation came straight from Long Lance, as did much of the chapter content. That same year, historian Frank Anderson published *Almighty Voice* in the Frontier Book series (#25), which was distributed at highway stops throughout the rural west. In the foreword to the booklet, Anderson blamed Almighty Voice—yes, blamed Almighty Voice—for "creat[ing] a situation which lends itself admirably to (slight) exaggerations. We only hope we have not been guilty of too many of these in our own attempt."[11] It was wishful thinking. The cow that Almighty Voice slaughtered was evidently for Small Face and their wedding

Frank Anderson's *Almighty Voice* was part of the
Frontier Book series sold at highway stops throughout
western Canada. ANDERSON, *ALMIGHTY VOICE*

feast. When Colebrook's body was retrieved, Small Face was
still there, calmly cooking her breakfast over a fire. And Dublin,
one of the two young men with Almighty Voice in the bluff, was
apparently the person who had told the police about the killing
of the cow. One wonders what Anderson might have written if he
had not promised to avoid distorting the story. Tiffany Shrimpton
faced a similar challenge in *The Search for Almighty Voice* (1999)
in the Gopher Book series (#31). She complained about "reading mounds of conflicting 'facts'" and "decided to approach the
topic from a different perspective." But she, too, made a number
of questionable claims. Perhaps her last sentence summed it up

best: "Funny how it is as difficult to find Almighty Voice in death as it was to find him in life."[12]

Almighty Voice was also a standard figure in collections about western outlaws. In fact, he and famed train robber Bill Miner jockeyed for top billing as the "most villainous" Canadian criminal. In *Outlaws of Western Canada* (1974), T. W. Paterson calculated that "the anonymous cow ... that Almighty Voice butchered must be one of the most expensive on record" because it had resulted in seven deaths. The "brave" was held to account when the mounted police put on a "command performance" at the bluff.[13] In *Pirates and Outlaws of Canada* (1984), on the other hand, Almighty Voice died a "redemptive death" by lifting himself out of his "drab and colourless" life to fight "the final battle of the four hundred years of war between the white man and red man in North America."[14] A similar message was found in *Outlaws of the Canadian West* (1999). M. A. Macpherson claimed Almighty Voice "thumbed his nose at white man's authority and so began one of the prairie's longest and bloodiest manhunts."[15]

Police literature, especially the spate of books that marked the force centennial (1873–1973), continued to portray Almighty Voice as a bad Indian who came perilously close to starting another rebellion. One author, drawing a link between the March 1885 Battle of Duck Lake and the October 1895 Colebrook murder, suggested that "there must have been something in the soil of that area." Almighty Voice and his two companions holed up in the bluff were "really no more than ghosts from the violent past."[16] *Maintain the Right*, a history of the early years of the force, offered a similar interpretation. Almighty Voice encapsulated the "spirit of restlessness" among Indians, a restlessness that caused the fugitive "to make up his mind to die" and take several policemen with him.[17] Stan Horrall, official RCMP historian, warned of the threat to civil society represented by the likes of Almighty Voice. "Unless such an open defiance of authority was quickly and effectively silenced," he cautioned, "others would follow his example."[18] Prairie historian R. C. Macleod regarded the threat as more sinister, more deadly. The Almighty Voice incident was "unusual" because the Cree man "did not hesitate to kill anyone who got in his way."[19] He appeared to be a new kind of criminal.

Then again, maybe the mountie code—a "mixture of reckless courage and self-confidence"—blinded Colebrook to the gravity of the situation and made him vulnerable. "Apparently Almighty Voice was not as impressed," writer Dan Francis drolly observed, "by Colebrook's display of resolution (or maybe he hadn't read any mountie stories)."[20]

Two very different assessments of the incident were offered by mounted police historians who had access to the same official

Almighty Voice also made an appearance in the British children's magazine *World of Wonder* in the 1970s. RONALD EMBLETON, *WORLD OF WONDER*

records. John Jennings studied the police and their dealings with Indigenous people (1873–1896) for his 1979 doctorate at the University of Toronto. In a subsequent article on Indian-police relations in the post-rebellion period, Jennings suggested that fear was at the root of the Almighty Voice affair. Indians had come to view the police as oppressors, their authority as restrictive. The police, in turn, imagined any unrest as a prelude to something much bigger, a worry that "showed how little they still trusted the Indians." Jennings was reluctant to pin the hero label on Almighty Voice. But he nonetheless found the fugitive's final hours "somehow fitting ... this last dramatic gesture of defiance of the Canadian Indian took place in a clump of scrub poplar that would not burn." Almighty Voice was "a symbol of a once proud race hurling futile defiance at the government's attempts to recycle them into wards of the state ... against the coercion of the Police and the Indian Department, against the systematic destruction of Indian culture."[21]

RCMP historian William Beahen and his predecessor Stan Horrall took dead aim at Jenning's conclusion in their official history of the force, *Red Coats on the Prairies*, for the period 1886 to 1900. "Such powerful imagery," they declared, "clouds rather than clarifies the facts concerning Almighty Voice, who bore individual responsibility for his actions." Like Jennings, Beahen and Horrall had access to the thick police files on the incident. And their account never strays too far from the official record. In the end, though, the pair dismissed the story for lacking any "wider significance." It was only worth including in their force history "because of the loss of so many lives and ... the unique nature of the final showdown." They did concede, though, that the mounted police had botched the case from the beginning and were forced to devote so much time and resources to finding Almighty Voice in order that "the authority of the police [was] not weakened in the eyes of the Indians."[22]

That the incident was unusual—or what one author described as "its relatively exceptional nature"[23]—might explain why Almighty Voice is largely missing from Native-newcomer academic literature.[24] When he is mentioned, it's to underscore how uncommon it was for the time. One study suggested that Almighty Voice represented "a momentary resort to weapons ... but for the most part Indians' resistance has been non-violent."[25] Another echoed this interpretation: "following 1885 ... growing repressions were accepted without violence. When it did erupt, it was on the part of individuals."[26] Only one scholar connected Almighty Voice's protest with "the policies and practices ... that restricted the basic freedoms of ... Indians." His brutal death directly challenged "the idea of Canada's kinder and gentler history."[27]

It's surprising that Almighty Voice didn't get more attention in the scholarly literature. Yes, the Cree were an administered people in the latter part of the nineteenth century, subject to a concerted program of coercion, control, and interference. But formal policy and actual practice were sometimes quite different. Indian people, ever resilient and resourceful, creatively found ways to evade, undermine, or ignore government restrictions and regulations.[28] Almighty Voice was not, then, the only person to defy authority. And these acts of resistance warrant greater study, if only to answer the question of why only a few led to violence. Almighty Voice was also the kind of Indian that settlers feared. As long as the prairie west remained largely unsettled—and that was the case until the early twentieth century—white society viewed the Indigenous population with unease, if not suspicion, and expected a possible third rebellion.[29] That, too, is worthy of scholarly examination.

The academy's general neglect of Almighty Voice has been counterbalanced by his emergence as a popular cultural figure. He is found in song. Bruce Cockburn's 1987 *Waiting for a Miracle* compilation album refers to Almighty Voice in the lyrics to "Stolen Land":

From Tierra del Fuego to Ungava Bay
the history of betrayal continues to today
the spirit of Almighty Voice ...
so now we've all discovered the world wasn't only
    made for white
what step are you gonna take to try and set things right
in this stolen land[30]

He is also found in poetry. Andrew Suknaski wrote "Almighty Voice" in response to a January 1975 *Globe and Mail* story about a pack of stray dogs mauling to death a three-old-boy in La Ronge, Saskatchewan. The same pack, in the form of the mounted police, had hunted the Cree fugitive:

a tragedy of misunderstanding
the scent of blood
alerting the wild dog pack
howling for revenge

in the name of white justice
almighty voice escaping[31]

Suknaski's poem mentioned Indian hunger, the killing of a
government cow, and the threat of hanging, similar to elements
in Métis writer Maria Campbell's traditional Michif story, "Big
John," from her acclaimed Road Allowance collection. But her
story also talked about life under treaty and the repressive Indian
Affairs department:

Anyways
dey kill Almighty Voice over a damn cow
Hees jus not right how dey can do that
Jus kill a man for killing hees own cow
Dats how bad dat Indian Department he use to be in
dem days[32]

Almighty Voice also headlined a special exhibit, curated by
his great-great nephew, singer-actor Tom Jackson, at Calgary's
Glenbow Museum in 2000. And he stares down today from an
expansive wall mural on the side of a Duck Lake building. Artist
Ray Keighley has placed Almighty Voice, rimmed in yellow, in the
centre of the canvas. To his left the white settler understanding of
the story is depicted, to his right the Indian perspective.

The most inventive treatment of the story—and the most unsettling—was the Great Canadian Theatre fall 1991 production of
Daniel David Moses's two-act play *Almighty Voice and His Wife*.
The play did much to cement Moses's standing in Indigenous
theatre in Canada. But it also pointed the way to reconciliation,
even though reconciliation was probably not a word associated
with the play in the early 1990s. The play ironically facilitates
the healing process by making Almighty Voice, in Moses's words,
"a rather obviously and intentionally theatrical creature."[33] The
big difference from past inventions, though, is that it is Almighty
Voice, as Almighty Ghost in white face, who has turned the situation on its head and has his white audience on the run. He never
lets them rest, never lets them find refuge because of what they
have done to Indigenous people and the threat they continue to
represent.

The Almighty Voice mural by artist Ray Keighley on the side of a Duck Lake building. BILL WAISER

Moses, a Delaware from the Six Nations Reserve on the Grand River in southwestern Ontario, first encountered Almighty Voice in the late 1970s: "I knew as soon as I came across the story that someday I would do something about it." Moses tried to find out more, especially how a "dark-skinned delinquent" could die for killing a cow? It seemed, in his words, "the epitome of overkill." But in the search for "some other angle" to the story, Moses kept encountering "shifting historical facts." He took this finding as creative permission to come up with another version of the story, one that "sidestep[ped] some of those so-called historical facts." He didn't want his play, though, "to serve up" yet another Indian tragedy. "What I intended to do," Moses imagined, "was to stop the story the moment after Almighty Voice and his friends get cornered in the poplars. I thought I could leave them there [in the first act]."[34]

But what would come next? Moses initially planned to surprise the audience "by forcing their attention away from Almighty Voice and in the direction of all his pursuers." He would create police and settler characters and use the second act to explore their attitudes towards Indigenous peoples and Almighty Voice in particular. Then, he came up with his "coup de theatre" idea of a travelling minstrel show; act two would poke fun at Native stereotypes through the songs, jokes, dances, and parodies that entertained white audiences at the time. Moses also reduced the number of actors to two, both playing two parts. Act one would be a more traditional drama, telling the story of the incident through the relationship between Almighty Voice and his wife, White Girl, who had spent time in a residential school. In act two, Almighty Voice has become Almighty Ghost, while White Girl assumes the role of Interlocutor. Both actors revisit the story as a raucous minstrel show that parodies white racist attitudes. The Native characters, in white face, see the world as white society sees it. "White as a colour exists," Moses reasoned, "only because some of us are told that we're black or yellow or Indians. I think my ghosts exist to probe this white problem."[35]

Moses's research for his play clearly reflected much of the pop literature on Almighty Voice. In fact, it would be surprising if he did not repeat many of the "untruths" associated with the story: that it was a government cow, that it was killed for a wedding feast, that the mountie guard threatened Almighty Voice with hanging, and so on. But what makes act one of *Almighty Voice and His Wife* so different is that Moses jettisons the renegade Indian approach in favour of making it a romance. As Almighty Voice and White Girl flirt on stage, their courtship develops into a deep, loving relationship that is threatened by white settler society and its drive to assimilate, educate, and Christianize the Indigenous population. And that's the other interesting feature of act one. Instead of simply focusing on the conflict between Almighty Voice and the Indian Affairs department and the mounted police, Moses deftly contrasts the two worlds—but from the Indigenous perspective.

Act one, titled "Running with the Moon," opens with White Girl, bathed in moonlight, lying asleep on the ground, breathing

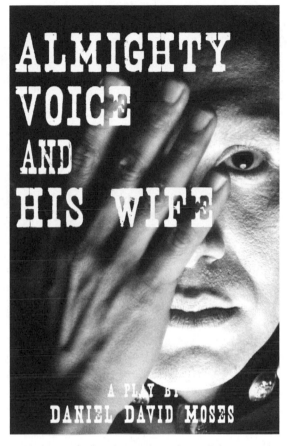

Book cover of *Almighty Voice and His Wife* (cover photo
of Michael Greyeyes by Nadya Kwandibens). PLAYWRIGHTS
CANADA PRESS, 2009

deeply to the slow beat of a drum. She is startled awake by rapid
drumming followed by a gunshot. Temporarily blinded by a flash,
she hears three more shots in rapid succession and then peers
through a teepee-shaped cone of light to see the silhouette of
Almighty Voice before the moon. At the sound of more gunfire,
Almighty Voice crumples. White Girl drops to her knees and the
moon bleeds. Moses uses the moon and its sacred place in Cree
spiritualism in opposition to the ever-seeing gaze of the settler
"glass" god. The audience learns in the play's early scenes, for

example, that thirteen-year-old White Girl has spent time in a residential school and found herself shielded from the world she knew by the glass walls (windows). "I have bad medicine in me," she tells Almighty Voice about her school days. "They said I could live forever but I had to marry their god." She also confidently predicts his death: "He's going to kill you. He's a jealous god."[36]

Act one explores these contrasting worlds against the backdrop of the Almighty Voice incident. When Almighty Voice escapes from custody and returns to the One Arrow reserve, he tells White Girl that he has gone from one prison to another: "They even turn the prairie into a jail." White Girl disagrees: "They can't put the wind in prison." And when Almighty Voice is being pursued by the mounties, he observes that their telescopes ("clear beads they look through") distort the world. "Far away comes real close," he says. "All the walking in between seems to disappear." Sergeant Colebrook, meanwhile, is said to have a "glass eye" as he tracks down the couple to the camp in the Carrot River uplands. When Almighty Voice kills him with one shot, White Girl remarks, "I told you glass breaks."[37]

The remainder of act one revolves around Almighty Voice's flight from justice and his eventual showdown at the bluff. White Girl is an integral part of the storyline. She tells the mounted police that "the prayers you say to your glass eyed god" won't help find her husband. Nor will any reward—"a coin is not the moon"—get Indigenous people to assist their oppressors. "It's like a war but no one will say so," Almighty Voice adds. "So there's never any peace." White Girl has a baby, and Almighty Voice takes her and the infant boy to be with his mother. It's at this point that Almighty Voice and his two companions ride off "laughing … to hunt somewhere, the grass new, blue green." White Girl knows what's going to happen and begs to die with him. But Almighty Voice wants her to live on, to tell their son about their time together: "Tell him, wife, how good a season it was along the Saskatchewan the winter before he was born. Tell him I always found game, never got cold."[38] White Girl then recounts the numbing scene at the bluff, how she tried to forget the image of Almighty Voice against the moon before shots rang out. The act ends with White Girl, bathed in light, proudly showing the baby to Almighty Voice. The moon turns white and he dies.

Stanislaus (Almighty Voice Jr) with his sons Ernest (left) and Edward (right), circa 1940s. PROVINCIAL ARCHIVES OF SASKATCHEWAN S-B8546

This rather conventional treatment of the Almighty Voice story is disrupted by act two, "Ghost Dance," performed amongst a collection of discarded stools. Almighty Ghost, in white face, sits under a spotlight. White Girl, also in white face and wearing white gloves, has been transformed into the Interlocutor, master of ceremonies for the Red and White Victoria Regina Spirit Revival show. The pair share a fleeting glance, telling each other through their eyes that they know who they really are. But the show must go on. And it does through a series of fast-paced, at times frantic, scenes, introduced by placards that the pair take turns putting up.

Almighty Ghost, at first, is a reluctant participant. He appears stone-faced, as if in a trance, and speaks in Cree when the Interlocutor tries to stop the dance he is performing on stage. "What's the meaning of this," she stammers. "Come on, use the Queen's tongue, or I'll send you to a cigar store." The Interlocutor then harangues Almighty Ghost, calling him "Chief" repeatedly and insisting that he is supposed to say, "How." These and other white insults are accompanied by slaps on his face and a threat to break his leg, the one that was not wounded in the bluff siege, if he continues to dance. Almighty Ghost then asks what's going on? "These fine, kind folks want to know the truth," the Interlocutor addresses the audience. "They also want to be entertained and enlightened and maybe a tiny bit thrilled, just a goose of frightened ... They want to know the facts. And it's up to you and me to try and lie that convincingly." Almighty Ghost responds that he won't dance. "But you have to toe the line, Chief," she retorts.[39]

The next few scenes are a mixture of short skits, songs, and monologues, all interspersed with the Interlocutor's stupid puns, comic putdowns, and sarcastic asides to what happened in the bluff. At one point, Almighty Ghost asserts that he'll be remembered by his people. "One must always strive for accuracy," she shoots back. "Do you have documentation?" When Almighty Ghost persists that his death mattered, the Interlocutor answers, "We do remember you, Mister Almighty Ghost. The angry young man, the passionate lover, the wild and crazy Indian kid." The dialogue then shifts to a general evaluation of Indigenous peoples. The Interlocutor, speaking as a "loyal citizen of our territory," observes that "we have ourselves a problem, dear friends, an Indian problem ... the pampered redskins, they are the bad ones ... and this gives weight to the wise adage, friends, that the only good Indians are the bad ones." Almighty Ghost thanks her for bringing this threat to the audience's attention, noting, "Dead Indians would be even better, sir, if they didn't stink that way."[40]

The Interlocutor decides that it's time for some excitement and calls on Almighty Ghost to reprise the bluff showdown with the mounted police and civilian volunteers. "Fuck you," he tells her. "I'm not going through that again for your entertainment." But he does agree to join her in a song about the ongoing war against "the blood thirsty redskins":

> We are the men, well let's say it again, to get them
> heathen Indians
> We are the ones, oh let's do it with guns, let's kill them
> stinking Indians
> We are the ones, well let's do it with rum, let's get them
> redskin Indians
> We are the men, of let's say it again, to kill them
> damn dead Indians

The scene then changes abruptly to a recitation of the uplifting policies of the Indian Affairs department as enthusiastically outlined in the regional newspapers. "Did you read how we're teaching our primitive friends agriculture?" the Interlocutor asks. "And we're giving them the benefit of our modern tongue." She continues, "Did you read how tranquil and subordinate they've become under our wise and humane government?" Almighty Ghost pretends to fire his gun. A shaken Interlocutor asks if it was a shot. "Likely not," he replies. "The Indian Agent won't give them any more ammunition until they put in a crop."[41]

Towards the end of act two, the Interlocutor's disguise begins to slip and Almighty Voice takes over the questioning. He calls on her to look into his eyes and tell him how she feels. "I feel this evening like the moon," she answers. "The Moon's an old woman," Almighty Ghost explains. "A very wise old woman—She's made of light!" But the Interlocutor fights the urge to reveal her true identity and going back into character, poses the bizarre question, "Do you know, sir, how many Indians it takes to screw in a light bulb?" When Almighty Voice asks what's a lightbulb, she unleashes a torrent of hate-filled invective: "You're primitive, uncivilized, a cantankerous cannibal! Unruly redman, you lack human intelligence! Stupidly stoic, sick, demented, foaming at the maws! Weirdly made and dangerous, alcoholic, diseased, dirty, filthy, stinking, ill-fated degenerate race, vanishing, dying, lazy, mortifying, fierce, fierce, and crazy, crazy, shit, shit, shit, shit … who the hell are you?" A subdued Almighty Ghost admits, "I'm a dead Indian." The Interlocutor is pleased, "That's good. That's very good."[42]

The closing scene opens with the Interlocutor asking Almighty Ghost, "Who am I? Do you know?" He lovingly responds, "I recognized you by your eyes."[43] She imploringly asks twice more and each time Almighty Voice emphatically answers, "White Girl." Now under a spotlight, she wipes the white makeup from her face, gradually revealing her identity. Almighty Ghost briefly embraces her and then helps her remove her white gloves. He resumes his dance from the opening scene, while she picks up a baby bundle to show the audience. The final moments are awash in moonlight, then darkness.

Almighty Voice and His Wife helped reclaim the Almighty Voice story for Indigenous people. For decades, it had been essen-

Members of the extended Almighty Voice family: Stanislaus or
Almighty Voice Jr (second from left) and Prosper John, brother of
Almighty Voice (standing, far right), circa 1940s. PROVINCIAL ARCHIVES
OF SASKATCHEWAN S-B8548

tially told as a law-and-order parable: how a young, misguided
Indian outlaw had openly challenged Canadian authority and
met a defiant but deserved death at the hands of the Queen's
soldiers. Now, the other side, the Indigenous perspective, was
being forcefully addressed. It was an uncomfortable reckoning,
but one that was both intentional and necessary. White Canadian
smugness—that they knew what was best, that they could do no
wrong—needed to be openly questioned, maybe even mocked as
in the case of the Moses play, to get people's attention and get them
thinking about how racism informed Canada's relationship with
its treaty partners and shaped its Indian policies. Only then could
they begin to understand and appreciate what pushed Almighty
Voice to do what he did: why he fled captivity, why he refused to
surrender to Sergeant Colebrook, why he remained a fugitive for
so long, and why he finally chose to die in a poplar bluff rather
than at the end of a rope. The concentrated shelling of Almighty
Voice's makeshift hideout was brutal testimony to how Indigenous
resistance was to be snuffed out by any means necessary. But it

also was a poignant reminder that the Cree were not a cowed people. Family and friends may have watched in silent disbelief at the bluff, but they were there, there as witnesses, to ensure that Almighty Voice was not alone when he died—and to remember. "[It's] like a purging or exorcism," Daniel David Moses reflected. "It feels like it gets a lot of the poison out."[44] Getting the poison out was long overdue. But it was only the beginning. Healing and recovery take time, especially when the wound had festered, without being properly attended, for nearly a century.

EPILOGUE

Bring Me Home

No sooner had the ceremonial pipes been lit than the cathedral bells suddenly rang out over the graveyard. Everyone momentarily stopped to look up. Even the graveside singing died down. Everything had been meticulously planned for the exhumation, everything solemnly steeped in spiritualism. But the pealing bells were an unexpected interruption, embraced by the Willow Cree as yet another sign that they were doing the right thing. Chief One Arrow had been sentenced to three years in Manitoba's Stony Mountain penitentiary for his apparent role in the 1885 North-West Rebellion. When he was released early—after eight months of incarceration—he immediately let it be known that he wanted to return to his reserve in the Saskatchewan country. But the elderly chief, likely battling pneumonia, was too ill to make the five-hundred-mile trip and was taken instead to St. Boniface hospital in Winnipeg. He was soon transferred to the nearby archbishop's residence to spend his final days with the Roman Catholic priests. As One Arrow lingered near death, he was baptized, something he had resisted in the penitentiary. He died Easter Sunday morning, at 8 a.m. on 25 April 1886, and was buried two days later in the St. Boniface cathedral cemetery grounds. "There is no doubt," argued *Le Manitoba*, "that his detention was fatal to his health and that had he been released sooner it would have been possible to heal him."[1]

≈

The One Arrow band would be without a chief for fifty years—until 1936. It would be another fifty years before a future chief, Richard John (Standing Growling Bear), contemplated bringing his great-great grandfather One Arrow home. Chief John initially thought One Arrow had been buried somewhere on the reserve. But research for the band's Treaty Land Entitlement application revealed that the grave was in St. Boniface. John visited the cathedral cemetery in the mid-1990s but gave up on doing anything more on the advice of Elders who warned that the body should not be disturbed. Then, in 2006, the spirit of One Arrow seemed to be present in sweat lodges. John held a shaking tent ceremony that summer at which One Arrow appeared briefly, spoke about how he had been badly treated, and said, "Bring me home." The band was divided on the matter, but John decided to go ahead and fulfil his ancestor's request.[2]

In September 2006, John submitted a formal application to the Manitoba government to have One Arrow's remains returned to his reserve. Two family Elders also submitted a letter of support later that fall, expressing their desire to have the body repatriated and confirming Richard John as next of kin to the deceased (with an accompanying genealogical chart). John was worried that St. Boniface church officials might prove uncooperative, but they were accommodating and gave their consent, especially after he explained why he was doing it. A provincial government order authorizing disinterment of Marc Kapeyakwaskonan (Chief One Arrow) was approved June 2007.

John turned to his friend Butch Amundson to handle the exhumation.[3] The senior archaeologist at Stantec Consulting in Saskatoon, Amundson had dealt with the removal and relocation of human remains, particularly in rural graveyards. He had also been the lead investigator in two major projects in the province: the discovery of the S.S. *City of Medicine Hat,* a sternwheeler that wrecked on Saskatoon's Traffic Bridge in June 1908; and the excavation of a nine-thousand-year-old bison kill site along the north bank of the South Saskatchewan River near St. Louis. Nothing had prepared him, though, for this "life-changing experience." Amundson knew the One Arrow people from his field work in the area, most recently helping the band find the hill where Chief Beardy had wanted to sign Treaty Six. During that time, he became immersed in Cree spiritualism through his guide, the late Gerry Prosper, and participated in various ceremonies. The disinterment of the chief was consequently something special for Amundson, something he did on his own time. And whenever he talks about it, he can feel the hairs on his neck standing up.

The One Arrow gravesite in St. Boniface cathedral cemetery was marked by a stone monument. But it was not certain
whether the headstone stood above the actual grave shaft. In
1950, the cemetery had been hurriedly bulldozed in a failed effort
to strengthen the levee holding back the waters of the devastat-
ing Red River flood. Then, in 1968, cemetery records were lost
when fire destroyed the cathedral (today's basilica is built within
the exterior walls of the ruins). This uncertainty over the exact
location of One Arrow's grave could have stymied the repatriation
project. But on the morning of 8 August 2007, a glorious summer
day, Kirby Littletent took a red stick with an eagle feather fastened
by rawhide to one end and walked over the area where One Arrow
was presumably buried. Every time he passed over a particular
spot, the feather vibrated. Amundson then had colleague David
McLeod of Stantec's Winnipeg office perform a geophysical
survey, using an electromagnetic conductivity machine (collo-
quially known as the "dig here" machine) that pinpointed the
casket, running north-south, and four other graves, at right angles,
protruding into the One Arrow grave shaft.[4] Two weeks later, in
preparation for the exhumation, Elders Eddie Baldhead, George
Sutherland, Gerry Prosper, and Stewart Prosper held a pipe ceremony on the spot. That's when the cathedral bells started chim-
ing—to the surprise of everyone in the cemetery, including the
resident priests.

Amundson had initially proposed the removal of all grave
contents, from wood and hardware to clothing and bones, and
then sifting the removed soil through a mesh to ensure that nothing was missed. But a standard exhumation was not possible. For
spiritual reasons, he was not to touch the skeleton nor disturb the
remains in any neighbouring grave. That increased the difficulty of
the exhumation for Amundson, but he would not know how big
a challenge it would be until he entered the grave shaft. Before he
started to dig down, though, one of the Elders anointed his forehead with berries. The Willow Cree trust in him was evidenced
by the traditional name given to him on a previous occasion: "He
Who Walks through the Spirit Wall."

Amundson had dug down only a few feet before he encount=

tered his first surprise. He found the remains of a baby. It was not unusual for a child to be buried into an already occupied grave, but John now wondered if they were digging in the wrong place. The baby was disinterred, after proper protocol had first been observed, and put into the care of the priests who had been watching the exhumation with rapt attention. Amundson's next surprise was the depth of the grave shaft. He did not hit the top of a casket until he was down six feet; it was now little more than a wood stain in the soil. But the good news, as he carefully excavated around the casket, was that it was probably from the 1880s: it was toe-pincher in shape, dovetailed at the joints, and contained no metal except for handmade nails. By the time Amundson had managed to expose what remained of the casket, he was nine feet down in the ground. And it was only because of his small, wiry stature that he was able to work in the narrow grave shaft and not disturb the other remains.

Amundson's task the second day, 24 August, was to get One Arrow's remains and the casket out of the ground without it falling apart. He recommended that dry ice be used to freeze everything solid, but that was not acceptable to the Cree. He then came up with the idea of temporarily wrapping the body and coffin in chicken wire covered with wet strips of gauze, much like a palaeontologist prepares specimens for transport from the field. This process created a protective frame; for added measure, Amundson applied duct tape selectively here and there. He then dug three small trenches under the bottom of the coffin through which he placed planks with tow straps, at both ends and in the middle; these transverse planks served as the base of a wooden crate that Amundson built around and above the jacketed remains for extra protection. Lifting the archaeologist's handiwork through the narrow excavated passageway required herculean effort by several men. But once safely above ground, One Arrow, still encased in silty soil, was placed on the base of a breakdown birch casket that had been built by Amundson's father. The casket was assembled around the chief's remains and then placed with great difficulty into the back of a van that had been driven onto the cemetery grounds. That left one remaining duty: to re-bury the baby, adopted and named Earth Child by

A traditional feast was held for One Arrow in the community hall prior to his re-burial on the reserve. DENNIS FISHER

One Arrow's remains were taken to the reserve cemetery by a wagon drawn by two Indian ponies. DENNIS FISHER

One Arrow's funeral was held on 28 August 2007—131 years to the day that the Willow Cree entered Treaty Six. DENNIS FISHER

The One Arrow basalt headstone in the cemetery (left foreground); the Almighty Voice red granite memorial is visible on the right horizon. BILL WAISER

the Willow Cree, through prayers and smudging. The priests in attendance performed the last rites, using a cross that had been fashioned from roots removed from the grave during exhumation. Everyone present participated in the funeral.

It was mid-afternoon when brothers Gerry and Ross Prosper began the drive back to the Saskatchewan reserve. They talked constantly to One Arrow throughout their journey, assuring him that he was finally getting his wish: he was going home. They also stopped four times to make tobacco offerings before reaching the reserve late that evening. There was no one there to welcome him home.

Over the next few days, the band came together in making preparations for his re-burial, especially in ensuring that proper protocol was observed. Several hundred attended the funeral in the community hall on Tuesday, 28 August. The choice of the date was deliberate: 131 years to the day that the Willow Cree entered treaty. A replica Treaty Six medal—the original had been confiscated in 1885 and never returned—and a Union Jack were placed on a blanket atop the new casket. The formal service, led by Elder A. J. Felix of the Sturgeon Lake First Nation, featured smudging, songs and drumming, a pipe ceremony, and speeches by Saskatchewan First Nations leaders. What made the day particularly special, though, was the traditional feast at which band members and guests shared a last meal with the chief. One Arrow's remains were then taken to the cemetery by a wagon drawn by two Indian ponies. Mourners followed on foot, many offering prayers in Cree. At the gravesite, as One Arrow was being laid to rest, a huge gust of wind swirled across the cemetery. The chief had come home.[5]

One Arrow's new grave sits at the front of the cemetery, in a prominent place, marked by a large basalt headstone. It purposefully stands out in a graveyard populated with simple white crosses, many at odd angles. But on a rise at the rear of the cemetery is another memorial in red granite, this one to One Arrow's grandson Almighty Voice and his two companions who died in May 1897 when the North-West Mounted Police shelled the bluff where they had taken refuge. The names of the three men appear in English, Cree, and syllabics, along with some of their

The One Arrow memorial to Almighty Voice and his companions from the bluff fight. BILL WAISER

The provincial historical marker for Almighty Voice, on the reserve's main road, has several bullet holes. BILL WAISER

last words. But there is no other information except for the brief, albeit incorrect, passage: "On this site three braves died." There is no mention of how they met their deaths or why. Nor is there any reference to how Almighty Voice was a fugitive for nineteen months in the mid-1890s, how other Indians kept him hidden and safe, or how his one-man fight assumed heroic, even legendary, proportions in the region. Any information about the Almighty Voice incident is found on a 1981 Government of Saskatchewan historical marker, placed on the reserve's main road and sporting bullet holes.

The similarities between One Arrow and Almighty Voice are quite striking. Like his grandfather, Almighty Voice was a hunter and not interested in the settled life of a farmer. He also ran into trouble with the law over the killing of livestock. And he died off-reserve. There, the similarities would appear to end. Whereas One Arrow faced Canadian justice in a Regina court, Almighty Voice fiercely resisted Canadian authority, at the cost of several lives, including his own.

But there were parallels between grandfather and grandson and the path they chose. In August 1881, several Cree chiefs, including One Arrow, voiced their frustration with Canada's delayed and limited fulfilment of its treaty obligations when they met with Canada's governor general, the Marquess of Lorne, at Fort Carlton. The Cree leaders believed they could speak candidly to Lorne because he was Queen Victoria's son-in-law (married to Princess Louise) and that the Queen Mother would want to know how her "children" were faring under treaty. The governor general, on the other hand, listened to their needs and complaints, even saying at one point that he wanted "to see how by keeping treaties I can help them [the Cree] to live."[6]

Too ill to stand, One Arrow had to address the governor general through a band headman at the meeting. He asked Lorne for more cattle for his hungry people. He also wanted "some clothing for the children to keep them warm … [and] something to eat today and some food to take home with me." And he wanted help "for children unborn."[7] That One Arrow would be seeking assistance for himself and his followers, then and into the future, underscored how dramatically life had changed for the Willow

Cree over the past decade. At one time, the band had thrived on the northern plains—was beholden to no one—but now it was suffering. The chief's plea for help from the Marquess of Lorne was also testimony to how much Canada had failed its treaty partners; how Indian Affairs had created a climate of ill will. Had not the Crown's representative at the 1876 treaty negotiations held out his hand to the Cree, pledging that it was "full of the Queen's bounty"?[8] But Canadian government officials blithely dismissed One Arrow's requests as those of a tired, old man at the head of a difficult, if not backward, band that stubbornly adhered to traditional ways. This reputation would only worsen when the One Arrow people were swept up into rebellion in the spring of 1885 and their sickly chief found guilty of treason-felony.

Almighty's Voice's defiance was directly linked to his grandfather's experience. He was just eleven years old at the time of One Arrow's arrest and imprisonment and came to the cold realization that he should be wary of government people, whether Indian Affairs officials or the mounted police. This mistrust was reinforced after the rebellion, when the Canadian government tried to starve the band into submission and force it to abandon its reserve—exactly what One Arrow feared during the last days of his life. But when the One Arrow people refused to give up their land, Indian Affairs sought to establish ultimate authority over them through a number of repressive and interfering measures in contravention of the spirit and intent of Treaty Six. Indian Commissioner Hayter Reed insisted that government assistance was the path to dependency and had to be kept to an absolute minimum, if not eventually discontinued. Those who dared step out of line—if only to protest government parsimony—were dismissed as chronic whiners and troublemakers and threatened with the withholding of rations. Some even faced possible arrest by the mounted police and sometimes incarceration at the hands of Indian agents acting as justices of the peace.

Almighty Voice was not prepared to suffer this kind of mistreatment under treaty, not prepared to accept control over his life, even if it meant killing a stray settler's cow for food and facing the consequences. He had seen what had happened to his grandfather and was not going to let it happen to him when

The remains of a sun dance lodge on the One Arrow reserve.
BILL WAISER

Sergeant Colebrook rode forward, calling on him to surrender, ignoring the repeated warnings to leave him alone. As a senior mounted policeman and future commissioner had conceded only a few years earlier, the Cree had come to "fear the police ... we have developed into the men who arrest them."[9] The shooting of the mounted policemen had nothing to do with any supposed hanging threat. That was too convenient an excuse and diverted attention away from Indian Affairs complicity in the affair. Nor was Almighty Voice trying to recapture some glory days of the past. That, too, belittled his actions and the reason for them. Allowing Colebrook to arrest him meant surrender to a stultifying existence where the One Arrow reserve was little better than a prison farm, where band members faced punishment and hunger unless they followed the directives of the Indian agent and farm instructor, and where there was no independence of movement. It's a wonder that more young men did not attempt to throw off the yoke of government control.

That the graves of One Arrow and Almighty Voice lie today within sight of one another is only fitting, and a constant reminder of the failed treaty relationship with Canada in the late nineteenth century. Indeed, Almighty Voice remains on the lips of One Arrow band members. There's a quiet respect for the young man that includes the naming of the local education centre in his honour. But his story has been largely forgotten beyond the reserve over the past few decades and is generally unknown to Canadians today. Just the mention of his name elicits questioning looks. That's a shame.

There can be no reconciliation without memory.

APPENDIX

One Arrow and the Sutherland Connection

According to the Stony Mountain penitentiary inmate admission book for 1885–91, One Arrow was born in the vicinity of Rocky Mountain House (in west-central Alberta) around 1815.[1] That's quite possible because the Cree in the nineteenth century regularly travelled up the North Saskatchewan River to hunt and trade. His father is said to have been George Sutherland, a Hudson's Bay Company servant who was instrumental in introducing the more durable, larger-capacity York boat to the fur trade in the mid-1790s. But even though company men often took Indian partners and Sutherland was stationed along the North Saskatchewan River (at Cumberland House and then Edmonton House), he retired from the trade *and* North America in 1798— almost two decades before One Arrow was born.[2]

There was another George Sutherland, though, who headed a Cree band active in the Saskatchewan forks area. According to the journal of North West Company clerk Daniel Harmon, he met a George Sutherland and his Indian wife during a visit to the nearby rival HBC post on the Assiniboine River on 23 December 1800. Harmon was "agreeably surprised" that the "Woman a Native of this Country could speak the English Language tolerably well and I understand can both read and write it also." But he found Sutherland to be "a great Drunkard and when he is in his cups a perfect mad-man."[3] The Willow Cree told a similar story to an Oblate priest at St. Michael's Indian Residential School at Duck Lake in 1930. Their tradition was that Sutherland, known as Akayasew (the Englishman), was fair-haired, blue-eyed, and hairy, with tattoos covering his body and arms up to his neck. (One of his sons, Moneas, had similar hair and eyes). They also provided the name of Sutherland's partner: Papâmikewis (She Follows Him Everywhere).[4]

This other George Sutherland is regularly listed as Indian, Native, or Halfbreed in the Carlton House accounts books in the early nineteenth century. He appears to have been well-treated, undoubtedly because of his parentage. When his family was short of supplies, he would send a note to the HBC that was always honoured. The post journal also recounts how the Indian George Sutherland travelled by canoe from Carlton to Cumberland House in April 1820 to seek medical help from Dr. John Richardson of the first Franklin overland expedition. He had lost his hand when his muzzle loader exploded while hunting and stoically had the arm amputated just above the wrist.[5]

Further evidence linking the mixed-descent Sutherland to the Willow Cree is provided by Anglican Cree priest Henry Budd who founded a mission at "Upper Nepowewin" on the north side of the Saskatchewan River, near the forks and directly across from the HBC Fort à la Corne. In the early 1850s, Budd reported that he was visited by a one-handed George Sutherland and his Indian band and told that they had once lived in a house in the area and tried to cultivate potatoes: "The party belongs to an old man named George Sutherland, called by the Indians 'Ahka-hyahscu,' 'Englishman.' He is the headman or chief ... the son of a Mr. Sutherland, formerly a gentleman in the Hudson's-Bay Company's service." Budd added that "he has a large family of his own—eight sons and eight daughters ... and all living ... with numerous families."[6] Among them was One Arrow, the son of Sutherland and his second wife Pasikus. Two other band members and future leaders, Beardy (Kamīyistowesit) and Cutnose (Saswaypew), had married into the family.[7]

ENDNOTES

PREFACE

1. The descendants of Almighty Voice spell their last name as one word (Almightyvoice).

2. *Saskatoon StarPhoenix*, 23 September 1992.

3. https://www.cbc.ca/news/politics/truth-and-reconciliation-report-brings-calls-for-action-not-words-1.3096863 (accessed 4 February 2019). Senator Sinclair also commented during an interview on CBC's *As It Happens* on 29 August 2017: "Reconciliation is really about trying to find a balance in telling the history of this country ... [it] is about establishing a relationship of mutual respect." https://www.cbc.ca/radio/asithappens/as-it-happens-tues-day-edition-1.4266662/debate-over-john-a-macdonald-s-name-not-what-reconciliation-is-all-about-says-murray-sinclair-1.4269327 (accessed 4 February 2019).

4. When asked whether non-Indigenous writers should stay away from Indigenous topics, acclaimed Indigenous writer Tomson Highway bluntly responded: "I don't have time for it." See A. Lamey, "The 'C' Word," *Literary Review of Canada*, July/August 2018, p. 32. Lamey concludes the article, "The more we allow it [appropriation] to set the terms of debate, the poorer everyone's culture will be."

INTRODUCTION

1. At the time of the first western treaties, each family head received a metal check with a number that corresponded with the number on the treaty pay list. This system was supposed to facilitate the payment of annuities, but the metal checks were often lost or used for gambling. In 1879, a numbered ticket was introduced for annuity payments. It, too, assigned a number to the family head, as well as indicated where and when each year's treaty payment was made. Canada, *Sessional Papers*, n. 4, 1880, "Annual Report of the Department of Indian Affairs for 1879," p. 101.

2. Before treaty payment day, the NWMP would deliver uncut sheets of one-dollar bills to the Indian agent. These sheets came in a small chest. A.J. Looy, "The Indian Agent and his Role in the Administration of the North-West Superintendency, 1876–1893," unpublished Ph.D. thesis, Queen's University, 1977, p. 223.

3. The names of Indigenous individuals come from the original documents. Fluent Cree and Saulteaux speakers have been consulted about the spelling and meaning of the Indigenous names and their English translation, but it proved difficult to reach a consensus in several instances. The matter was further complicated by errors in the recording of the names in official sources.

4. In *The North-West Mounted Police and Law Enforcement, 1873–1905* (Toronto: University of Toronto Press, 1976), R.C. Macleod argued that the police were successful because of their "benevolent despotism."

5. "Indian" has been used throughout the book because it was the word for First Nations people during the period under consideration. The term "First Nations" did not come into use until the 1970s.

6. Macleod, *The North-West Mounted Police*, p. 3.

7. On 17 November 1879, Constable Marmaduke Graburn was found murdered—shot in the back—in the Cypress Hills. Star Child, a Blood Indian, was charged two years later but acquitted at trial.

8. A.J. Looy, "The Indian Agent," p. 69.

9. Library and Archives Canada [LAC], RG10 (Indian Affairs), v. 3719, f. 22,685, W. Palmer Clarke to J.A. Macdonald, 31 July 1880.

10. Quoted in S.A. Gavigan, *Hunger, Horses, and Government Men: Criminal Law on the Aboriginal Plains, 1870–1905* (Vancouver: University of British Columbia Press, 2013), p. 126.

11. RG10, v. 3719, f. 22,685, E. Dewdney to L. Vankoughnet, 16 August 1880.

12. Quoted in I. Andrews, "Indian Protest Against Starvation: The Yellow Calf Incident of 1884," *Saskatchewan History*, v. 28, n. 2, Spring 1975, p. 46.

13. RG10, v. 3692, f. 13990, L. Crozier to E. Dewdney, 25 June 1884.

14. R.C. Macleod and H. Rollason, "'Restrain the Lawless Savages': Native Defendants in the Criminal Courts of the North-West Territories, 1878–1885," *Journal of Historical Sociology*, v. 10, n. 2, June 1997, pp. 157–83.

15. For an examination of post-1885 federal Indian policies, see B. Stonechild and B. Waiser, *Loyal till Death: Indians and the North-West Rebellion* (Calgary: Fifth House Publishers, 1997), pp. 192–237 and appendix 3.

16. LAC, RG18 (Royal Canadian Mounted Police), v. 1009, f. 628; Canada, *Sessional Papers*, no. 153, 1885, "Report of the Commissioner for the North-West Mounted Police for 1884," p. 6.

17. E.B. Titley, *The Indian Commissioners: Agents of the State and Indian Policy in Canada's Prairie West* (Edmonton: University of Alberta Press, 2009), p. 106.

18. RG10, v. 3788, f. 43943, V.-J. Grandin to J.A. Macdonald, 23 August 1886.

19. E.B. Titley, "Hayter Reed and Indian Administration in the West," in R.C. Macleod, ed., *Swords and Ploughshares: War and Agriculture in Western Canada* (Edmonton: University of Alberta Press, 1993), p. 113.

20. G.F.G. Stanley, *The Birth of Western Canada: A History of the Riel Rebellions* (London: Longmans, Green and Co., 1936), p. 270.

21. Canada, House of Commons *Debates*, 26 April 1882, p. 1186.

22. Quoted in W. Beahen and S. Horrall, *Red Coats on the Prairies: The North-West Mounted Police, 1886–1900* (Regina: Centax Books, 1998), p. 71.

23. RG18 B1, v. 1038, f. 68, A.B. Perry to A.G. Irvine, 19 February 1886.

24. Ibid.

25. During his visit to the area in August 1772, Hudson's Bay Company servant Matthew Cocking walked southwest from the Birch Hills toward the Minichinas Hills and referred to them as the Birch Hills' "younger brothers."

26. RG10, Duck Lake letterbooks, April to November 1895, R.S. McKenzie to A.E. Forget, 24 July 1895.

27. Ibid., R.S. McKenzie to A.E. Forget, 21 May 1895.

28. RG18, v. 1347, f. RCMP 1895, n. 226, pt. 1, G.B. Moffatt to NWMP Commissioner, 13 March 1896.

29. Ibid., v. 10038, f. 301, Harry Keenan personnel file, 18 November 1895 disciplinary hearing transcript. See revised regulations for prisoners in police guard rooms, v. 108, RCMP 1895, n. 311.

30. Ibid., v. 121, f. RCMP 1896, n. 269, R.C. Dickson, 24 October 1895 disciplinary hearing transcript.

CHAPTER ONE: MISERABLE BEYOND DESCRIPTION

1. Provincial Archives of Saskatchewan [PAS], D.G. Mandelbaum papers, transcript disc 135, John Sounding Sky interview, 17 July 1934.

2. Please see appendix for genealogical history of Willow Cree.

3. M. Weekes, *The Last Buffalo Hunter* (Calgary: Fifth House Publishers, 1994), pp. 19–20, 44–5.

4. S. Krasowski, *No Surrender: The Land Remains Indigenous* (Regina: University of Regina Press, 2019), p. 204; See also J.R. Miller, *Compact, Contract, Covenant: Aboriginal Treaty-Making in Canada* (Toronto: University of Toronto Press, 2009).

5. K.J. Taylor, "Kā-peyakwāskonam" in F.G. Halpenny, ed., *Dictionary of Canadian Biography*, v. XI, (1881–1890) (Toronto: University of Toronto Press, 1982), p. 461.

6. Library and Archives Canada [LAC], RG10 (Indian Affairs), v. 3719, f. 22,685, W. Palmer Clarke to J.A. Macdonald, 31 July 1880.

7. Canada, *Sessional Papers*, n. 5, 1883, "Annual Report of the Department of Indian Affairs for 1882," p. 209.

8. *Sessional Papers*, n. 4, 1884, "Annual Report of the Department of Indian Affairs for 1883," p. 120.

9. M. Lux, *Medicine that Walks: Disease, Medicine, and Canadian Plains Native People, 1880–1940*, (Toronto: University of Toronto Press, 2001), p. 51.

10. RG10, v. 3697, f. 15, 773, pt. 1, E. Dewdney to M. Dumas, 15 September 1884.

11. For a history of the rebellion, with particular emphasis on the Indigenous perspective, see B. Stonechild and B. Waiser, *Loyal Till Death: Indians and the North-West Rebellion* (Calgary: Fifth House Publishers, 1997).

12. D. Lee, "The Métis Militants of 1885," *Canadian Ethnic Studies*, v. 21, n. 3, 1989, pp. 9–12.

13. RG10, v. 3697, f. 15423, J.A. Macrae to E. Dewdney, 25 August 1884.

14. LAC, John A. Macdonald papers, v. 212, pp. 90617–21, L.W. Herchmer to E. Dewdney, 10 February 1886.

15. *Sessional Papers*, n. 4, 1886, "Annual Report of the Department of Indian Affairs for 1885," p. xxxix.

16. D. Morton and R. Roy, eds., *Telegrams of the North-West Campaign, 1885* (Toronto: Champlain Society, 1972), F. Middleton to A.P. Caron, 25 May 1885. Middleton said he would treat One Arrow the same way he had treated Beardy—namely, take away his treaty medal.

17. B. Beal and R. Macleod, *Prairie Fire: The 1885 North-West Rebellion* (Edmonton: Hurtig Publishers, 1985), pp. 306–07.

18. The three other chiefs (Poundmaker, Big Bear, and Whitecap), charged with treason-felony, were photographed individually in Regina, but apparently not One Arrow. In May 2019, Prime Minister Justin Trudeau exonerated Poundmaker and formally apologized for the chief's treason-felony conviction. For an examination of the Indian trials, see B. Waiser, "The White Man Governs: The 1885 Indian Trials" in Wright and Binnie, eds., *Canadian State Trials, v. III: Political Trials and Security Measures, 1840–1914* (Toronto: Osgoode Society for Canadian Legal History, 2009), pp. 451–82.

19. B. Beal and R.C. Macleod, *Prairie Fire: The 1885 North-West Rebellion* (Edmonton: Hurtig Publishers, 1984), p. 309. Father Louis Cochin, a keen observer of the proceedings, lamented: "The poor old man didn't understand a word of it." T. McCoy, "Legal Ideology in the Aftermath of the Rebellion: The Convicted First Nations Participants, 1885," *Histoire sociale/ Social History*, v. 42, n. 83, May 2009, p. 185.

20. S.E. Bingaman, "The North-West Rebellion Trials," unpublished M.A. thesis, University of Regina, 1971, p. 15.

21. Ibid., pp. 32–33.

22. Quoted in McCoy, "Legal Ideology in the Aftermath of the Rebellion," p. 176.

23. LAC, Inmate Admission Books, 1885–1891, Stony Mountain penitentiary.

24. *Sessional Papers*, 1887, n. 4, "Report of the Minister of Justice as to the Penitentiaries in Canada," p. 84 (Catholic Chaplain's Report, 5 July 1886).

25. Quoted in McCoy, "Legal Ideology in the Aftermath of the Rebellion," p. 195.

26. Ibid., p. 196.

27. Glenbow Archives [GA], Edgar Dewdney papers, box 4, f. 57, pp. 1232–39, H. Reed to E. Dewdney, 29 August 1885.

28. *Sessional Papers*, 1886, n. 8, "Report of the Commissioner of the North-West Mounted Police for 1885," appendix O.

29. D. Lee, "Almighty Voice and His Stories," *Native Studies Review*, v. 10, n. 2, 1995, pp. 58–59.

30. RG10, v. 3584, f. 1130, Hayter Reed, "Memorandum for the Honourable the Indian Commissioner relative to the future management of Indians," 13 July 1885.

31. *Sessional Papers*, n. 4, 1886, "Department of Indian Affairs Annual Report for 1885," part 1, p. 219.

32. Prince Albert Historical Museum [PAHM], Duck Lake letterbooks, May 1885–June 1886, J.M. Rae to E. Dewdney, 8 October 1885.

33. RG10, v. 3585, f. 1130, pt. 8, A.R. Cuthbert to A.B. Perry, 20 January 1886.

34. GA, Dewdney papers, box 2, f. 38, pp. 589–90, E. Dewdney to J.A. Macdonald, 20 December 1885.

35. LAC, Macdonald papers, v. 213, pp. 90438–42, L.W. Herchmer to E. Dewdney, 21 January 1886.

36. RG10, v. 3719, f. 22, 817, "Petition, August 1885."

37. Quoted in J.B.D. Larmour, "Edgar Dewdney, Commissioner of Indian Affairs and Lieutenant Governor of the North-West Territories, 1879–1888," unpublished M.A. thesis, University of Saskatchewan, 1969, p. 47.

38. LAC, RG18 B1 (Royal Canadian Mounted Police), v. 1038, f. 68, E. Dewdney to A.G. Irvine, 1 February 1886.

39. RG10, v. 3598, f. 1411, C. Adams to E. Dewdney, 30 March 1886.

40. PAHM, Duck Lake letterbooks, May 1885–June 1886, C. Adams to E. Dewdney, 5 April 1886, 8 April 1886.

41. RG10, v. 3598, f. 1411, Adams to Dewdney, 30 March 1886.

42. *Le Manitoba*, 22 April 1886 (translation).

43. RG10, v. 3598, f. 1411, C. Adams to H. Reed, 18 June 1886.

44. Quoted in T. White, *Facts for the People: The Northwest Rebellion* (Ottawa: Department of the Interior 1887), p. 13.

45. RG10, v. 3598, f. 1411, C. Adams to H. Reed, 18 June 1886.

46. Ibid., H. Reed to C. Adams, 12 July 1886.

47. *Sessional Papers*, n. 6, 1887, "Annual Report of the Department of Indian Affairs for 1886," C. Adams to Superintendent General of Indian Affairs, 30 August 1886, p. 125.

48. *Sessional Papers*, n. 6, 1887, "Department of Indian Affairs Annual Report for 1886," part 1, p. 171.

49. F.L. Barron, "Indian Agents and the North-West Rebellion" in F.L. Barron and J. Waldram, eds, *1885 and After: Native Society in Transition* (Regina: Canadian Plains Research Center 1985, pp. 142–43.

50. RG10, v. 3785, f. 41,783-1, T.P. Wadsworth to E. Dewdney, 7 June 1887.

51. Quoted in Looy, "The Indian Agent," p. 318.

52. *Sessional Papers*, n. 16, 1889, "Annual Report of the Department of Indian Affairs for 1888," p. lix.

53. RG10, v. 1596, H. Reed to R.S. McKenzie, 28 October 1890.

54. Ibid., Duck Lake Agency letterbooks, March to July 1895, R.S. McKenzie annual report March 1895.

55. RG10, v. 9995, "Financial Statement of Expenses, Duck Lake Agency, 1887–1889."

56. RG18, v. 1398, f. RCMP 1987, no. 186, Pee-yeh-chee witness statement, n.d.

57. RG18, v. 10039, C.C. Colebrook personnel file, service #605, J.B. Allen to G.B. Moffatt, 4 November 1895; RG10, v. 8618, f. 1/1-15-2-1, pt. 1, J.H. Gordon to R.S. McKenzie, 6 November 1895.

58. RG10, v. 9423-30, "Treaty Annuity Paylists," One Arrow, 1890–97.

59. RG10, v. 9995, "Register of Births and Deaths for One Arrow Band, 1889-1895"; Lee, "Almighty Voice and His Stories," *Native Studies Review*, p. 60, 65.

60. *Sessional Papers*, n. 16, 1889, "Department of Indian Affairs Annual Report for 1888," part 1, p. 84; RG10, Duck Lake Agency letterbooks, July 1894 to March 1895, R.S. Mackenzie to A.E. Forget, 25 July 1894.

61. RG10, Duck Lake letterbooks, April–November 1895, R.S. McKenzie to A.E. Forget, 25 May 1895.

62. RG18, v. 48, f. 115-91, L.W. to Controller, 18 January 1891.

63. RG10, Duck Lake Agency letterbooks, April to November 1895, R.S. McKenzie to Indian Commissioner, 21 May 1895.

64. House of Commons *Debates*, 25 June 1895, pp. 3279–3294.

65. *Debates*, 14 June 1895, pp. 2690–98, 25 June 1895, pp. 3282–94; J.R. Miller, "Cultural Insecurity in the Peaceable Kingdom: Assimilation Policy and Government Propaganda," unpublished paper presented before British Association for Canadian Studies, 2011.

66. *Sessional Papers*, n. 14, 1892, "Department of Indian Affairs Annual Report for 1891," part 1, p. 241.

67. T.J. Williams, "Compulsive Measures: The Resistance to Indian Residential Schools at One Arrow Reserve, 1889–1895," *Canadian Journal of Native Studies*, v. 34, n. 2, 2014, pp. 197–222.

68. Ibid. As early as February 1885, Indian Commissioner Edgar Dewdney had recommended arresting troublesome Indians to limit their influence over others. RG10, v. 3576, f. 309, E. Dewdney to J.A. Macdonald, 12 February 1885.

69. RG18, v. 1347, f. RCMP 1895, n. 226, pt. 1, J. Allan to G.B. Moffatt, 23 February 1896.

70. RG10, v. 3788, f. 43943, V.-J. Grandin to J.A. Macdonald, 23 August 1886. Bishop Grandin had told Prime Minister Macdonald that Indians "say they would rather live ten years in freedom than twenty in slavery [on reserves]."

CHAPTER TWO: COME ON, OLD BOY

1. *Fort Benton Record*, April 1877.

2. Library and Archives Canada [LAC], RG18 (Royal Canadian Mounted Police), v. 10039, C.C. Colebrook personnel file, service #605, G.B. Moffatt to L.W. Herchmer, 26 October 1895.

3. Prince Albert Historical Museum [PAHM], Duck Lake agency letterbooks, R.S. McKenzie to A.E. Forget, 9 July 1890. Marion recommended that Dumont be allowed to rejoin the band because he could be useful.

4. Colebrook file, medical examination, 16 October 1895.

5. Ibid., Frank Dumont and Small Face testimony, coroner's inquest. All quotations and description of Colebrook shooting are taken from this source.

6. "The closed rock" likely refers to the stone weirs near the outlet to Barrier Lake.

7. Colebrook file, G.B. Moffatt to L.W. Herchmer, 30 October 1895.

8. Ibid., J.H. McIllree to Divisions, 31 October 1895.

9. Ibid., J.B. Allan to G.B. Moffatt, 19 November 1895; J.B. Allan, "A Chapter in the RNWMP Annals," *Scarlet and Gold*, 4th annual, 1922, pp. 69–70.

10. Ibid., G.B. Moffatt to L.W. Herchmer, 3 November 1895.

11. Ibid.

12. LAC, RG10 (Indian Affairs), Duck Lake agency letterbooks, R.S. McKenzie to J.H. Gordon, 12 November 1895.

13. RG10, v. 8618, f. 1/1-15-2-1, pt. 1, R.S. McKenzie to A.E. Forget, 1 November 1895.

14. See, for example, Canada, *Sessional Papers*, n. 15, 1888, "Department of Indian Affairs Annual Report for 1887," pt. 1, p. 188.

15. A succession of fur trading posts had been located in the area since the 1750s; the HBC had re-established Fort à la Corne in 1851 and continued to operate the post into the 1900s.

16. RG10, v. 1596, no f., J.H. Gordon to R.S. McKenzie, 31 October 1895.

17. R.B. Deane, a rival for the position, claimed Herchmer was named commissioner because he was "a bosom friend of Hon. Edgar Dewdney, and Dewdney had John Macdonald's ear." R.B. Deane, *Mounted Police Life in Canada: A Record of Thirty-One Years' Service* (London: Cassells, 1916), p. 30.

18. R. Macleod, *Sam Steele: A Biography* (Edmonton: University of Alberta Press, 2018), p. 145; W. Beahen and S. Horrall, *Red Coats on the Prairies: The North-West Mounted Police 1886–1900* (Regina: Centax Books, 1998), p. 8.

19. Colebrook file, L.W. Herchmer to G.B. Moffatt, 2 November 1895.

20. RG18, v. 121, f. 269, R.C. Dickson to President of the Privy Council, 23 March 1896; Dickson to Privy Council, 4 May 1896; L.W. Herchmer to F. White, 18 May 1896; White to Privy Council, 30 June 1896. Dickson died in Vancouver in August 1936.

21. Ibid., Dickson to President of the Privy Council, 23 March 1896.

22. Colebrook file, Colebrook discharge certificate, signed 9 December 1895.

23. Ibid., J.H. McIllree to G.B. Moffatt, 4 November 1895.

24. RG10, v. 8618, f. 1/1-15-2-1, pt. 1, J.H. Gordon to R.S. McKenzie, 6 November 1895.

25. Colebrook file, J.B. Allan to G.B. Moffatt, 4 November 1895.

26. RG10, v. 8618, f. 1/1-15-2-1, pt. 1, J.H. Gordon to R.S. McKenzie, 6 November 1895.

27. Colebrook file, J.B. Allan to G.B. Moffatt, 4 November 1895.

28. Ibid., G.B. Moffatt to L.W. Herchmer, 6 November 1895.

29. Ibid., J.B. Allan to G.B. Moffatt, 4 November 1895.

30. Ibid., G.B. Moffatt to L.W. Herchmer, 6 November 1895.

31. RG10, v. 8618, f. 1/1-15-2-1, pt. 1, Gordon to McKenzie, 6 November 1895.

32. Ibid., Duck Lake agency letterbooks, R.S. McKenzie to G.B. Moffatt, 6 November 1885.

33. Ibid., v. 8618, f. 1/1-15-2-1, pt. 1, R.S. McKenzie to A.E. Forget, 7 November 1895.

34. Quoted in T.J. Williams, "Compulsive Measures: The Resistance to Indian Residential Schools at One Arrow Reserve, 1889–1895," *Canadian Journal of Native Studies*, v. 34, n. 2, 2014, p. 219.

35. RG10, v. 1596, no f., A.E. Forget to R.S. McKenzie, 8 November 1895.

36. Ibid., A.E. Forget to R.S. McKenzie, 8 November 1895 (different letter).

37. Colebrook file, G.B. Moffatt to J.H. McIlree, 9 November 1895.

38. RG10, v. 1596, no f., J.H. Gordon to R.S. McKenzie, 15 November 1895.

39. Colebrook file, J.B. Allan to G.B. Moffatt, 19 November 1895.

40. Ibid., G.B. Moffatt to L.W. Herchmer, 10 November 1895.

41. RG18 B1, v. 1038, f. 68, A.B. Perry to A.G. Irvine, 19 February 1886.

42. Colebrook file, J.B. Allan to G.B. Moffatt, 19 November 1895.

43. Ibid., G.B. Moffatt to L.W. Herchmer, 10 November 1895.

CHAPTER THREE: REGARDED AS A HERO

1. Canada. *Sessional Papers*, n. 15, 1896, "Annual Report of the North-West Mounted Police for 1895," p. 4.

2. *Saskatchewan Herald*, 1 November 1895.

3. Moose Jaw *Times*, 8 November 1895.

4. Regina *Standard*, 31 October 1895.

5. Post-1885 political cartoons in Canada's *Grip* magazine reinforced this sentiment. C.J. Nielson, "Caricaturing Colonial Space: Indigenized, Feminized Bodies and Anglo-Canadian Identity, 1873–94," *Canadian Historical Review*, v. 96, n. 4, December 2015, p. 503.

6. *Saskatchewan Times*, 12 November 1895.

7. Reprinted in Regina *Standard*, 14 November 1895.

8. Regina *Leader*, 14 November 1895.

9. *Saskatchewan Times*, 19 November 1895.

10. Manitoba *Free Press*, 28 November 1895.

11. Keenan was the oldest original member of the force when he died in 1934.

12. Library and Archives Canada [LAC], Government Archives Division RG18 (Royal Canadian Mounted Police), v. 10039, C.C. Colebrook personnel file, service #605, L.W. Herchmer to Editor Winnipeg *Free Press*, 17 November 1895.

13. Ibid., Small Face testimony, coroner's inquest, 24 November 1895.

14. Chakastaypasin is rumoured to be buried on the One Arrow reserve. Personal communication, Chief T. Sutherland to B. Waiser, 2 April 2019.

15. *Sessional Papers*, n. 13, 1893, "Annual Report of the Department of the Interior for 1892," p. 59.

16. Dale Russell, "The Fort a la Corne Forest Area: A Survey of the Historical Documents," unpublished report of Western Heritage Services, August 2007, pp. 39–41.

17. Colebrook file, J.B. Allan to G.B. Moffatt, 19 November 1895.

18. Stewart Prosper interview, 7 October 2015.

19. LAC, Government Archives Division (Indian Affairs), RG10, v. 8618, f. 1/1-15-2-1, pt. 1, R.S. McKenzie to A.E. Forget, 7 November 1895. Forget to McKenzie, 12 November 1895.

20. Colebrook file, G.B. Moffatt to L.W. Herchmer, 23 November 1895.

21. Ibid., L.W. Herchmer to G.B. Moffatt, 27 November 1895.

22. RG18, v. 1347, f. 226/95, pt. 1, G.B. Moffatt to L.W. Herchmer, 4 December 1895.

23. Ibid., L.W. Herchmer to G.B. Moffatt, 7 December 1895.

24. Ibid., G.B. Moffatt to L.W. Herchmer, 13 December 1895.

25. Ibid., R.B. Beatty to G.B. Moffatt, 5 December 1895.

26. RG10, v. 1596, A.E. Forget to R.S. McKenzie, 27 December 1895.

27. D. Lee, "Almighty Voice and His Stories," *Native Studies Review*, v. 10, n. 2, 1995, p. 65.

28. RG18, v. 1347, f. 226/95, pt. 1, J.B. Allan to G.B. Moffatt, 22 December 1895.

29. Ibid., G.B Moffatt to L.W. Herchmer, 22 December 1895.

30. Ibid., J.B. Allan to G.B. Moffatt, 22 December 1895.

31. Ibid., G.B. Moffatt to R. Vickers, 19 December 1895.

32. Ibid., G.E. Pulham to A.B. Perry, 6 January 1896.

33. Ibid., J.B. Allan to G.B. Moffatt, 14 January 1896.

34. Ibid., G.B Moffatt to L.W. Herchmer, 15 January 1896.

35. Ibid., J.B. Allan to G.B. Moffatt, 17 February 1896.

36. Ibid. F. White to L.W. Herchmer, 25 January 1896.

37. Ibid., J.B. Allan to G.B. Moffatt, 14 January 1896.

38. Ibid., G.B Moffatt to L.W. Herchmer, 13 March 1896.

39. Ibid., J. Hourston to R.S. McKenzie, 9 February 1896.

40. Ibid., R.S. McKenzie to A.E. Forget, 24 February 1896.

41. Prince Albert *Advocate*, 25 February 1896.

42. RG18, v. 1347, f. 226/95, pt. 1, G.B. Moffatt to L.W. Herchmer, 26 February 1896.

43. Regina *Leader*, 5 March 1896.

44. RG10, v. 8618, f. 1/1-15-2-1, pt. 1, H. Reed to T.M. Daly, 16 March 1896; T.M. Daly to H. Reed, 18 March 1896.

45. Ibid., T.M. Daly to M. Bowell, 24 March 1895.

46. Ibid., M. Bowell to T.M. Daly, 25 March 1896.

47. Canada. *Proclamation*, 20 April 1896.

48. RG18, v. 1347, f. 226/95, pt. 1, J.B Allan to G.B. Moffatt, 15 March 1896.

49. RG18, v. 1347, f. 226/95, pt. 2, G.E. Pulham to A.B. Perry, 30 March 1896.

50. Ibid., J.B Allan to G.B. Moffatt, 25 March 1896.

51. RG18, v. 1347, f. 226/95, pt. 1, J. Carroll to G.B. Moffatt, 3 March 1896.

52. RG18, v. 1347, f. 226/95, pt. 2, R.S. McKenzie to G.B. Moffatt, 22 August 1896.

53. Ibid., A Macdonald to A.E. Forget, 14 May 1896.

54. Ibid., G.E. Pulham to A.B. Perry, 21 June 1896.

55. Ibid., W.J. Bowdridge to G.B. Moffatt, 19 September 1896.

56. Letter, Rick Gamble to author, 1 December 2018. At least one Mennonite settler in the Batoche area also apparently assisted Almighty Voice. See C.A. Krause, "Emilia Wieler and Almighty Voice," *Saskatchewan Mennonite Historian*, v. xiii, n. 2, July 2007.

57. RG18, v. 1347, f. 226/95, pt. 2, J.A. Wilson to G.B. Moffatt, 19 October 1896.

58. Ibid., J.A. Wilson to G.B. Moffatt, 18 October 1896.

59. RG18, v. 1347, f. 226/95, pt. 1, J.A Wilson to G.B. Moffatt, 7 November 1896.

60. Ibid.

61. Ibid., v. 1398, f. 186, A.H. Griesbach to L.W. Herchmer, n.d.

62. See H.A. Dempsey, *Charcoal's World* (Saskatoon: Western Producer Prairie Books, 1978).

63. *Sessional Papers*, n. 15, 1897, "Annual Report of the North-West Mounted Police for 1896," p. 1.

64. Ibid., G.B. Moffatt to S. Hildyard, 13 January 1897.

CHAPTER FOUR: OTHER THINGS TO DO BESIDES DANCING

1. Library and Archives Canada [LAC], RG18 (Royal Canadian Mounted Police), v. 138, f. 395, D. Venne to T.O. Davis, 1 June 1896 [sic].

2. RG18, v. 1398, f. 186, S. Hildyard to S. Gagnon, 20 March 1897.

3. Ibid., L.W. Herchmer to A.E. Forget, 30 March 1897.

4. Ibid., J.A. Wilson to S. Gagnon, 13 May 1897.

5. Ibid., W.J. Bowdridge to S. Gagnon, 2 June 1897. This letter serves as his official report about the incident.

6. Ibid., J.A. Wilson to S. Gagnon, 27 May 1897. By an order-in-council dated 20 October 1897, David and Napoleon Venne were paid five hundred dollars for information leading to the finding of Almighty Voice. Napoleon was also granted a small pension of twenty-three cents per day for his wound.

7. RG18, v. 1398, f. 186, S. Gagnon to L.W. Herchmer, 28 May 1897.

8. In December 1897, then ex-Constable Ascott asked for the reward but was flatly turned down.

9. RG18, v. 137, f. 376, J.B. Allan to S. Gagnon, 27 July 1897. The letter recounts Inspector Allan's rush of the bluff.

10. J.N. Jennings, "The North-West Mounted Police and Indian Policy, 1874–1896," unpublished Ph.D. thesis, University of Toronto, 1979, p. 359 (appendix).

11. RG18, v. 10043, William Hume personnel file, service #2259, W. Hume to A.E. Snyder, 20 March 1908.

12. Ibid., v. 137, f. 376, J.B. Allan to S. Gagnon, 27 July 1897.

13. O'Kelly's report is found in RG18, v. 1398, f. 186, A. O'Kelly to S. Gagnon, 2 June 1897.

14. LAC, Government Archives Division, RG10 (Indian Affairs), v. 8618, f. 1/1-15-2-1, pt. 1, R.S. Cook to E.F. Stephenson, 6 June 1897.

15. RG18, v. 2480, f. RCMP Court Cases A, pt. 1., J.H. McIllree to L.W. Herchmer, 4 June 1897.

16. This second assault on the bluff led by Corporal Hockin is described by Constable O'Kelly in RG18, v. 1398, f. 186, O'Kelly to Gagnon, 2 June 1897.

17. Superintendent Gagnon's account of the bluff siege is found in Ibid., S. Gagnon to L.W. Herchmer, 3 June 1897.

18. J.F. Dunn, *The North-West Mounted Police, 1873–1885* (Calgary: Jack Dunn, 2017), pp. 454–5.

19. RG18, v. 1398, f. 186, L.W. Herchmer to F. White, 10 June 1897 [L.W. Herchmer to S. Gagnon telegram, 28 May 1897]. The telegrams exchanged between Regina and Duck Lake during these hours are cited in a report that Commissioner Herchmer sent to NWMP comptroller Fred White.

20. Ibid., S. Gagnon to L.W. Herchmer telegram, 29 May 1897.

21. Ibid., A.B. Stewart to L.W. Herchmer telegram, 29 May 1897.

22. Ibid.

23. Quoted in Jennings, "The NWMP and Indian Policy," p. 344.

24. RG18, v. 1398, f. 186, Herchmer to White, 10 June 1897 [S. Gagnon to L.W. Herchmer telegram, 29 May 1897].

25. Assistant Commissioner McIlree's report is found in RG18, v. 2480, f. RCMP Court Cases A, pt. 1., McIllree to Herchmer, 4 June 1897.

26. RG18, v. 1398, f. 186, L.W. Herchmer to S. Gagnon, 28 May 1897.

27. Ibid., v. 2480, f. RCMP Court Cases A, pt. 1., McIllree to Herchmer, 4 June 1897; D.P. Payment, "The Free People–Otipemisiwak": Batoche, Saskatchewan 1870–1930 (Ottawa: Canadian Parks Service, 1990), pp. 72–73.

28. Ibid., v. 1398, f. 186, L.W. Herchmer to A.E. Forget, 29 May 1897.

29. Ibid., v. 2480, f. RCMP Court Cases A, pt. 1., McIllree to Herchmer, 4 June 1897.

30. R. Macleod, Sam Steele: A Biography (Edmonton: University of Alberta Press, 2108), p. 142.

31. Quoted in Dunn, NWMP, p. 114. McIllree had been part of the police escort for the 1876 treaty commission and signed Treaty Six as a witness at Fort Carlton.

32. Ibid., v. 1398, f. 186, L.W. Herchmer to J.H. McIllree, 29 May 1897.

33. Canada. Sessional Papers, 1898, n. 15, "Annual Report of the North-West Mounted Police for 1897," appendix A, pp. 23–24.

34. Quoted in W.A. Fraser, "Soldier Police of the Canadian Northwest," McClure's Magazine, July 1899, p. 231.

35. The bombardment of the bluff on Sunday, 30 May, is found in RG18, v. 1398, f. 186, F. Smith to L.W. Herchmer, 1 June 1897. Smith left the force shortly thereafter because of a drinking problem and died the following spring en route to the Klondike.

36. Regina Leader, 3 June 1897.

37. RG18, v. 1398, f. 186, A.C. Macdonell to L.W Herchmer, 1 June 1897.

38. NWMP Commissioner Herchmer called for an explanation of the reported comment, but Indian Agent McKenzie vehemently denied saying any such thing. RG10, v. 8618, f. 1/1-15-2-1, pt. 1, R.S. McKenzie to A.E. Forget, 9 June 1897.

39. RG18, v. 2480, f. RCMP Court Cases A, pt. 1., McIllree to Herchmer, 4 June 1897.

40. Ibid., v. 1398, f. 186, Herchmer to White, 10 June 1897

41. Ibid., v. 2480, f. RCMP Court Cases A, pt. 1., McIllree to Herchmer, 4 June 1897.

42. The author found the skull fragment in a Manila envelope in a filing cabinet at the RCMP Heritage Centre in Regina. Heather Devine of the University of Calgary had the same experience during a research trip there. H. Devine to B. Waiser, email communication, 23 April 2018.

43. RG10, v. 8618, f. 1/1-15-2-1, pt. 1, R.S. McKenzie to A.E. Forget, 1 June 1897.

44. According to his diary entry for 31 May 1897, Marion spent the day making coffins for the three dead.

45. RG18, v. 265, f. 378, T.O. Davis to R.J. Cartwright, 16 June 1897 [petition attached].

46. Prince Albert *Advocate*, 8 June 1897.

47. Edmonton *Bulletin*, 7 June 1897.

48. RG18, v. 1398, f. 186, J.A. Wilson to L.W. Herchmer, 2 June 1897.

49. Ibid., J.H. McIllree to S. Gagnon, 8 July 1897.

50. Ibid., L.W. Herchmer to NWMP divisional headquarters, 29 May 1897.

51. Ibid., Wilson to Herchmer, 2 June 1897.

52. Ibid., H.J. Thompson to S. Gagnon, 27 June 1897.

53. RG10, v. 8618, f. 1/1-15-2-1, pt. 1, R.S. McKenzie to A.E. Forget, 13 June 1897.

54. Ibid., A.E. Forget to Deputy Superintendent General of Indian Affairs, 15 June 1897.

55. *Sessional Papers*, n. 14, 1898, "Annual Report of the Department of Indian Affairs for 1897," p. xxv.

56. Ibid., n. 15, 1898, "Annual Report of the North-West Mounted Police for 1897," pp. 2–3; Canada. House of Commons *Debates*, 14 June 1897, p. 4079.

57. Edmonton *Bulletin*, 21 October 1882.

58. Quoted in C. Reimer, "Gordon, Daniel Gordon" in R. Cook and R. Belanger, eds., *Dictionary of Canadian Biography*, v. XV, 1921–1930 (Toronto: University of Toronto Press 2005), p. 414.

59. Quoted in T. Longstreth, *The Silent Force* (London: P. Allan 1928), p. 220.

CHAPTER FIVE: THE WORST OF THE BAD

1. Qu'Appelle *Vidette*, 2 June 1897.

2. *Saskatchewan Times*, 29 May 1897, 1 June 1897.

3. Prince Albert *Advocate*, 1 June 1897.

4. Regina *Leader*, 3 June 1897 [various editions].

5. Regina *Standard*, 3 June 1897.

6. Quoted in Edmonton *Bulletin*, 7 June 1897.

7. Qu'Appelle *Vidette*, 2 June 1897.

8. Moose Jaw *Times*, 4 June 1897.

9. *Saskatchewan Herald*, 4 June 1897; 11 June 1897.

10. Edmonton *Bulletin*, 10 June 1897. The *Bulletin* mistakenly claimed that one of Almighty Voice's companions was the Saulteaux Tom Lamack, another fugitive from the law, wanted for murder in the Fort Qu'Appelle area in 1894. Lamack was not apprehended until 1902.

See I. Cowie, *The Company of Adventurers* (Lincoln: University of Nebraska Press, 1993), pp. 195–96.

11. *The New York Times* (1 June 1897), for example, reported that the "Manitoba police" had avoided a repetition of the trouble of 1885 by killing Almighty Voice.

12. Winnipeg *Free Press*, 31 May 1897.

13. Ottawa *Journal*, 15 January 1898.

14. Toronto *Globe*, 1 June 1897.

15. Toronto *World*, 29 May 1897, 31 May 1897, 1 June 1897, 3 June 1897.

16. For an examination of Native representation in newspapers, see M.C. Anderson and C.L. Robertson, *Seeing Red: A History of Natives in Canadian Newspapers*; J.M. Coward, *The Newspaper Indian: Native American Identity in the Press, 1820–1890*; M.A. Weston, *Native Americans in the News: Images of Indians in the Twentieth Century Press*; and R. Harding, "Historical Representations of Aboriginal People in the Canadian News Media," *Discourse and Society*, v. 17, n. 2, 2006, pp. 205–35.

17. G. Colpitts, *Game in the Garden: A Human History of Wildlife in Western Canada to 1940* (Vancouver: University of British Columbia Press, 2002), pp. 65–67; D.J. Hall, *From Treaties to Reserves: The Federal Government and Native Peoples in Territorial Alberta, 1870–1905* (Montreal: McGill-Queen's University Press, 2015), pp, 156–59.

18. See B. Waiser, *Saskatchewan: A New History* (Calgary: Fifth House Publishers, 2005), p. 178.

19. Quoted in J.R. Miller, *Shingwauk's Vision: A History of Native Residential Schooling* (Toronto: University of Toronto Press, 1996), p. 135. In 1898, the Liberal government repealed the provision in the 1885 Franchise Act that granted the vote to qualified Indian males living east of Manitoba.

20. Edmonton *Bulletin*, 31 May 1897; Regina *Leader*, 3 July 1897.

21. Winnipeg *Free Press*, 1 June 1897.

22. Prince Albert *Advocate*, 13 July 1897.

23. Ibid., 1 June 1897.

24. Quoted in S.D. Hanson, "Kitchi-Manito-Waya" in F.G. Halpenny, ed., *Dictionary of Canadian Biography, v. 12, 1891–1900* (Toronto: University of Toronto Press, 1990), p. 499.

25. Regina *Standard*, 24 June 1897.

26. Quoted in Edmonton *Bulletin*, 7 June 1897.

27. Winnipeg *Free Press*, 4 June 1897; Regina *Leader*, 17 June 1897.

28. London *Times*, 31 May 1897.

29. Prince Albert *Advocate*, 6 July 1897.

30. Toronto *World*, 29 May 1897; Winnipeg *Free Press*, 31 May 1897, 1 June 1897; Toronto *Globe*, 31 May 1897, 1 June 1897; Regina *Standard*, 3 June 1897; *Saskatchewan Herald*, 4 June 1897; Edmonton *Bulletin*, 7 June 1897.

31. This phrase was evidently first used by NWMP comptroller Fred White in 1896. See T. Longstreth, *The Silent Force* (London: P. Allan, 1928), p. 220.

32. W.A. Fraser, "Soldier Police of the Canadian Northwest," *McClure's Magazine*, July 1899, pp. 225–26, 228–32.

33. E.J. Chambers, *The Royal North-West Mounted Police: a corps history* (Ottawa: Mortimer Press, 1906), pp. 117–19.

34. A.L. Haydon, *The Riders of the Plains* (London: Melrose, 1910), pp. 174–81.

35. W.B. Cameron, "Almighty Voice–Outlaw," *Scarlet and Gold*, Second Annual, 1920, pp. 46–49.

36. J.N. Jennings, "The North-West Mounted Police and Indian Policy, 1874–1896," unpublished Ph.D. thesis, University of Toronto, 1979, pp. 337, 349 (n. 26).

37. R.G. MacBeth, *Policing the Plains* (London: Hodder and Stoughton, 1921), p. 92.

38. Longstreth, *The Silent Force*, p. 216.

39. C.E. Denny, *The Law Marches West* (Toronto: J.M. Dent, 1939). W.B. Cameron edited and arranged the memoirs for publication.

40. J.B. Allan, "A Chapter in RNWMP Annals," *Scarlet and Gold*, Sixth Annual, 1924, p. 36; C.C. Raven, "Reminiscences," Scarlet and Gold, v. 22, 1940, p. 73.

41. H. Dempsey, ed., *William Parker: Mounted Policeman* (Calgary: Glenbow Alberta Institute, 1973), pp. 84–88.

42. R. Jefferson, "Fifty Years on the Saskatchewan," *Canadian North-West Historical Society Publications*, v. 1, n. 5, 1929, pp. 94–95.

43. W.M. Graham, *Treaty Days: Reflections of an Indian Commissioner* (Glenbow Museum, 1991), pp. 94–96.

44. Prince Albert *Times*, 23 May 1907 [reprinted in Saskatoon *Phoenix*, 31 May 1907].

45. A search of the pre-1895 Prince Albert and Duck Lake field day results did not turn up Almighty Voice's name. Email communication, Prince Albert Historical Museum Archives to author, 11 July 2018.

46. M.H. Anson, "Last Stand of Almighty Voice," *Chicago Record Herald*, 1907 [reprinted in Saskatoon *Phoenix*, 23 December 1908].

47. G. Abrams, *Prince Albert: The First Century, 1866–1966* (Saskatoon: Modern Press 1966), pp. 155, 165, 379.

48. The Anson article was reprinted in the Saskatoon *Phoenix*. A typescript of the article was also found in the A.S. Morton papers in the University Archives and Special Collections, University of Saskatchewan.

49. B.M. Bower, *The Flying U's Last Stand* (Boston: Little Brown, 1915), p. 19.

50. B.C. D'Easum, "The Killing of Almighty Voice," *The Quaker*, v. 6, n. 1, August 1899, pp. 1–5.

51. E. Murphy, *Janey Canuck in the West* (Toronto: Cassell, 1910), p. 201.

52. N.F. Black, *History of Saskatchewan and the Old North West* (Regina: North West Historical Company, 1913), pp. 588–89.

53. J. Hawkes, *The Story of Saskatchewan and its People* (Regina: S.J. Clarke, 1924), pp. 157–61.

CHAPTER SIX: ON THE WARPATH

1. Long Lance's rebellion article appeared first (see *Saskatoon StarPhoenix*, 15 September 1923) and prompted a stinging rebuke from the Prince Albert Historical Society for its gross inaccuracies. T.N. Campbell to Long Lance, 31 October 1923. Copy of letter kindly provided by D.B. Smith.

2. The standard work on Long Lance is D.B. Smith, *Chief Buffalo Child Long Lance: The Glorious Imposter* (Red Deer: Red Deer Press, 1999). See also the Long Lance chapter in R. Heidenreich, *Literary Impostors: Canadian Autofiction of the Early Twentieth Century* (Montreal: McGill-Queen's University Press, 2018).

3. Glenbow Archives, M6426, S.C. Long, "Interview with Clear Sky & Spotted Calf," May 1923. All transcript quotes in text are from this source.

4. El Paso *Times*, 6 January 1924.

5. Winnipeg *Tribune* on 6 January 1924. All newspaper quotes in text are from this source. The same story also appeared under a different title in *Maclean's*, 1 January 1924 and Montreal *Family Herald*, 5 January 1924.

6. J. Hawkes, *The Story of Saskatchewan and its People* (Regina: S.J. Clarke, 1924), p. 160.

7. Chief Buffalo Child Long Lance, *Long Lance* (New York: Cosmopolitan Book Corporation, 1928), p. xiv.

8. *Maclean's*, 1 February 1929.

9. *Long Lance*, pp. 273, 301.

10. Ibid., p. 274.

11. Ibid., p. 276.

12. Ibid., p. 281.

13. Ibid., p. 306.

14. The author wishes to thank Henry Kloppenburg for providing several references to the use of the term "unring the bell" in Canadian case law decisions.

15. Provincial Archives of Saskatchewan [PAS], D.G. Mandelbaum papers, transcript disc 135, John Sounding Sky interview, 17 July 1934.

16. Royal Canadian Mounted Police Heritage Centre library [RCMPHCL], Almighty Voice file, J.J. Atherton, "Notes on the Almighty Voice Incident," 1956.

17. H.S.M. Kemp, "Almighty Voice–Public Enemy No. 1," *RCMP Quarterly*, v. 23, n. 1, July 1957, p. 4.

18. R.L. Neuberger, *Royal Canadian Mounted Police* (New York: Random House, 1953), p. 67.

19. R. Moon, *This is Saskatchewan* (Toronto: Ryerson Press, 1953), pp. 148–49.

20. A. Cooper, "The Brave They Fought With Cannons," *Maclean's*, 1 July 1953, pp. 16–17, 34, 36.

21. J. Prebble, "Almighty Voice," *Lilliput*, v. 40, n. 1, January 1957, p. 21.

22. J. Prebble, *My Great-Aunt Appearing Day, and Other Stories* (London: Secker and Warburg, 1958).

23. Prebble, "Almighty Voice," pp. 21–22.

24. N. Shipley, *Almighty Voice and the Red Coats* (Toronto: Burns and MacEachern, 1967), pp. 4, 13–14.

25. P.H. Godsell, "The Scarlet Trail of Almighty Voice," *Fury*, January 1949, pp. 12–15, 63–66.

26. H. O'Hagan, "the warpath of almighty voice," *True*, March 1954, pp. 29–31, 79–84.

27. *Saskatoon StarPhoenix*, 30 May 1957.

28. Regina *Leader-Post*, 18 February 1932.

29. The *Minot Daily News*, 17 October 1970.

30. RCMPHCL, "Almighty Voice file," R. Lobb to RCMP, Regina, 17 January 1948.

31. Ibid. A.S. Band to Officer Commanding, Depot Division, 5 August 1958; E.C. Oliver to RCMP, Regina, 25 January 1961. See also F. Osipoff, "Almighty Voice's Rifle," *Canadian Journal of Arms*, v. 2, n. 2, 1964, p. 33.

32. Regina *Morning Leader*, 15 July 1926.

33. RCMPHCL, R. van Vleuten to Superintendent, Duck Lake Indian Agency, 23 April 1957.

34. Ibid., A.S. Band to Officer Commanding, Depot Division, 14 February 1964; D. Stone to Superintendent, Duck Lake Indian Agency, 19 January 1967.

35. PAS, Richard Mayson papers, III, 2b. *Pioneer Trails*, "Almighty Voice, part 1–3."

36. Library and Archives Canada, Manuscript Division, MG29-E69, v. 1, J.H. Wilson papers, "An account of the pursuit and capture of Almighty Voice."

CHAPTER SEVEN: SPECTATOR SPORT

1. The most influential expression of this clash of cultures interpretation was George Stanley's *The Birth of Western Canada* (London: Longmans Green, 1936).

2. The Department of Indian Affairs deliberately cultivated and promoted a positive image of itself and its policies. See J.R. Miller, "Cultural Insecurity in the Peaceable Kingdom: Assimilation Policy and Government Propaganda," unpublished paper presented before British Association for Canadian Studies, 2011.

3. A.L. Haydon, *The Riders of the Plains* (London: Melrose, 1910), p. 156.

4. Quoted in J.R. Miller, *Skyscrapers Hide the Heavens: A History of Native-Newcomer Relations in Canada* (Toronto: University of Toronto Press, 2018), p. 267. Miller should be consulted for the story of the Canadian post-war search for a new federal Indian policy.

5. L.B. Peterson, *Almighty Voice* (Agincourt: Book Society of Canada, 1974), pp. vi–ix, xiii–xv.

6. University of Calgary Archives and Special Collections [UCASC], L.B. Peterson papers, f. 358.85.4.1.17B, L. Peterson, "Almighty Voice," n.d.

7. Ibid., f. 358.85.4.1.16, "Rehearsal Notes," n.d.

8. Peterson, *Almighty Voice*, pp. 10–11.

9. Ibid., pp. 12, 17–18.

10. Ibid., p. 20.

11. Ibid., pp. 23, 25, 27.

12. Ibid., pp. 28, 30.

13. Ibid., pp. 34, 38, 48–49.

14. Peterson papers, f. 358.85.4.1.17A, "Reviews," n.d.

15. Peterson, *Almighty Voice*, p. 48.

16. Claude Fournier interview, 5 November 2018.

17. Ibid.

18. UCASC, W.O. Mitchell papers, f. MsC 19.15.5, tape 4 transcript, p. 4.

19. Ibid., tape 1 transcript, p. 1.

20. Ibid., tape 1 transcript, pp. 6–7.

21. Ibid., tape 5 transcript, pp. 1, 8; tape 6 transcript, p. 1.

22. Ibid., tape 2 transcript, pp. 2–3, 7; tape 7 transcript, p. 6.

23. UCASC, W.O. Mitchell papers, f. MsC 19.16.4, "Alien Thunder," Onyx Films, 1972, pp. 3, 12–13, 17.

24. Bud Sillinger interview, 10 November 2018.

25. All dialogue is from *Alien Thunder*.

26. W.O. Mitchell, *Jake and the Kid* (Fredericton: Goose Lane Editions, 2008), pp. 73–74.

27. UCASC, W.O. Mitchell papers, f. MsC 19.15.5, tape 7 transcript, p. 9.

28. *Maclean's*, 1 April 1974; Vancouver *Sun*, 16 March 1974.

29. Calgary *Herald*, 27 April 1974.

30. Fournier interview.

31. Ned Powers interview, 7 November 2018.

CHAPTER EIGHT: CAN'T PUT THE WIND IN PRISON

1. Library and Archives Canada [LAC], RG10 (Indian Affairs), f. 27107-1, J. Lestock to T.O.

Davis, 1 June 1897.

2. R. Wiebe, "Where Is the Voice Coming From?" in D. Helwig and T. Marshall, eds., *Fourteen Stories High* (Ottawa: Oberon Press, 1971), pp. 112–21.

3. *Western Producer*, 16 November 1972.

4. Chief Tricia Sutherland of the One Arrow First Nation has formally asked the RCMP Commissioner for the return of the Almighty Voice skull fragment to the Willow Cree people.

5. Glenbow Archives, H.A. Dempsey to S. Boyer, 22 June 1972. The correspondence is in a file for photograph NA-2310-1.

6. Victoria *Times*, 20 November 1971; Victoria *Times*, 14 June 1972; "The Case of Almighty Voice," *Community Schools*, v. 4, n. 4, 1974, p. 28.

7. D. Kennedy, *Recollections of an Assiniboine Chief* (Toronto: McClelland and Stewart, 1972), pp. 81–82.

8. J.F. Dion, *My Tribe, The Crees* (Calgary: Glenbow-Alberta Institute 1979), pp. 85–87; see also R. Jefferson, "Fifty Years on the Saskatchewan," *Canadian North-West Historical Society Publications*, v. 1, n. 5, 1929, pp. 94–96.

9. P. Berton, *The Wild Frontier: More Tales from the Remarkable Past* (Toronto: McClelland and Stewart, 1978), pp. 209–33.

10. G. MacEwan, *Portraits from the Plains* (Toronto: McGraw Hill, 1971), p. 201.

11. F.W. Anderson, *Almighty Voice* (Saskatoon: Frontier Books, 1971), p. 1; A slightly revised version of the Anderson account appeared under the title, "Death Song from the Poplars" in A. Downs, ed., *The Law and the Lawless: Frontier Justice on the Canadian Prairies* (Victoria: Heritage House Publishing, 2014), pp. 106–32.

12. T. Shrimpton, *The Search for Almighty Voice* (Humboldt: Gopher Books, 1999), pp. 9–10, 70.

13. T.W. Paterson, *Outlaws of Western Canada* (Toronto: Mr. Paperback, 1982), p. 55.

14. H. Horwood and E. Butts, *Pirates and Outlaws of Canada* (Toronto: Doubleday, 1984), p. 207.

15. M.A. Macpherson, *Outlaws of the Canadian West* (Edmonton: Lone Pine Publishing, 1999), p. 119.

16. D.A. Young, *The Mountie* (1973), pp. 59–60.

17. R. Atkin, *Maintain the Right: The Early History of the North-West Mounted Police* (London: Macmillan, 1973), pp. 286, 297.

18. S.W. Horrall, *The Pictorial History of the Royal Canadian Mounted Police* (Toronto: McGraw-Hill Ryerson, 1973), p. 108.

19. R.C. Macleod, *The North-West Mounted Police and Law Enforcement, 1873–1905* (Toronto: University of Toronto Press, 1976), pp. 117–18.

20. D. Francis, *The Imaginary Indian* (Arsenal Pulp Press, 1992), p. 67.

21. J. Jennings, "The North West Mounted Police and Indian Policy After the 1885 Rebellion"

in F.L. Barron and J.B. Waldram, eds., *1885 and After: Native Society in Transition* (Regina: University of Regina Press 1986), pp. 235–36.

22. W. Beahen and S. Horrall, *Red Coats on the Prairies: The North-West Mounted Police 1886–1900* (Regina: Centax Books, 1998), pp. 73–77.

23. A. Graybill, *Policing the Great Plains: Rangers, Mounties, and the North American Frontier, 1875–1900* (Lincoln: University of Nebraska Press, 2007), p. 23.

24. The exception is D. Lee, "Almighty Voice and His Stories," *Native Studies Review*, v. 10, n. 2, 1995, pp. 57–76.

25. N. Dyck, *What Is the Indian 'Problem': Tutelage and Resistance in Canadian Indian Administration* (Institution for Social and Economic Research, 1991), p. 87.

26. O.P. Dickason, *Canada's First Nations: A History of Founding Peoples from Earliest Times* (Toronto: McClelland and Stewart, 1992), p. 315.

27. S. Carter, *Aboriginal People and Colonizers of Western Canada to 1900* (Toronto: University of Toronto Press, 1999), p. 175

28. See J.R. Miller, "Owen Glendower, Hotspur, and Canadian Indian Policy" in J.R. Miller, *Reflections on Native-Newcomer Relations: Selected Essays* (Toronto: University of Toronto Press, 2004), pp. 107–39.

29. See, for example, C.J. Nielson, "Caricaturing Colonial Space: Indigenized, Feminized Bodies and Anglo-Canadian Identity, 1873–94," *Canadian Historical Review*, v. 96, n. 4, December 2015, pp. 503.

30. B. Cockburn, "Stolen Land," *Waiting for a Miracle* (1987)

31. A. Suknaski, "Almighty Voice," *Dreadnaught 52* Pickup 39, 1975.

32. M. Campbell, *Stories of the Road Allowance People* (Penticton: Theytus Books, 1995), p. 79.

33. D.D. Moses, "How My Ghosts Got Pale Faces" in S.J. Ortiz, ed., *Speaking for Generations: Native Writers on Writing* (Tuscon: University of Arizona Press, 1997), p. 135.

34. Ibid., pp. 137–39.

35. Ibid., pp. 139, 147.

36. D.D. Moses, *Almighty Voice and His Wife* (Stratford: Williams-Wallace Publishers, 1992), pp. 19–20.

37. Ibid., pp. 26, 31, 34–35.

38. Ibid., pp. 38–39, 49.

39. Ibid., pp. 54, 57.

40. Ibid., pp. 62–63, 67–69.

41. Ibid., pp. 75–76, 78–79.

42. Ibid., pp. 92–95.

43. Ibid., pp. 95–96.

44. Moses, "How My Ghosts Got Pale Faces," p. 145.

EPILOGUE

1. *Le Manitoba*, 29 April 1886 (translation).

2. Interview with Richard John and Butch Amundson, 11 April 2016.

3. The story of the exhumation and repatriation of One Arrow is based on the John and Amundson interview. Additional information was generously provided by Stewart Prosper.

4. K.D. McLeod, "Chief One Arrow Repatriation: Geophysical Surveying, St. Boniface Cemetery," Stantec report, March 2008.

5. D. and J. Fisher, "One Arrow comes home," newsletter, 28 August 2007.

6. Library and Archives Canada [LAC], RG10 (Indian Affairs), v. 3768, f. 33642, "Report to the Minister of the Interior on the Governor General's Tour," 4 November 1881.

7. Ibid.

8. Quoted in A. Morris, *The Treaties of Canada with the Indians of Manitoba and the North-West Territories* (Saskatoon: Fifth House Publishers, 1991), pp. 205, 208.

9. LAC, RG18 B1 (Royal Canadian Mounted Police), v. 1038, f. 68, A.B. Perry to A.G. Irvine, 19 February 1886.

APPENDIX

1. Library and Archives Canada [LAC], Inmate Admission Books, 1885–1891, Stony Mountain penitentiary. The author wishes to thank Kris Inwood for providing a copy of the register in spreadsheet format. Other sources claim that One Arrow was born in 1810 but this date cannot be substantiated.

2. D.G. Mandelbaum, *The Plains Cree: An Ethnographic, Historical, and Comparative Study* (Regina: Canadian Plains Research Center, 1979). p. 10. Other authors have repeated the Mandelbaum claim. See also J.S.H. Brown, "Sutherland, George" in F.G. Halpenny, ed., *Dictionary of Canadian Biography*, v. iv (1771–1800) (Toronto: University of Toronto Press, 1979), pp. 726–27.

3. D.W. Harmon, *Harmon's Journal* (Victoria: New Caledonia House Publishing, 2006), p. 30.

4. University of Saskatchewan Archives and Special Collections, A.S. Morton papers. Unknown to A.S. Morton, 25 September 1930.

5. Dale Russell, "The Fort a la Corne Forest Area: A Survey of the Historical Documents," unpublished report of Western Heritage Services, August 2007, pp. 39–41. Russell kindly provided a copy of this report and drew attention to the confusion over George Sutherland; Morton papers, Unknown to Morton, 25 September 1930.

6. Quoted in Ibid., p. 41. Fort à la Corne was also known as nicawakihcikanisihk or Little Garden, probably because of the presence of the George Sutherland house and garden in the immediate area.

7. According to Willow Cree oral tradition, Sutherland had eighteen children (ten boys and eight girls) from three wives. He had four children with Papâmikewis: two boys, Tchimanaskat (The Short Leg) and Napikew, and two girls, Mittimoyew (Old Woman) and Yakatsus (The Light Woman); nine children with Pasikus: four boys, One Arrow, Moniah, Istchaw, and Mistikwetahaw (Knocked with a Stick [also known as Neanomitanow (Fifty)], and five girls, Skwew (The Woman), Apakusis (The Mouse), Kanisopaminew (Calling for Water), Pawistik (The Fall) and Kanawapukayus (Keeping the Gate) [also known as Mistaskaogan (Big Raw Back)]; and five children with Ka Neotototosimiw (Four Breasted): four boys, Kanamatchit (Left Handed), Yamaskin, Pakustikwan (Bald Head) and Kappimuttak, and one girl, Kananwasew (Lighting here and there). Morton papers, Unknown to Morton, 25 September 1930.

INDEX

220–226; portrayal of in *Alien Thunder*, 202–210, 212; portrayal of in histories, 147–148, 149, 151–152, 218–**219**; presumed stealer of Colebrook's horse and rifle, 63, 73; R. S. Cook's concocted memories of, 152–155; R. Wiebe's essay on, 213–218; radio programs on, 183–184; reason for escape from barracks, 19, 45–46, 221, 247–248; reasons given for killing the cow, 41, 151, 152, 161, 220, 222–223; reward for his capture, 89, 90–91, **95**; rumour that he committed no crime, 88; seen as hero, 74, 81, 194, 195; seen as spiritual shape shifter, 80; and shooting of N. Venne, 105, 162; shoots Colebrook, 52–54, 57; shoots J. Allan in bluff, 108–109; sightings of while on the run, 82–83, 94–95, 100; significance and galvanizing force of, 4–5, 247–249; similarities with Chief One Arrow, 176, 246, 247; skull fragment of, 123, 163, 182, 214, 216–217, 263n42, 270n4; songs about, 227; story he was told he'd hang for killing cow, 45, 158, 159, 165–166, 171, 177, 184, 190, 193–194, 200, 205, 215, 216, 220, 221; sympathetic newspaper coverage of, 138–139, 140; sympathetic portrayals of in plays/tv/film, 186, 192–195, 228–237; threatens to kill R. S. McKenzie, 40, 66–67; treatment of in scholarly studies, 226–227; trips home to see new son, 84, 94; view of as cold-blooded killer, 76, 109, 140, 166, **178**; view of F. Dumont, 50; W. Fraser article on, 142–146; as young man, 30, 40–41

Almighty Voice (booklet), 222–**223**

Almighty Voice (play), 186, 189, 195–196

Almighty Voice and His Wife (play), 228–237

Almighty Voice and the Redcoats (Shipley), 176–177

Almightyvoice, Peter, 2

Amundson, Butch, 239–241

Anderson, Frank, 222–223

Anderson, Fred, 218

Angelique (Almighty Voice's sister), **184**

Anson, Mae Harris, 152–153

Arcand, Jean-Baptiste, 85

Ascott, Alfred, 106, 262n8

Atherton, J. J., 171

B

Badger, Joseph, 42

Bain, Hugh U., 62, 63, 123, 125

Baldhead, Eddie, 240

Ballendine, Robert, 84

Ballendine, Sam, 40

Beahen, William, 226

Beardy, Chief: arrested for cattle killing, 9; background, 21; family of, 251; and North-West Rebellion, 25, **26**; and Treaty Six, 22, 239

Beatty, Reginald, 82

Berton, Pierre, 220–222

Big Bear, Chief, 50, **51**

Birch, J. C., 141

Black, N. F., 157–158

bluff siege: Almighty Voice at, 105–107, 108–109, 117, 119, 123; bodies found after, 122–123; burial for those who died at, 125; cannon shelling of, 117, 119–122; final attack at, 119–122; first attack by NWMP, 107–108; gravesite for Indians who died during, 128; how it started, 105–107, 111; Indians fortify position at, 111; J. B. Allan and C. Raven's memories of, 150–151; lack of investigation after, 127; memorial for, 244–

ACKNOWLEDGEMENTS

In Search for Almighty Voice greatly benefited from the generous support and encouragement of many people over many years.

The One Arrow community embraced the project and provided guidance and inspiration. I'm particularly indebted to Chief Tricia Sutherland and Elders Stewart Prosper and Richard John, both former chiefs of the band, who shared their insights into the story, often leavened with smiles and laughter.

The research for the project was funded by a grant from the Social Sciences and Humanities Research Council of Canada. Jennie Hansen, Merle Massie, Dustin McNichol, Blaine Wickham, and especially Alex Deighton, served as research assistants at various stages in the project. The amount of material they turned up about Almighty Voice was truly amazing. Jennie also steered me clear of a train wreck in my first attempt at a draft manuscript.

Butch Amundson, Rick Gamble, Jim Miller, Mary Ellen Turpel-Lafond, and Glenn Wright offered critical comment on the project and the manuscript. I'm extremely fortunate to have friends who willingly give of their time and experience—and their opinions! Naturally, any errors are my own.

David Meyer and Dale Russell helped me sort out locations and their late nineteenth century names—and answered many questions along the way. Lorena Cote, Keith Goulet, and Arok Wolvengrey shared their linguistic skills in trying to make sense of garbled Cree and Saulteaux names and/or English renderings in the official documents. Doug Chisholm and his Cessna plane made it possible to secure an aerial view and assessment of the Saskatchewan terrain covered in the book.

Articulate Eye Design of Saskatoon expertly prepared the maps. Research materials, including photographs, were secured at the Provincial Archives of Saskatchewan (Tim Novak), the RCMP Heritage Centre (Jodi Ann Eskritt), the University of Calgary library special collections (Allison Wagner), the University of Saskatchewan archives and special collections (Patrick Hayes), the Prince Albert Historical Museum (Jamie Benson), Library and Archives Canada, and from Dennis Fisher.

Charlene Dobmeier was a gentle but thorough editor who smoothed out the rough edges and brought some consistency to the style. Tuesdays are not the same without a call from her.

Robin Mitchell Cranfield of hundreds & thousands produced a clean, accessible design that places the focus on the story.

My publisher Sharon Fitzhenry has been a constant supporter and advocate of my writing—sprinkled with shouts of "hot damn."

Finally, my bride Marley (forty-four years and counting) understood the importance of this book as it took shape and was always there to talk about the story and why it matters. She read each chapter as it was drafted and provided helpful and insightful feedback. It's been quite the journey together.

Bill Waiser
Saskatoon 2020

ABOUT THE AUTHOR

Historian Bill Waiser lives in Saskatoon. He is the author of *A World We Have Lost: Saskatchewan before 1905*, winner of the 2016 Governor General's Literary Award for Non-fiction. He is also the recipient of the 2018 Governor General's History Award for Popular Media (the Pierre Berton award). Please visit Bill's website www.billwaiser.com or follow him on twitter @billwaiser. He can be reached at bill.waiser@usask.ca.

©Daniel Hallen, University of Saskatchewan

OTHER TITLES BY BILL WAISER

A World We Have Lost: Saskatchewan before 1905
winner of the 2016 Governor General's Literary Award for Non-Fiction

Saskatchewan: A New History
"Saskatchewan has certainly found its historian."
—The Globe and Mail

Loyal till Death: Indians and the North-West Rebellion (with Blair Stonechild)
1997 short-list finalist for Governor General's Literary Award for Non-Fiction